THE

PATRIARCHS AND LAWGIVERS

OF

𝕮𝖍𝖊 𝕺𝖑𝖉 𝕮𝖊𝖘𝖙𝖆𝖒𝖊𝖓𝖙.

THE
PATRIARCHS AND LAWGIVERS

OF

The Old Testament.

A SERIES OF SERMONS PREACHED IN THE CHAPEL
OF LINCOLN'S INN.

BY

FREDERICK DENISON MAURICE, M.A.,

PROFESSOR OF MORAL PHILOSOPHY IN THE UNIVERSITY OF CAMBRIDGE.

WIPF & STOCK · Eugene, Oregon

Wipf and Stock Publishers
199 W 8th Ave, Suite 3
Eugene, OR 97401

The Patriarchs and Lawgivers of the Old Testament
A Series of Sermons Preached in the Chapel of Lincoln's Inn
By Maurice, Frederick D.
ISBN 13: 978-1-60899-712-1
Publication date 6/29/2010
Previously published by Macmillan & Co., 1892

TO THE

REV. JAMES SHERGOLD ANDERSON,
PREACHER OF LINCOLN'S INN

THESE SERMONS ARE DEDICATED,

IN GRATEFUL RECOLLECTION OF THE UNVARYING KINDNESS

WHICH HE HAS SHEWN TO THE AUTHOR

DURING THE FIVE YEARS IN WHICH HE HAS HAD

THE PLEASURE AND PRIVILEGE

OF KNOWING HIM,

AND

IN WHICH HE HAS BEEN PERMITTED TO WORK WITH HIM

CONTENTS.

                                                                 PAGE

ADVERTISEMENT.
PREFACE TO SECOND EDITION i
PREFACE TO FIRST EDITION xv

SERMON I.
THE CREATION OF MANKIND, AND OF THE FIRST MAN.

GENESIS II. 1.—Thus the heavens and the earth were finished, and all the host of them 33

SERMON II.
THE FALL AND THE DELUGE.

GENESIS VI. 5, 6, 7.—And God saw that the wickedness of man was great in the earth, and that every imagination of the thoughts of his heart was only evil continually. And it repented the Lord that he had made man on the earth, and it grieved him at his heart. And the Lord said, I will destroy man whom I have created from the face of the earth; both man, and beast, and the creeping thing, and the fowls of the air; for it repenteth me that I have made them 50

SERMON III.
NOAH AND ABRAHAM.

GENESIS XII. 1, 2, 3.—Now the Lord had said unto Abram, Get thee out of thy country, and from thy kindred, and from thy father's house, unto a land that I will shew thee. And I will make of thee a great nation, and I will bless thee, and make thy name great; and thou shalt be a blessing: And I will bless them that bless thee, and curse him that curseth thee: and in thee shall all families of the earth be blessed 68

CONTENTS.

SERMON IV.
ABRAHAM AND ISAAC.

GENESIS XXII. 7, 8.—And Isaac spake unto Abraham his father, and said, My father: and he said, Here am I, my son. And he said, Behold the fire and the wood: but where is the lamb for the burnt offering? And Abraham said, My son, God will provide himself a lamb for a burnt offering: so they went both of them together 83

SERMON V.
ESAU AND JACOB.

GENESIS XXVIII. 10-17.—And Jacob went out from Beer-sheba, and went toward Haran. And he lighted upon a certain place, and tarried there all night, because the sun was set; and he took of the stones of that place, and put them for his pillows, and lay down in that place to sleep. And he dreamed, and behold a ladder set up on the earth, and the top of it reached to heaven: and behold the angels of God ascending and descending on it. And, behold, the Lord stood above it, and said, I am the Lord God of Abraham thy father, and the God of Isaac: the land whereon thou liest, to thee will I give it, and to thy seed; and thy seed shall be as the dust of the earth, and thou shalt spread abroad to the west, and to the east, and to the north, and to the south: and in thee and in thy seed shall all the families of the earth be blessed. And, behold, I am with thee, and will keep thee in all places whither thou goest, and will bring thee again into this land; for I will not leave thee, until I have done that which I have spoken to thee of. And Jacob awaked out of his sleep, and he said, Surely the Lord is in this place; and I knew it not. And he was afraid, and said, How dreadful is this place! this is none other but the house of God, and this is the gate of heaven . 100

SERMON VI.
THE DREAMS OF JOSEPH.

GENESIS XLII. 8, 9.—And Joseph knew his brethren, but they knew not him. And Joseph remembered the dreams which he dreamed of them 118

CONTENTS.

SERMON VII.

JOSEPH AND HIS BRETHREN.

GENESIS XLV. 7, 8.—God sent me before you to preserve you a posterity in the earth, and to save your lives by a great deliverance. So now it was not you that sent me hither, but God: and he hath made me a father to Pharaoh, and lord of all his house, and a ruler throughout all the land of Egypt 137

SERMON VIII.

THE MISSION OF MOSES.

EXODUS V. 22, 23.—And Moses returned unto the Lord, and said, Lord, wherefore hast thou so evil entreated this people? why is it that thou hast sent me? For since I came to Pharaoh to speak in thy name, he hath done evil to this people; neither hast thou delivered thy people at all 154

SERMON IX.

THE MIRACLES OF MOSES, AND THE HARDENING OF PHARAOH.

EXODUS X. 20.—But the Lord hardened Pharaoh's heart, so that he would not let the children of Israel go 172

SERMON X.

THE PASSOVER.

EXODUS XIV. 13, 14.—And Moses said unto the people, Fear ye not, stand still, and see the salvation of the Lord, which he will shew to you to-day: for the Egyptians whom ye have seen to-day, ye shall see them again no more for ever. The Lord shall fight for you, and ye shall hold your peace 186

SERMON XI.

THE REBELLION OF KORAH.

NUMBERS XVI. 3.—And they gathered themselves together against Moses and against Aaron, and said unto them, Ye take too much upon you, seeing all the congregation are holy, every one of them, and the Lord is among them: wherefore then lift ye up yourselves above the congregation of the Lord? 204

SERMON XII.

THE PROPHECY OF BALAAM.

NUMBERS XXIII. 11, 12.—And Balak said unto Balaam, What hast thou done unto me? I took thee to curse mine enemies, and, behold, thou hast blessed them altogether. And he answered and said, Must I not take heed to speak that which the Lord hath put in my mouth? 221

SERMON XIII.

PROSPERITY AND ADVERSITY.

DEUT. V. 33.—Ye shall walk in all the ways which the Lord your God hath commanded you, that ye may live, and that it may be well with you, and that ye may prolong your days in the land which ye shall possess 241

SERMON XIV.

THE NATION AND THE CHURCH.

DEUT. VII. 22–26.—And the Lord thy God will put out those nations before thee by little and little: thou mayest not consume them at once, lest the beasts of the field increase upon thee. But the Lord thy God shall deliver them unto thee, and shall destroy them with a mighty destruction, until they be destroyed. And he shall deliver their kings into thine hand, and thou shalt destroy their name from under heaven: there shall no man be able to stand before thee, until thou have destroyed them. The graven images of their gods shall ye burn with fire: thou shalt not desire the silver or gold that is on them, nor take it unto thee, lest thou be snared therein: for it is an abomination to the Lord thy God. Neither shalt thou bring an abomination into thine house, lest thou be a cursed thing like it: but thou shalt utterly detest it, and thou shalt utterly abhor it; for it is a cursed thing 256

SERMON XV.

THE TEST OF PROPHECY AND MIRACLE.

DEUT. XXIII. 1–8.—If there arise among you a prophet, or a dreamer of dreams, and giveth thee a sign or a wonder, and the sign or the wonder come to pass, whereof he spake unto thee, saying, Let us go after other gods, which thou hast not known, and let us serve them; thou shalt not hearken unto the words of that prophet, or that dreamer of dreams: for the Lord your God proveth you, to know whether ye love the Lord your God with all your heart and with all your soul 274

SERMON XVI.

PENTECOST.

DEUT. XXX. 19, 20.—I call heaven and earth to record this day against you, that I have set before you life and death, blessing and cursing: therefore choose life, that both thou and thy seed may live: that thou mayest love the Lord thy God, and that thou mayest obey his voice, and that thou mayest cleave unto him: for he is thy life, and the length of thy days: that thou mayest dwell in the land which the Lord sware unto thy fathers, to Abraham, to Isaac, and to Jacob, to give them 289

SERMON XVII.

JOSHUA AND ST. JOHN.

JOSHUA XXIII. 1, 2, 3.—And it came to pass a long time after that the Lord had given rest unto Israel from all their enemies round about, that Joshua waxed old and stricken in age. And Joshua called for all Israel, and for their elders, and for their heads, and for their judges, and for their officers, and said unto them, I am old and stricken in age: and ye have seen all that the Lord your God hath done unto all these nations because of you: for the Lord your God is he that hath fought for you 305

SERMON XVIII.

THE BOOK OF JUDGES.

JUDGES V. 1, 2. —Then sang Deborah and Barak the son of Abinoam on that day, saying, Praise ye the Lord for the avenging of Israel 320

SERMON XIX.

ELI AND SAMUEL.

1 Samuel III. 14.—And therefore I have sworn unto the house of Eli, that the iniquity of Eli's house shall not be purged with sacrifice nor offering for ever 336

ADVERTISEMENT.

THE First Edition of this book was published under the following title: "*The Old Testament: Nineteen Sermons on the First Lessons, for the Sundays from Septuagesima Sunday to the Third Sunday after Trinity. Preached at the Chapel of Lincoln's Inn.*" The following note then appeared at the end of the Preface:—

"There is no Sermon in this Volume on the fifth Sunday after Easter, as I was absent on that day from Lincoln's Inn. I had thought of introducing a Sermon which I preached at Oxford, on the 9th of Deuteronomy: but I determined on the whole that a discourse addressed to a different congregation would confuse the course rather than complete it. Happily the Church has selected so many chapters from the book of Deuteronomy, that the omission of two is of less consequence. The Sermon on Whit-Sunday is taken from one of the lessons for Whit-Tuesday. There are none on Trinity Sunday, as the lessons for that day are taken from the book of Genesis, on which I had preached already."

PREFACE

TO THE SECOND EDITION.

CIRCUMSTANCES obliged me nearly two years ago to write a pamphlet on the meaning of the word Eternal. Various answers were made to this pamphlet, as containing a doctrine which was inconsistent with the popular notion of future punishment. There was one, in which the subject was contemplated from an entirely different point of view. An accomplished member of the University of Oxford, Mr. Mansel, of St. John's, in a letter to a friend,[1] pointed out the relation in which my argument stood to our whole belief respecting *Revelation*. He saw that what I had said involved the assumption, that the Eternal Being has actually unveiled or discovered Himself to his creature man. With much courtesy to me, and much philosophical ability, Mr. Mansel explained his reasons for rejecting that assumption. 'Revelation,' he says (pp. 15, 16), ' does not tell us what God is in Himself, but only under what accommodations He has vouchsafed to

---

[1] "Man's Conception of Eternity; an Examination of Mr. Maurice's Theory of a Fixed State out of Time, in a Letter to the Rev. L. T. Bernays, by Rev. H. L. Mansel, B.D., Fellow and Tutor of St. John's College, Oxford." J. H. Parker.

'represent Himself.' And again (pp. 9, 10), 'Ideas 'and images which do not represent God as He is, may 'nevertheless represent Him as it is our duty to regard 'Him. They are not in themselves true; but we must 'nevertheless believe and act as if they were true. A 'finite mind can form no conception of an infinite Being, 'which shall be *speculatively* true, for it must represent 'the infinite under finite forms; nevertheless, a concep- 'tion which is *speculatively* untrue may be *regulatively* 'true. A regulative truth is thus designed not to satisfy 'our reason, but to guide our practice; not to tell us 'what God is, but how He wills that we should think 'of Him.'

It will be obvious to the reader of these Sermons, that this statement has a far more direct bearing upon them, than upon the particular question which called forth Mr. Mansel's remarks. My chief object in preaching and writing upon the Old Testament, has been to show that God has created man in His image; that being so created he is capable of receiving a revelation of God,—of knowing what God is; that without such a revelation he cannot be truly a man; that without such knowledge he cannot become what he is always feeling that he ought to become. I believe, as little as Mr. Mansel does, that man's conceptions of God can be true. I believe that history shows them not only to be limited, but to be false. I believe also, that unless man can rise above his own conceptions, he can know nothing of nature or of himself any more than of God. The history of the Bible, as I read it, is the history of the way in which

God has raised men above their own conceptions, has educated them to believe in Him, to trust in Him, to know Him; a history also of the way in which men have determined to judge Him according to their conceptions, and so have become idolaters of things in heaven, and on earth, and under the earth, framing God outwardly according to the likeness of that which they see and handle,—inwardly, according to the habits and tendencies of their own minds. The education of man by God is, it seems to me, the education into a knowledge of that which is, not of that which it behoves us to think or believe. Just so far as a man submits to that education, he is brought under the government of the true God; his thoughts and words and acts are regulated according to His true law, are in conformity with His true will: just so far as he does not submit to it, he continues the victim of ever fresh delusions, the utterer and begetter of ever fresh falsehoods. To his mind 'nothing is, but all things seem.' The world about him is as much a phantom world as the world beyond him; he himself becomes the centre of both, reconstructing both in his own image, turning the realities of earth and heaven equally into shadows.

I do most entirely agree with Mr. Mansel, that this is a practical question, and ought to be considered on practical grounds and in reference to its practical issues. That it has the most direct bearing on the history of philosophy I have endeavoured to show elsewhere; here I am much more anxious to speak of its bearing upon the morality of individuals and of nations. That subject is very fully discussed in one of the books on which I have commented in this volume, the book of Deuteronomy. The whole principle of that book, it seems to me, is this, that a Nation is only a wise and understanding nation when it confesses a God who is,—a God who has made Himself known as the ground of all human righteousness, fidelity, veracity; that when it ceases to believe in such a God, and that He is its actual present King, the Director of its counsels, the Lord of its hosts, it becomes an idolatrous, stupid, slavish nation. Would to God that our statesmen, our philosophers, the teachers in our schools, the divines who give out oracles from our pulpits, would meditate upon the words of that divine and terrible book, and would try whether they cannot regulate their thoughts, their speech, and their acts according to it! The history of all the nations of the world since it was written,—of the nations of Christendom quite as much as of those before the Incarnation, is a commentary upon it. Oh that England may not supply the most luminous, and yet also the darkest commentary of all!

I can well exercise towards Mr. Mansel the same tolerance which he has manifested towards me, and ' am ' conscious how little justice can be done to all the ' higher features of his teaching, by a dry, formal ex- ' amination of one particular proposition.' I have no doubt that he is a more truthful man than I am, and could less endure any equivocation in practice than I do. But I cannot help perceiving, that the maxim which he has so clearly and logically announced is the suppressed premiss in a multitude of minds which possess little of his learning, and would perhaps be even startled by his statement if it was suddenly and broadly presented to them. The notion of a revelation that tells us things which are not in themselves true, but which it is right for us to believe and to act upon as if they were true, has, I fear, penetrated very deeply into the heart of our English schools, and of our English world. It may be traced among persons who are apparently most unlike each other, who live to oppose and confute each other. Those who speak most of the old Catholic creeds seem to love them because they have been handed down to us, not because they utter the Name in which we are living, and moving, and having our being, the name of the Father of an infinite Majesty, of his true and honourable Son, and of the Holy Ghost the Comforter. If we speak of them with joy and thanksgiving, as telling us the thing we most crave to know, we are answered, 'Oh, then you mean, you 'believe them because you like them, not because the 'Church has told you to believe them.' In other words, you are to believe them because they ought to be believed, not because they tell the thing as it is. And if we turn for protection against this hard dogmatism, to those who declare themselves the members of an Experimental, or Evangelical, rather than of a Catholic school, if we speak with them in the language which their fathers spoke, of the struggles through which patriarchs and prophets passed, while they were learning to rise above their own poor thoughts, and were coming

to the knowledge of God, we are answered, 'Oh, then
'you only receive the Bible because it corresponds to
'human experience, not as an authoritative message
'from Heaven.' In other words, you are to believe the
Bible because you ought to believe it, not because it
shows you the way to the knowledge of what you are,
and of what God is. Both our religious schools are
unconscious plagiarists from the canons of Mr. Mansel's
philosophical school.

But their differences are not in the least likely to be
adjusted by the discovery of this common ground. How
the atmosphere is to be regulated by the regulative
Revelation; at what degree of heat or cold this constitution or that can endure it; who must fix,—since
the language of the Revelation is assumed not to be
exact, not to express the very lesson which we are to
derive from it,—what it does mean; by what contrivances its phrases are to be adapted to various
places and times: these are questions which must, of
course, give rise to infinite disputations; ever new
schools and sects must be called into existence to settle
them; there is scope for permissions, prohibitions, com-
promises, persecutions, to any extent. The despair which
these must cause will probably drive numbers to ask for
an infallible human voice, which shall regulate for each
period that which the Revelation has so utterly failed to
regulate.

There are some who have observed these things, and
have suffered from them more than words can tell.
They have seen the great plausibility and convenience

of Mr. Mansel's formula; how much of what the world calls Mysticism it might save them from; how easily, if they could be content with it, they might take up with any of the popular systems of Christianity, and pass as creditable religious men. But they have found it impossible. They have been driven to ask if there is not a Revelation which means revealing; if God has not revealed Himself; if there is not that in man which can receive this Revelation, and be moulded in conformity with it. It is not that their minds do not crave to be regulated as well as to be impelled,—to be regulated in the daily events of life, as well as in its most serious and trying emergencies; but, neither in the one nor in the other, have they found that such a Revelation as Mr. Mansel conceives of, serves their purpose. They cannot recollect the rules just at the moment when the little occasions arise which set their minds ajar; the habits which are formed for one set of circumstances are found not to fit in another; in great crises and revolutions, the machinery for keeping the soul in order refuses to work,—its wheels become clogged, —the safety-valve is stopped. And then the man asks, ' Were not those old words, *Be ye perfect, as your* ' *Father in heaven is perfect,*—high and discouraging as ' they once sounded,—more practical, more comforting, ' than all the regulative motives and maxims into which ' they have been reduced,—because they speak of an ' actual Revelation of a Father to His children,—of an ' actual power by which He can mould them, however ' reluctant, into His likeness ?'

Those who try to meet any of these doubts and questions, will, of course, be accused of raising them, and of inventing a new Theology to displace that which their fathers found sufficient. All such accusations must be patiently borne. When they proceed from earnest men, the answer, I hope, will be found in due time, not in my books, but in a better than mine and than all others. If they are proposed by frivolous men, neither that Book nor any other will help them; they will not find the truth, for they do not seek it. I have endeavoured here to lead my readers back to the old theology, which I am afraid some of our popular notions, and some of our scholastic notions, are sadly concealing from us. I have endeavoured to maintain here, as elsewhere, that the most literal meaning of Scripture is the most spiritual meaning; that if we follow it faithfully we shall not be led to the worship of it, but of God; that if we trace the revelation which the Book sets forth as it gradually unfolds itself, we shall find that we are drawn away from letters to life; from sounds that are conveyed to the ear, to living words that are conveyed with mighty power to the conscience and the heart; from those words, to Him who speaks them; from the manifestations which came through the right and wrong acts of men, through their blessings and their punishments, to the perfect manifestation of the Son of God. In these discourses I have had to encounter that which I believe to be the great denial of our time,—the one which is most at variance with the express letter of the Bible, and with its whole object and history,—the denial, I mean, that man continued to be in the image of God after the Fall, with the denials which correspond to this, and grow out of it, that man was originally created in the Divine Word, and that apart from Him, neither Adam nor any of his descendants either had, or ever could have, any righteousness or any life.

While we cling to this disbelief we shall, I think, read ourselves more and more into the Bible, and find it less and less the corrector of our ignorance, the guide of our thoughts. For while we are most anxious to plead the Fall as an excuse for our folly and sinfulness, while we give it a prominence in our discourses which the Apostles never gave it,—for they were sent to preach the Gospel of the kingdom of God,—we are very indignant when we are told that Protestant England may have the same low and dark conceptions of the character of God which there were among Egyptians or Assyrians. If we really believed that we carry about with us the same fallen nature which Egyptians and Assyrians had, this would seem to be a very obvious consequence; and our inward experience would tell us that we do not like to retain God in our knowledge, that we have a tendency to worship the creature more than the Creator, just as the heathens had. But because we make the Fall a reason for denying them the conscience of good, the craving for it, the search after it with all that is promised to those hereafter who have pursued it here, we are afraid to confess how much the conscience of evil, the readiness to embrace it and to sink into it, may belong to us, when our privileges and our religious pretensions are the greatest. In like manner, we cut ourselves off from communion with the great men in the Old Testament. We suppose that God did not speak to them as He speaks to us; that they heard certain syllables sounding in their ears; that it was not with the real man,—with the spirit of the man,—that the Lord of the heart and reins carried on His wonderful intercourse. Augustine, and Luther, and Knox, delighted to read their own temptations in the temptations of Noah and Abraham. We set these men at an immeasurable distance from us, sometimes dreaming that they had advantages which we do not possess, though He, whose day they saw and rejoiced in, had not yet taken flesh and dwelt among men; sometimes supposing that because He has come to us we are further from Him and them, though the Apostle says, He has brought us into the general assembly and church of just men made perfect. All these miserable contradictions which affect our daily lives, our conduct to each other, which cut us off from the past and the future, which make our religion a mixture of bitterness and of trifling, our study of the Scriptures a wearisome duty, our worship of God a profane routine, must go on, it seems to me, and become wider and deeper, unless we grasp more than men have ever grasped yet, the truth which is contained in the first chapter of St. John's Gospel; unless we tell our scholars plainly that they may regard it as a piece of Alexandrian mysticism if they like, but that we want it and will have it for our common daily lives; unless we tell our divines that they may explain it away lest it should prove to be a Revelation for mankind, but that we want such a Revelation; the Revelation of a Word who was with God, and was God, and who took upon Him the nature of all men, and died the death of all men, that not the scholar or the divine, but the *man* might be God's child, and might see Him as He is.

I have reconsidered and revised these Sermons; but I have not found more than a sentence or two which I cared to change,—and this for the sake of making the meaning more clear, not for the sake of modifying it in the least. I brought the subject down to the period of history which is embraced in my "Prophets and Kings," of which a new edition has lately appeared. Some portions of the ground I have travelled again, in my "Sermons on Sacrifice," especially the part referring to Noah and Abraham. But I do not think that I have exactly repeated myself; and though my convictions on the subject of Sacrifice have been far more fully developed in the later volume, I am sure I have not contradicted anything I said in the earlier. In both I have endeavoured to show, that the Old Testament is not contrary to the New; that the New is not a mitigation or softening of the acts and the maxims which are exhibited to us in the Old, but the complete unfolding of the principles involved in those acts and maxims; that St. John is not more of a sentimentalist, not less of a warrior, than Joshua; that both alike hold forth rewards only to those who overcome; that each, in his own way, presents to us a Captain of the hosts of the Lord,—a Word of God,—whose garments are dipped in blood. I have striven to prove that selfishness is the curse which both Testaments are setting forth as the destruction of mankind, because it is the separation of men from God and from each other; that Sacrifice is revealed to us in both as the only means by which the great enemy of the Creator and the creature can be vanquished. I have maintained that Sacrifice, according to the teaching of both Testaments, involves Death,—the death of the person who presents it, which is symbolised by the death of animals, though *that* could never take away sins. I have spoken of the death of the Cross, the death of the Son of God, as the only interpreter of the facts of the world; as the only solution of the meaning of all previous Sacrifices; as the only ground of all future Sacrifices; as that, without which all the example and all the blessed life of the Son of God would have been nothing; as that which was necessarily attended with agony and horror unspeakable, with the sense of separation between the Father and the Son, which the darkening of earth and heaven could but feebly typify. I have maintained that His death alone could take away the sin of the world, because it alone could satisfy the perfectly loving mind of God; because it could alone unite mankind to God in the person of His Son and our Lord, who was known before the foundation of the world, but who was manifested in the latter day on Calvary; because it alone could draw the minds of all men, each wandering in his own way, seeking his own ends, to the one centre. I have striven, lastly, to show that neither Testament sets before men the doctrine, that the selfishness which all God's righteous and terrible punishments have been contending with on this earth, which God's mighty sacrifice has been redeeming us from, is to be the law of a future state; that we are to expect in that state the gratification of self, the repeal of the law of sacrifice I have maintained that the vision of such a state is the vision of a Hell, in which the Devil is reigning supreme and absolute; and that the Heaven which the Bible, in both its portions, would lead us to think that God has prepared for them that love Him, is a society, from which selfishness, and self-seeking, and self-indulgence shall be entirely banished; where the Lamb that was slain shall be the standard of the life, the object of the adoration, of all creatures; where not a self-concentrated, self-glorifying Being, but the Father, the Son, and the Holy Ghost, shall be the new name that is written on all hearts, shall be confessed as the foundation of the divine city, the New Jerusalem.

July, 1855.

PREFACE

TO THE FIRST EDITION.

The Author of these Sermons has been recently charged in a dissenting Review with 'not suffering men 'in general to hold converse with the Bible, unless the 'Church in some way be present at the interview, like 'the jailor when the prisoner receives a visit from his 'friends.'* Whether this statement is true respecting an individual Clergyman, is a question of immense importance to him, of little to the world. But I am supposed to be afraid of the Bible, because the Church of which I am a minister is afraid of it. In many other instances, the Reviewer says that my 'relations' with the Church are 'unfriendly;' in this part of my conduct, he believes I am its too faithful representative. This accusation therefore concerns us all. It has nothing to do with the sins or the follies of me, or of any who may happen to agree with me. Every Clergyman of the English Church ought to be prepared to prove by his words and his acts whether he pleads guilty to it or not.

I will merely set down a few notorious facts. I find myself obliged by my position to read each day to

* *Eclectic Review*, September 1851, p. 269.

my Congregation certain chapters from the Old and the New Testament. These chapters are called 'Lessons.' They are not chosen at random, but follow each other continuously. No hint is given about interpretations of them to be obtained from doctors old or new. On Sundays we read in our Communion Service an Epistle and a Gospel. These taken alone might lead us to fancy that the Bible was to be cut up into portions, each containing some particular moral; not to be treated as a history. Lest we should go away with that impression, the regular order of lessons in the New Testament is preserved, and a special set of lessons is appointed from the Old Testament. These last can by no possibility have been selected for the purpose of teaching a certain set of maxims or notions. They often consist of passages which modern teachers stumble at, and which fastidious parents desire their children to pass over. They must have been appointed because the compilers of our Services held the Bible to be an orderly historical revelation.

This statement I leave to the consideration of every honest Dissenter. If he knows any religious body here or elsewhere, which has expressed its desire that the Bible,—the whole Bible,—should be presented 'to men in general,' in a more formal, decisive, and practical manner than the English Church has done, I shall be rejoiced to hear the name of that body. But if he supposes that in saying so, I am striving to make out a case for myself or for the English Clergy, he is entirely mistaken. I think we are laid under a heavy responsibility by our position in a Church which has given these distinct and emphatical intimations of her meaning. I do not think that we have in any satisfactory degree acquitted ourselves of that responsibility. I do not think we have had courage to bring out the Scriptures of the Old and New Testament in their simple clear sense, as a revelation of God to Man, or as a lamp to the feet of us Englishmen in the nineteenth century.

The cause of this failure is, I think, not far to seek. The religious world has adopted a certain theory respecting the Old Testament. The polity we read of there, we are told, was constructed upon principles entirely peculiar, entirely different from those under which we are living. God was the King of the Hebrews, in a literal actual sense; He is the King of the people of England, in an imaginary metaphorical sense. This is the assumption with which we begin our studies; we announce it or imply it continually in our sermons; it leavens all our thoughts. Consequently, the whole scheme of Old Testament history must be resolved into a scheme of irregular interferences. It cannot be brought to bear,—we have no right to bring it to bear,—upon the actual condition and relations of our English population. It cannot, in any honest sense of the words, be looked upon as a history or revelation for *us*. It must be treated as a mere collection of religious notions and maxims, as supplying a set of texts upon which we are to make edifying remarks, and from which we are to deduce what are called practical applications. At the same time, it is a part of our business to tell our congregations, that the religious teaching of the Old Testament does not strictly belong to us, seeing we are Christians, and have been brought into a much more spiritual economy. Nay, we are to inform them that the doctrine of a future state and the way of preparing for it, which are taken to be the main subjects of divine communications, can be learnt but very imperfectly and indistinctly from these records. What then can remain of them? What is the foundation for the reverence which we are taught to entertain for them? Can you maintain it by speaking of them as merely typical, or the likenesses of something else? Can you maintain it, by drawing from them certain rules of conduct, which in the same breath you say are superseded by other and higher rules?

These are questions which men are asking themselves everywhere. Would to God they were asking them more earnestly, with more determination to obtain an answer! If they were, I should not care how much they heard of neological doubts or neological solutions. I believe the first might be a means of leading them to look again into the Bible, for a real and simple history; that the others would afford them scarcely a temporary resting-place. What makes one tremble, is not the active, but the passive unbelief of our day; not the vehement words, 'like the east-wind,' of men who declare that they cannot be content with conventions, and must have something solid to rest on; but the placid scepticism which takes it for granted that religious men in general are standing upon a reef of sand, and has not interest to ask whether there is any rock beneath upon which we all might stand. Let us confess it plainly and simply. It is not Neologians or Rationalists who have taught men that the Bible is a collection of incoherent fragments,—an old oriental document with which modern civilization has nothing to do. *We* have taught them that. The religious world has been inculcating the lesson upon all classes amongst us. And then we are shocked and startled when we see it brought out openly before us, dressed in critical formulas: and we fly hither and thither for defence against the evil spirit we have ourselves raised; now begging help of some orthodox German, who, we suppose, has more knowledge about documents than ourselves; now entreating some Genevan divine to furnish us with a new theory of inspiration, which will settle all doubts, and which must be received as if it was itself inspired.

But there is an *earnest* infidelity abroad, that will certainly not be settled by the school-arguments, which we childishly suppose may be effectual to convert the *lazy* infidelity of our upper and professional classes into solid faith. Toiling and suffering men want to know, not how the world was governed thousands of years ago, but how it is governed now; whether there is any order in it, whether there is any one who can and will rectify its disorders. They must have plain straightforward answers to these questions. They will listen to no talk about a future state, unless we can tell them something about their present state. They will listen to no arguments from Paley, or Watson, or Hengstenberg, or Gaussen, to prove that such a book must be inspired or divine. 'If it is,' they say, 'what 'message does it bring to us? Is it one of despair or 'of hope, of bondage or of emancipation? Speak it 'out if you know what it is. We will listen if it is 'what we want, however little we may trust you who 'speak it. We will not listen if you bring ever so 'many arguments to prove your powers, your right to 'dictate, or your skill to argue, unless you make known 'to us that which will show us the path in which we are 'to walk, more clearly, which will explain why we were 'sent into this world, and how we are to live in it.'

This tune goes manly. To words like these I believe we can make answer. The Bible, as I think, *is* a friend who comes to men in their prison; the Church, as I think, *does* stand by during the interview, whether as a jailer to hinder intercourse or not, I will try to explain. The Church, it seems to me, exists in the world as a witness to mankind that there is a continual, divine, gracious government over it; as a witness to each nation that God is not less a King over it than He was over the Jews: that there has been a more complete revelation of His government, of the mode in which it is carried on, of the purposes which it designs to accomplish, than that which was made in the old time; but one which does not in the least set that revelation aside, or make it obsolete for us. The Church is to tell men, that the more completely divine any government is, the more human it is; that it belongs to all common circumstances, ordinary interests, actual business. The Church is to tell men, that if God was a Redeemer of old, He is a Redeemer now; that if He was the Judge of kings, priests, nobles, in old times,—if He called them to account for their cruelties, punished them for their superstitions, reproved them for their exactions,— He does so still. The Church is to tell men, that if God in other days took cognizance of the bag of deceitful weights and of the sins of the employer who kept back by fraud the wages of the labourer, He does so still. The Church is to teach men, that society exists for the sake of the human beings who compose it, not to further the accumulation of the capital, which is only one of its instruments. The Church is to declare, that any civilization which is not based upon this godly principle, will come utterly to nought; that all the real blessings which have flowed from it, have proceeded from the acknowledgment of this principle; all the curses which have accompanied the growth of wealth and luxury, from the forgetfulness of it. The Church is to declare, that the spiritual and eternal kingdom which God has prepared for them that love Him, is about men now, and that they may enter into it; and that His government of this spiritual and eternal world does not make Him less interested for the earth which He has formed for the habitation of man, in which He watches over him and blesses him, and which He desires that he should till and subdue, according to the command which He gave him on the creation-day.

To bring these truths practically home to the minds

and hearts of human beings, is, it seems to me, the great function of a Church. And this function, I believe, the Church of England has in some respects a special call to perform, and can, if she will, perform most effectually. For the very causes which lead to some of her greatest dangers, are signs to her of the work which God means her to do, and which, if she trusts in Him, He will enable her to do. The religious men, and the irreligious men too, of her own community, complain of her as earthly and secular. She is in most imminent danger of becoming all that they accuse her of being. She has stooped to rank and wealth, and trampled upon the poor; she often does so now. She has fancied that her strength lay in her revenues; she is still beset every day and hour with that temptation. But, on the other hand, every circumstance in her position teaches her that she is not merely to be a preacher about the world to come; that she is to be a witness for God's righteous dominion over the world that is. The relations with the State which Romanists and Protestant Dissenters taunt her with, are relations of infinite peril, of infinite responsibility. She has abused them to immoral purposes. She is bound to use them for the most glorious and holy purposes. She is bound to feel that she is set in high places, and has a voice to reach all classes of society, not that she may utter cant phrases about religion and the Church, in the ears of those who think that these phrases signify the maintenance of their possessions, by what are called 'religious sanctions;' not to preach servility to the lower classes;

but to tell all by words and acts, that they are members of one body; that they exist in their different relations as servants one of another, in His immediate presence, under His awful eye, who became the servant of all. and died for all.

This is a function which a 'religious world' can never discharge, never even tries to discharge. A religious world is a society by itself, witnessing for itself, for its own privileges, for its difference from the rest of mankind. It acknowledges no vocation from God; it has no living connexion with the past; it is subject to all the accidents and mutations of public opinion. Yet it has no hold upon human life in any of its forms. It treats politics, science, literature, as secular; but it dabbles with them, pretends to reform them by mixing a few cant phrases with them, is really affected by all the worst habits which the most vulgar and frivolous pursuit of them engenders. It trembles at every social movement, at every thought which is awakened in human hearts, at every discovery which is made in the world without. But it does not tremble at its own corruptions. It can see its members indifferent to all the precepts of the Bible in their daily occupations as shopkeepers, employers, citizens; yet if they put the Bible on their banners, and shout about the authority of the inspired book at public meetings, it asks no more; it boasts that we are 'sound at heart;' it congratulates itself that spirituality is diffusing itself throughout the land. Meantime, each of its sections has its own Bible. The newspaper or magazine, which keeps that section in conceit with itself, and in hatred of others, is to all intents and purposes its divine oracle, the rule of its faith, the guide of its conduct. For this religious world is an aggregate of sections, a collection of opinions about God and about man; no witness that there is a living God, or that He cares for men. Its faith is essentially exclusive, and so is its charity; for though it devises a multitude of contrivances for relieving the wants of human beings, nearly all these seem to proceed upon the principle, that they are creatures of another race, on behalf of whom religious people are to exercise their graces; not creatures who have that nature which Christ took, as much sharers in all the benefits of His incarnation and sacrifice, as their benefactors * are.

There has been a consciousness for many years past among the members of the English Church, that they are not meant to be mere portions of a religious world; that they utterly belie their high vocation, when they act as if they were. 'We must be churchmen,' we have said; 'we must claim a calling from God, and 'a connexion with the past; we cannot acknowledge 'ourselves to be mere nominees of the civil power; we 'cannot admit that we have merely formed a set of 'opinions, or established a certain fellowship, for our-'selves.' But in the endeavour to escape from this position, and to find a more safe and tenable one, we have, I fear, shown how much the low notions

---

* 'And He said unto them, The kings of the Gentiles exercise lordship over them, and they that exercise authority upon them are called benefactors. *But ye shall not be so.*' Luke xxii. 25, 26.

and habits of a religious world are cleaving to us. Trying to be something more than a sect, we have exhibited much of the narrowness of a sect; nay, those who exult in what they call their feelings of brotherhood to all Christian people, have been able to represent us as narrow and exclusive beyond all others. So far as I can see, the English Church must either lose itself in the mass of sects, and perish when the sentence, of which there are so many precursory tokens, so many trumpets of warning, goes forth for their destruction; or else must sink into a portion of the popedom,—and bring down upon itself a portion of that judgment which miserable sufferers in the dens of Naples and Rome join with the saints beneath the altar, in invoking against a power which has usurped the name of Christ, and counterfeited the government of the Father, for the support and propagation of fraud and cruelty,—a power which no visitations of God have been able to teach wisdom and righteousness; unless we believe that our peculiar standing ground has only been given us, that we may be witnesses of God's blessings to mankind, that we may claim the members of all sects as portions of God's great family, that we may bring the members of all churches to understand, that when they lose their Pope, they only exchange a reality for a phantom, the government of a present High Priest and King for that of an usurping vicar.

But when we speak of a church taking up a position, what do we mean? Must we wait till the English Church recovers what we hear so much about in newspapers, its 'synodical action?' That will come, I doubt not, when it is good for us. May God prevent it from coming a moment before! Are we to wait for some decrees or decisions of the rulers of the Church? Thank God for the mercy which has made those decrees so few, which has hindered our bishops from pronouncing judgments in deference to public opinion, or in conformity with the wishes of any faction! So the Church has been prevented from sinking into a sect, so its ministers have been obliged to learn, in spite of themselves, that when God brings them into a church, He becomes their teacher; He provides them with the means of learning His will and doing it; He gives them a living lore, for which the dead lore of decrees never can be a substitute; which it may crush and stifle. Thus they are taught that when God brings them into a church, He wishes them not to shut out the light which is pouring in on all sides, from members of partial sects, from artists, from scientific men, from political experience, from the conflicts and contradictions of the time; but that all these are their lesson-books, which His great lesson-book may enable them to understand, to appropriate, to harmonize. Thus they are forced to learn that their business is not to seek for themselves a quiet regulated atmosphere, where they may be safe from the intrusion of perplexities, where no wind of heaven may visit their faces too roughly; but that their place is in the dusty highway of the world, or on the open sea; that they are to be exempt from no vulgar interests or temptations to which others are exposed;

that they are to be acquainted with all shoals and tempests, since only by such experience can they understand the might of a present God, or be fit to deliver His gospel to men. I am sure that we have not too many of what are called the difficulties and dangers of our time; that it is cowardly and ignominious to wish them less; that in doing so, we wish that God had robbed us of some of the instruments which He has given us for knowing His mind, and entering into the sense of His revelation.

Therefore, I say, that every minister of our Church is bound for himself, without waiting for any further guidance than he has, though thankful for all, to consider how he may take up that position which he would wish to see the whole Church taking up. If he thinks that the Church has a message for mankind, he is to try, let his lips be ever so stammering, to deliver that message. If he thinks that the Church ought to meet men as men,—not according to their rank or social privileges, not according to the degree or measure of their faith, not according to the nature of their opinions,—but of whom Christ is the Lord, whether they acknowledge Him as such or not, for whom Christ died, whether they feed upon His sacrifice or not, for whom He lives to make intercession, whether they draw nigh to the Father of all through Him or not;— then, he is bound, so far as in him lies, to meet them in that way and on that ground: insisting upon no punctilios, asking for no deference, claiming no acknowledgment of powers but such as he claims for himself by the words which he utters, or the acts which he does. If he thinks that the Church is bound to deal with all the common conditions of human society for the sake of bringing them into conformity with God's law, he must endeavour individually to take that course. If he thinks that the Church should acknowledge obligations to all that are most hostile to it, he should gladly confess when he has received a benefit from any, should be ready to sit at the feet of any, but should feel at the same time that he has the power as a Churchman of returning the obligation, and that this is the very highest privilege God can confer upon him.

The reader of these Sermons will perceive that I have come to the study of the Old Testament with no philological lore; with no belief that I have any new interpretations to offer of its history; with the conviction that the most commonplace view of that history is the truest. I believe that philology is of unspeakable value, and should be applied manfully to Scripture. But I believe also, that the experience of life and of our own wants furnishes an organon for this investigation, more precious than the largest critical apparatus can ever be. I am satisfied that my clerical brethren who have no greater resources of learning than I have, will one and all be rewarded if they approach the Scripture in the spirit in which the Church teaches them to approach it, asking the great Teacher who has provided it for our use, to clear their minds of preconceptions and anticipations, and to let them feel what the blessing is of having a common book to correct their narrow, individual judgments, to raise them into the apprehension of permanent and universal truths.

In asserting this as the privilege and the duty of English Churchmen, I am not, consciously at least, interfering with the rights, or duties, or powers of any other men whatsoever. A great portion of the Latin Church believes us to be heretics, utterly incapable of interpreting God's Word, and of understanding it. Well! If they have the key of knowledge, let them use it. If they have lights which we do not possess, let those lights shine forth that all may see them and be blessed by them. I think I have more faith in the powers which God has endued them with, than they have ever shown that they have themselves. If the Pope and the Cardinals would teach us what a righteous government upon earth is, I have no doubt that they would be wonderful interpreters of Scripture. If they exhibit no such divine order, but one most contrary to it, I believe that God will some day open the eyes of the Latin Clergy to see that fact, and that the Bible will be their helper in the work of reformation, as much as it was the helper of the Teutonic Clergy and Laity in the sixteenth century. I believe that many portions of the Scriptures which were dark to the students of that time will be clear to them; just because they are occupied with problems with which those men were not so consciously occupied, and therefore they will be able better to receive the solutions.

So again the German Protestants despise us as

ignorant, antiquated, uncritical. I do not ask them to withdraw those censures. Let them be as learned, modern, critical as they please! But they have found, in the course of the last two or three years, that Germany has a political existence as well as a school existence, and that there are certain very complicated social knots which neither schoolmen nor statesmen can untie. Surely it could not grieve the countrymen of Luther if the book which in his hands became the asserter of their national existence,—which determined their national language,—should prove the instrument of scattering clouds, which the rage of mobs, and the theories of sovereigns, have seemed only to make thicker.

Our own Dissenters say, that *we* can only look at the Bible through the mist of old traditions. *They* maintain its absolute, undivided authority. Be it so. Then I trust, that when they have done all that they think necessary in the work of denunciation, they will apply themselves manfully to the work of study. Let them set before us the meaning of those records which they believe are so full of meaning; let them confound the narrow views which we have formed of them. I have found my own views most narrow and imperfect; I have wished to be delivered from them, and to be enabled to see the thing as it is; not distorted by the qualities of the medium through which I look at it. I am not so well acquainted as many are with the traditions of the past; the notions of the present —the impressons which one receives from the current religious literature, from the popular religious dialect, —have been greater impediments to me in the search for the living and literal sense of Scripture, than any other influences whatsoever, always excepting the influence of my own self-conceit and presumption. The forms of my Church have seemed to me useful in getting rid of both these hindrances; therefore I have prized them. I do not ask or expect the Dissenter to prize them, or to use them for this purpose. Let him hold fast his own maxim— let him determine to learn from the Bible only. If he does so faithfully, I am sure it will teach him. And if he succeeds in breaking more fetters from the hearts and consciences of men than I have been able to break, he will be acting more in the spirit of my Church, and be carrying out its lessons better than I have done.

Lastly, the liberal teachers of our day say, that a written revelation is itself an imposition upon men's minds, which they have endured long, and must now shake off. The revelation of Nature is what they want. 'Let that be laid open to men fully and broadly; there 'will be no more fear of the priest; his occupation 'will be gone.' Yes, let that be tried. Open this revelation of Nature as fully as you can; let every artist, every scientific man, feel that it is his business and duty to translate, and, if he thinks fit, to illuminate its pages. Let them say, one and all, that these pages are meant for the poor and ignorant to read in; that the beauties and glories of the outward creation, as well as its secret depths, are intended not for connoisseurs and men of leisure, but for the toilers and sufferers of the earth. Let such words be spoken, and let acts be done in conformity with them. And then it will be seen, whether men can be satisfied with *this* revelation, glorious as it is; whether they will not *demand* another; whether they will not be miserable slaves, incapable of enjoying the good things which God has provided for their eyes and ears, the victims of every impostor, of every new superstition, unless they know what they themselves are, whence they came, whither they are going, whether He who made them wishes them to dwell in hopeless bondage, or to be the citizens of a divine kingdom.

October, 1851.

SERMON I.

THE CREATION OF MANKIND, AND OF THE FIRST MAN.

(Lincoln's Inn, Septuagesima Sunday.—Feb. 16, 1851.)

Lessons for the day, Genesis I. and II

GENESIS II. 1.

Thus the heavens and the earth were finished, and all the host of them.

ON Septuagesima Sunday we begin the Old Testament. I propose, if God permit, to take the subjects in order which the first Lessons for the Morning and Evening bring before us.

To-day the subject is *Creation*. I have chosen my text from a verse which speaks of Creation, not in progress, but as completed. I have done so advisedly, not because I wish to evade the questions which are suggested by the previous chapter, but because I believe we shall understand them better, if we examine them by the light which is thrown upon them from this.

When does the Historian say, '*that the heavens and the earth were finished, and all the host of them?*' The last paragraph of the former chapter leaves us in no doubt. The heavens and the earth were finished when '*God created man in His own image.*' Then the Universe was that which He designed it to be; then he could look, not upon a portion of it, but upon the whole of it, and say, *It is very good.*' Then it was a unity: such a unity as was implied in the existence of light and a firmament, a productive earth, a sun and moon, fishes, birds, beasts of the field; such a unity as none of these separately, nor all of them together, could constitute. They find their meaning and interpretation in Man; as man finds his meaning and interpretation in GOD.

If we start from any other principle than this, we may talk very learnedly about the cosmogony of Moses; we may attack it as unscientific, or defend it as divine; but we shall never know of what we are complaining, or for what we are apologizing. The principle, as I hope to show you hereafter, goes through the Bible; its records are incoherent if you do not recognise it; just so far as you do, they come into harmony with each other. If any one strives to speculate upon the different days of Creation, or the works which are said to be done in them, without referring them all to this final day and final work, and without referring that to the seventh day and the divine rest, he may construct a very ingenious theory, or a number of ingenious theories; but his thoughts will only have the most remote and accidental connexion with the book of Genesis or the Bible.

Now, supposing this to be the case, we ought to derive our idea of Creation,—at least we ought to determine what is the idea of Creation in the first chapter of the book of Genesis,—from what we are told respecting the creation of man. First of all, '*God made man in His own image; male and female created He them;*' afterwards it is said He made '*A man out of the dust of the ground, and breathed into his nostrils the breath of life.*' If we follow the letter of these passages and do not endeavour to put any notions of our own into them, we shall be led, I think, naturally to the conclusion, that the former words have to do with the *Species*, as we should say, if we must have logical phrases (which I would rather avoid if it were possible); and that the other has to do with an *individual*, with the first man of the race. This, I think, is the inference that we should all draw, if the mere words were set before us without any context: it gains strength the more we study the context. The two accounts are distinct, as all readers have perceived; the obvious difference between them has suggested a number of schemes to account for their introduction into the same narrative. One, it seems to me, is quite necessary to the other. If we had the first without the second, we should have the description of an ideal man, without being told that there was an actual man. If we had merely the second, we should have the history of the appearance of a solitary creature in the universe, without knowing what he was, or why he was put there, or what relation he bore to all the things about him. But what I wish you particularly to notice is, that the part of the record which speaks of man ideally, according to his place with reference to the rest of the universe, according to his position with reference to God, is the part which expressly belongs to the history of CREATION; that the bringing forth of man in *this* sense is the work of the sixth day.

You will perceive the necessity of this interpretation the more steadily you look at the words, ' *God created man in His own image, in the image of God created he him; male and female created he them.*' The difficulty in this sentence consists in the change from the singular to the plural. Now, if you try to express for yourself the formation of an Order, of a Race, and at the same time seek to convey the impression that the order or race were to be composed of real beings, you *must* drop into some language of this sort; you must involve yourself in this seeming contradiction. You may fancy that you escape from it by resorting to the phrases of the Realists, and affirming the species to have an existence apart from the individual. You may escape from it by adopting the phrases of the Nominalists, and saying, that the man is nothing but the single, separate atom, which you denote by a particular name. But if you wish to talk in the language of fact, and not in mere dialectical terms; if you wish to satisfy the conscience of mankind, and to express that which we know to be,—whether we can define it or not,—you must speak as Moses speaks; you must have the '*him*' and the '*them;*' that word which declares that the male and female are both comprehended in humanity; that word which declares that humanity equally implies their distinct individual existence. I do not like meddling with abstractions, so much as I have felt myself obliged to do, in order to show you how Moses has avoided abstractions; how he has risen above them. He has risen above them, I conceive, because he has contemplated the creation of man not from our point of view, but from God's. He has told us what man was in His mind; and how He brought forth the purpose and intent of His mind into act. If it is said that an invisible being created 'man in His own likeness,' *that* cannot mean that He invested him with something visible. He may have done so: we are told afterwards that He did; but this cannot have been the special, essential, act of Creation. Again, if we are told that a real Living Being, —the source of all being and all life,—created 'man in His own image;' *that* cannot mean that He created a mere phantom, without substance, without life. The Creation, in this highest sense, must mean the bestowing, under whatever limitations, a portion of His own life, that which corresponded to His own being. It must denote, therefore, in this its highest acceptation, not what we understand by putting together a material thing, but the communication of that inward power and substance, without which matter is but a dream,—apart from which we only conceive it as possible, because we have learnt, by terrible experience, the possibility of death.

Now, extend this thought, which seems to arise inevitably out of the story of the creation of *Man* as Moses delivers it, to the rest of that universe of which he regards man as the climax, and we are forced to the conclusion, that in the one case, as in the other, it is not the visible material thing of which the historian is speaking, but of that which lies below the visible material thing, and constitutes the substance which it shows forth.

We are told in the second chapter of '*a mist going up from the earth, and watering the face of the ground.*' It is clearly intimated that *then*, and not till then, did the plants and the herbs of the field appear. It is said at the same time, '*that the Lord God* HAD *created every plant of the field* BEFORE *it was in the earth, and every herb of the field* BEFORE *it grew.*' We are compelled then to consider the creation of herbs and flowers as well as the creation of beasts, and birds, and fishes, which is recorded in the previous chapter, as the bringing forth of kinds and orders such as they are according to the mind of God, not of actual separate phenomenal existences, such as they present themselves to the senses of man. The language of the historian is most strictly in accordance with this interpretation, '*Let the earth bring forth grass, the herb yielding seed, and the fruit-tree yielding fruit after its* KIND, *whose seed is in itself, upon the earth.*' Again, '*And God created great whales, and every living creature that moveth, which the waters brought forth abundantly, after their* KIND.' Again, '*Let the earth bring forth the living creature after his* KIND, *cattle and creeping thing, and beast of the earth after his* KIND.'

Perhaps the thought may occur to you, 'Yes! it is very
' true that we are told of a word going forth from God,
' saying, Let this be so; *that* may merely indicate the
' process in the Divine mind. But have we not the addi-
' tional sentence, *It was so;* and are we not reminded that
' the earth *brought forth* grass, &c.? Must not we take
' these sentences into account as much as the other? and if
' we do, shall we not arrive, after all, at the merely material
' notion of creation?' I am far indeed from wishing to overlook these passages, or from fancying that we can understand the others without them. But if you once admit that the going forth of God's Word,—the expression of his Will and Mind *is* Creation, these sentences which announce that His word was not an idle ineffective word, that what He purposed came to pass, will carry a very different force indeed, from that which we attribute to them when we start from a consideration of the things themselves. For the passages which say that the earth brought forth grass and fruits, are passages which, if you take them literally, must point not to a single moment, but to the whole life of the world down to the present hour. When a chair or a table leaves the hands of the carpenter, it passes into the hands of the person for whom it is made;

CREATION INVOLVES PRODUCTION.

the workman has no more concern with it. But when you hear of the earth bringing forth grass, the herb yielding seed, the fishes or beasts being fruitful and multiplying, you are told of living powers which were imparted once, but which are in continual exercise and manifestation; the Creative Word has been uttered once; the Creative Word is never for a moment suspended; never ceases to fulfil its own proclamation. That this was the belief of Moses I shall not stop to prove. I should have to quote half the Pentateuch if I did; the idea is worked into the whole tissue of his faith, and comes out in every phrase he uses; in subsequent discourses, I shall have to remind you of it continually. What seems most strange is, that this truth should have been practically so much forgotten by readers of the first chapter of Genesis; that they should have supposed the heavens and earth were finished and the host of them, in the same manner as any ordinary work of human hands in which there is no life, no productive power, is finished; whereas Moses speaks of that life and those productive powers as called forth, that they might work on from generation to generation under God's government.

This mistake has, I believe, originated in our reluctance to acknowledge the meaning which the sacred historian gives to the week of seven days. Some persons, I need not tell you, have supposed that they could only reconcile the Mosaic story with modern Geology, by supposing each day to mean a thousand years. But when they brought themselves to think that the Scripture language was pliable enough to endure an outrage which would have been intolerable in any other book, geologists would not be tied down by such a rule; their discoveries and speculations would not be limited within the terms which a purely arbitrary criticism had assigned, as the possible duration of the materials whereof our globe consists. The honesty of Scripture interpretation, as much as the honesty of Science, owes them thanks that they would not; if they had, humble men must have felt that the words of the Bible might mean anything, everything, or nothing; those who believe that there is in them spirit and life, must have submittted to see them tortured into a materialism, against which they bear the most deliberate and consistent protest.

No one will say that a literal construction of the first chapter of Genesis would lead to the notion, that the order of the week is an order determined by the Sun or the Moon. The most plausible and popular objection to the Mosaic history is, that it affirms the Sun and Moon to have been created on the fourth day. Then first we hear of signs, and seasons, and years; then we are told, that the day and night were to be divided by the lights in the heavens. Hence we are obliged to suppose that the week had an import in the mind of the historian, altogether distinct from that which he gave to the ordinary measures of time. The Jew had been told in his commandments, that it was to remind him of God's work and his own work; of God's rest and his own rest. It was to bring before him the fact of his relation to God, of his being made in the image of God; it was to teach him to regard the universe not chiefly as under the government of Sun or Moon, or as regulated by their courses; but as an order which the unseen God had created; which included Sun, Moon, Stars, Earth, and all the living creatures that inhabit them.

The week, then, was especially to raise the Jew above the thought of Time, to make him feel that though he was subject to *its* laws, he yet stood in direct connexion with an *eternal* law; with a Being, '*who is, and was, and is to come.*' The more faithfully he acted out the command, to work and rest, and connected it with the whole course and meaning of his own life, and the life of his fellows, the less would the external Universe be an oppression and burden to him; the more would he enter into an apprehension of its order; the more would he be sure that it was not his master. When then the great Lawgiver taught him to associate the different days of this week with different steps or stages in the creation of the world, he certainly never intended him to introduce those very notions into the history from which the commandment was to preserve him. He was not to thrust in narrow and idolatrous fancies, derived from the Egyptian astronomy, into his thoughts of the divine order; he *was* to acknowledge days and months and years as connected with the heavenly bodies; he was *not* to feel that the divine Word which had given them their place and their bounds was limited by them, or that the creature of whom it had been said, '*Let us make him in Our likeness*,' was limited by them. The more he meditated on the clear simple view of the Order of the Universe, as it unfolded itself in the mind of the divine Artist, and as it was set forth to man in his week of seven days,—the more would he be delivered from that worship of visible things to which all people on the earth were prone; the more manly and faithful would be his inquiries respecting that Universe, before which he did not tremble, which he might not worship, but which he confessed to be the work of the God of Abraham and Isaac and Jacob; the more certain would be his assurance that the glory of man consists in looking up directly to Him;

in beholding Him in His own proper nature, not through dim reflections or earthly images.

I apprehend, brethren, that the real earnest study of the Mosaic history of the Creation may serve just the same purpose to us, which I have said that it might have served to the Jews. We know very well, that it was not effectual in delivering them from material idolatry; what document, however precious, ever was? It was never intended to exercise any charm or power of its own; it *was* intended to lead them to God, who had declared Himself to be their deliverer, who could break every chain from off their necks. If, instead of seeking Him, they sought only the book which spoke of Him, it might be a new bondage to them; it might itself become one of the barriers between them and Him. But the fault lay in themselves, not in it. And I believe the fault lies in us, not in it, that after so many centuries, during which we have been familiar with the phrases and sentences of it, we are still groping for the sense of it; often putting it forward as if it were in opposition to truths which God has revealed to those who have honestly studied His Universe; continually making it a plea for idolatries, which we bring with us to the study of it. This is an error against which we have especial need to watch. Scientific men often say to us, 'You must find 'out some new interpretation of your book; you must get 'rid of the mere letter of it, otherwise you will be in 'continual conflict with our facts.' I am convinced the directly opposite assertion is true. If we had been less busy with our interpretations, if we had studied the letter of the book more faithfully, we should very rarely indeed have come into any conflict with them; we should have felt no suspicion of them; we should have believed that even their doubts and suggestions, when they were far removed from proofs, and might soon be confuted by new evidence, were yet to be heartily welcomed as helpful towards the discovery or elucidation of truth. But our minds being filled, —as the minds of all people in this world are, whether they call themselves religious, scientific, or by any other name,—with a great many crude materialistic, idolatrous notions, we have not brought them to be corrected and cured by that teaching which we acknowledge to be the highest, the purest, the most spiritual; but we have insisted that these first, so-called natural, impressions of ours *must* contain the sense of Scripture. We exclaim, ' This is the obvious meaning of the book. There may be ' some highflown conceit about it, no doubt, but all plain ' people must think of it as we do.' I have seldom known a person use language of this kind, who had the least right to put himself forward as representing the common sense or conscience of mankind; who did not show by many infallible tokens that he had been bred in a very artificial school, and that he had taken no pains whatever to clear himself of the habits of it, in order that he might come with an open free mind to receive the lessons of God's word. A divine author, we say, must be simple. Are we sure that His simplicity is not the great obstacle to the discovery of His meaning, by those who will spend no pains in seeking for it, who fancy that hasty and impatient conclusions which would be intolerable in the readers of another book, are reverent in the readers of this?

Scriptural readers and commentators have insisted that the Mosaic history of Creation shall be the history of the formation of the material earth, though there is not a single sentence in which the slightest allusion is made to that formation. They have insisted that the week must refer to time as measured by the sun, though distinct words and the whole context of the discourse negative such a supposition. Now these are precisely the notions which set the record at variance with the conclusions of physical science. A geologist may not feel that he has any interest in getting rid of such notions, for he can pursue his inquiries without caring whether they clash with this book or no. But *we* have the greatest interest in getting rid of them,—not in order to make peace with science, not even in order to assert the letter of Scripture, though both these objects are highly important,—but because, as long as these conceptions last, we cannot enter into that idea of Creation which the Scripture is in every page bringing out before us; because we cannot feel the beauty of that order of the Universe which Moses was permitted to reveal to us; because we shall be continually subjecting both the facts of the material world and the laws of the spiritual world to a hard and dry theory of ours, instead of rising gradually, by calm and humble investigations of nature and of God's word, to an apprehension of them and Him. And do not suppose that it is only now, in this 19th century, through the influence of civilization and scientific inquiry, that divines have been led to feel the mischief which may result from the rashness of interpreters of Scripture and apologists for Scripture, who set themselves in opposition to physical discoveries, even to physical speculations. 'It is a very disgraceful 'and pernicious thing, and one greatly to be watched 'against,' says Augustine, 'that any infidel should hear a 'Christian talking wild nonsense about the earth and the 'heaven, about the motions and magnitude and intervals 'of the stars, the courses of years and times, the natures of

'animals, stones, and other matters of the same kind, pre-
'tending that he has the authority of the Scriptures on his
'side. The other who understands these things from reason
'or experience, seeing that the Christian is utterly ignorant
'of the subject, that he is wide of the mark by a whole
'heaven, cannot refrain from laughter. What pain and
'sorrow these rash dogmatists cause to their wiser brethren,
'can scarcely be told; who, if they have been convicted of
'a foolish and false opinion by those who do not acknow-
'ledge the authority of our books, straightway produce
'these same sacred books, in proof of that which they have
'advanced with the most light-minded rashness and open
'falseness; nay, even quote from memory many words
'which they think will help out their case, understanding
'neither what they say, nor whereof they affirm.'

So spoke one of the most devout, reverential, and at the same time most courageous, expositors the Church has ever had, in his Commentary on the Book of Genesis according to the Letter. His words are strictly and minutely applicable to the present day. Only that the pride and sin of setting the language of Scripture against the investigation of Nature, is a thousand times greater, when that investigation proceeds, not, as it did in his day, upon rash anticipations; but upon careful induction of particulars, and that the injury which is done to Scripture by such courses, is not merely or chiefly the laughter which they excite in others; but the contemptuous, self-exalting assurance which they nourish in the minds of those who indulge in them,—an assurance that hinders them from attaining the faith of little children, as well as from rising to the intellectual stature of men.

There is one point to which I would allude, before I quit

this subject. You may think that if geological facts are not interfered with by this narrative, yet that it does, by its fundamental maxim as I have laid it down, interfere with the great astronomical principle which Newton affirmed and demonstrated. If Man is the highest object in the divine order, is it not most natural that he should look upon the earth as the centre round which all the heavenly bodies are revolving? And does not the record of the fourth day's work seem to affirm, that the sun and moon and stars exist to give light to our planet? Unquestionably this was a most natural conclusion for man to adopt. That he did adopt it everywhere is the proof *how* natural it was. But would you get rid of this natural tendency, by denying the plain fact, to which every one's senses give testimony, that the sun and moon *do* perform ministeries for this earth, and that the whole economy of our earth is affected by those ministeries? Or would you get rid of it, by denying the fact of which the human conscience testifies as strongly, that a creature endued with a will and a reason must be higher than all the things which his senses contemplate, which his mind can conceive of, that have *not* a will and a reason? Did any one ever free himself from the delusion that the earth was the centre of the universe, by either of these methods? Did any speculations about the sun or the moon, any reverence for them, any worship of them, destroy this delusion? Were not all these means of strengthening and deepening it in him? And how then can he, consistently with an acknowledgment of plain facts, consistently with the sense of the dignity and glory which has been put upon him, rise to the conviction, that neither the earth, nor he himself, can be looked upon as giving the law and order to Creation?

I answer, he will rise to this conviction, if he can be taught that he only realizes his own glory when he beholds it in God; if he can be taught that there are other creatures besides himself who share that distinction,—which separates him from all mere sentient and animal existences; if he can be taught upon whom it is that they and he and the whole order to which they belong depend. And these are just the lessons which these chapters of the book of Genesis open to us, and which the whole Bible continues more and more clearly to impress upon us. The chapter we have read this afternoon exhibits the first man beginning to exercise that lordship over the animals which God had given to his race; beginning to realize the meaning of the words, 'male and female created He them;' subjected to a restriction which told him that he was not an independent being, but made in the image of another. Next Sunday we shall hear how he trifled with that lordship, submitting to a creature whom he was meant to govern,—how the relation of fellowship was broken,—how he set up independence in place of obedience. As we trace the nature and consequences of that act, we are taught more clearly than any words can teach us, what man becomes when he is a centre to himself, and supposes that all things are revolving around him. But we learn at the same time, by fresh discoveries and revelations, why the words 'the Heavens' have always conveyed to the readers of this book, not merely or chiefly the notion of bright and luminous bodies on which they were to gaze, but much more, of Persons,—of Spirits,—dwelling in unknown regions, with reasons and wills like their own, standing in dutiful subjection to the Creator, or revolting against Him. Such a belief, so far as it was maintained, was a preservative against the disposition to look upon the earth, as if it were the highest and most glorious portion of the universe, though it might be the prize for which two mighty hosts were contending.

But most of all, these chapters prepare us for the announcement of that truth which all the subsequent history is to unfold,—that the Word who said, '*Let there be light,' and there was light*, who separated the firmament from the waste of waters, and made the dry land appear, and placed the sun and moon and stars in their orbits, and called all organised creatures into life, and who is in the highest sense, the light of men,—the source of their Reason, —the guide of their Wills,—is the head of all principalities and powers, the upholder of the whole universe.

It was, brethren, the recognition,—the partial recognition at all events,—of this truth, in the sixteenth century, the acknowledgment that the righteousness which dwells in this Word, is that in which alone man can find his own righteousness, which can alone raise him out of degradation and sin,—it was this which prepared men for the scientific discovery of the seventeenth century,—which enabled them to give up the self-exalting dream, that all surrounding worlds look to the earth as their centre, for the acknowledgment of the strange, seemingly monstrous, mystery. that the ball, which appeared to be intended only for its illumination, was that to which all its movements must be referred. A selfish material religion, which consists only of arrangements to secure our individual felicity hereafter, —a selfish material philosophy, which consists only of arrangements to secure our felicity here,—a selfish spiritual religion or spiritual philosophy, which glorifies man above God, may, sooner than we are aware, rob us of this scientific conviction; or, at least, make it incapable of bearing any newer and riper fruits hereafter.

For the sake then of physical science, it may be necessary that we should study, more earnestly and deeply, that Book which has been thought to contradict it, and yet which has never been hidden without peril to its existence; —has never been simply perused and heartily delighted in, without awakening new and livelier zeal in the pursuit of it. Not for the sake of cultivating such desires however, but for other ends more directly concerning our personal and social life, do I invite you to enter upon this study. I cannot give you an adequate explanation of these or of any chapters in the Bible. I would not if I could. We do not want adequate, self-satisfying explanations. We want to be stirred up to fresh discoveries of our ignorance, to fresh desires for light. I go to the Bible,—I would bid you go to it,—because I feel how much darkness surrounds you and me; because I believe that He, in whom all light dwells, is ready to meet us there; to reveal Himself to us; to guide us onward to the perfect day.

NOTE.

The passage of Augustine referred to in the text will be found in the Commentary *De Genesi ad Litteram*, lib. i. § 39, beginning 'Plerumque enim accidit.' In the previous part of the book the difficulty about 'time' is boldly stated, and the idea of a succession in the divine mind which is the ground of succession in our minds, not dependent upon its conditions is clearly indicated.

SERMON II.

THE FALL AND THE DELUGE.

(Lincoln's Inn. Sexagesima Sunday.—Feb. 23, 1851.*
Lessons for the day, Genesis III. and VI.

GENESIS VI. 5, 6, 7.

And God saw that the wickedness of man was great in the earth, and that every imagination of the thoughts of his heart was only evil continually. And it repented the Lord that he had made man on the earth, and it grieved him at his heart. And the Lord said, I will destroy man whom I have created from the face of the earth; both man, and beast, and the creeping thing, and the fowls of the air; for it repenteth me that I have made them.

THERE can be no doubt that the chapter we have read this afternoon was chosen because it was supposed to illustrate the one we read this morning. Milton makes the Deluge the most prominent object, in the vision by which Adam is instructed respecting the consequences of the Fall. All readers of Scripture have felt that there is a connexion between them, though they might not be able clearly to perceive the nature of it. Perhaps if we consider what it is, we may gain some light respecting the meaning of the first event as well as of the second.

'*God saw that the thoughts of men's hearts were only evil continually.*' He had said before, '*My Spirit shall not always strive with man.*' 'Here,' it will be said, 'we see

'the results of the fall. Adam, created innocent, trans-
' gressed. Hence the evil which had at this time spread so
' widely among his descendants.' I do not say that there
is anything erroneous in this statement, but I think that it
is vague. There are expressions in it, which are capable
of very different significations: some of them may be more
or less in accordance with the teaching of Scripture; some
may be quite at variance with it. I believe we must
ascertain the force of the words we use before we can be at
all sure that we are not, under seemly and orthodox phrases,
admitting serious practical heresies into our minds.

When we say that God made man *innocent*, what do we
mean? The sense often affixed to that language is this:
' that God gave to Adam, the first man, a certain inde-
' pendent power, an innocence of his own, which he parted
' with by eating the fruit of the tree of the knowledge of
' good and evil; that man fell when he lost this independent
' virtue, this innocency of his own; that as the first father
' lost it, all his descendants by the decree of God, or by
' some necessity of their relationship, lost it too; that
' thence arose the need for Divine Grace, and for men
' being made partakers of a righteousness which is not
' their own.'

Now I apprehend that the Scripture narrative, if we
follow it closely, not only affords no warrant for this
statement, but directly negatives it. So far from saying
that God endowed man with an independent righteousness,
with an innocency of his own, it tells us that God said,
' Let us make man in *our* image, after *our* likeness.'
Such words absolutely exclude the idea that man according
to his original constitution, possessed *any thing* of his own.
They affirm him to be good only in so far as he reflects

that which exists perfectly in another, so far only as he confesses Him to be *the* Good. Personal, self-existing righteousness is not only not imparted to him by the law of his creation; it is denied to him. God did not look upon the order He had made, and lo! it was very good— because each creature was standing in its own separate excellence—because the highest creature of all held that excellence in its fullest measure. He pronounced it very good because *no* creature was standing in itself; because each was formed according to its kind in relation to every other; because the highest creature, that to which all the others looked up, and in which they saw their own perfection, himself looked up to his Maker, and saw his perfection in Him.

We must thoroughly satisfy ourselves, that this is what the Scripture affirms of man; or all the after records will become a weary maze to us. If we take this principle with us, I do not think we shall wish to put anything into Scripture that we do not find there, or to take anything from it which we do find. There may be much which we do not understand, much which perplexes our understandings. I do not think there will be anything which outrages our consciences, anything which the higher spirit within us shrinks from recognising.

That divine order for man as the member of a race, as part of an order, which we read of in the first chapter of the book of Genesis, being laid down for him, we heard how a *certain* man was placed in a *certain* garden, surrounded by a certain number of trees and animals. Of the fruit of the trees he is to partake, all except one. Of the fruit of that tree he must not eat; in the day that he eats of it, he will die. He gives names to the creatures which are about him. A help-meet is needed for him. A portion of himself is taken from him, and becomes a woman. She is bone of his bone, and flesh of his flesh. They are naked and are not ashamed.

This is all that we are told of that first man and woman in their first condition. We may add what we please out of our fancies about their transcendent knowledge, or their seraphic virtues. Nothing of it is to be found in the Bible. No hint of any vast endowments, or wide-reaching thoughts, or great projects. Everything is simple, childlike, just as you would expect it to be. People wearied themselves in former days to find out where the garden was; what actual country was bounded by the four rivers mentioned in the narrative. They could arrive at no conclusion. Then they fell into mystical conceits. They supposed the rivers must be anything but rivers, that the garden must be anything but a garden. From the mystical, the transition was easy to the mythical. The whole was set down as a wonderful dream of later ages, about an imaginary golden age. Whereas if you look fairly at the record, there is no golden age at all; nothing but the simplest and most natural description,—the most natural and simple you can conceive, at least if you adopt the belief which a very large body of physiologers, not believers in the Bible, resolutely maintain, that we are all descended from one pair.

Why have we failed to perceive this simplicity? Whence has arisen the temptation to substitute theories and speculations for it? The cause is in the subject of the next chapter. We cannot persuade ourselves that the entrance of Sin into the world, can be anything but the most wonderful of all facts. If that chapter contains the history of its introduction, it must contain the most deep and awful metaphysics. Our consciences and hearts cannot be satisfied except we find them. Most undoubtedly I believe the deepest and most awful metaphysics are there. It is impossible that a creature who has a reason and a will, can ever do anything which does not involve an unutterable mystery, anything which is not either done in conformity with a law higher than that which keeps the planets in their courses, or else in transgression of it.

I can imagine nothing less strange, less prodigious, than the act of a woman taking the fruit of a tree and eating it, and giving it to her husband to eat. The question is, what did that act signify? What did it indicate as to the inner mind, the essential being of the persons who were concerned in it? You answer, 'they were innocent before, 'and they ceased to be innocent then.' True. And if it was further demanded, 'In what did the *innocence* which 'they previously had, consist? In what did the guilt 'which they now contracted, consist?' you would not hesitate to answer: 'They were *obedient* before. They 'were *disobedient* now.' To change the phrase, but not the sense: 'They were acting as dependent creatures before. 'They did an act which asserted independence now. They 'claimed to be something which they were not. They 'refused to be that which they were.' I need not remind you that this is no gloss of mine upon the Scriptures. The express language ascribed to the tempter is, '*Ye shall be as Gods knowing good and evil.*' Part of the pleasure of the act lay in the taste of the fruit; part of it, and the deepest part, lay in the assertion of independence, in showing that they could do what they liked. Every one who has had the least experience of children, understands this mixture of feelings, knows how one passes into the other, what a mighty delight in selfwill lies beneath any forbidden gratification of the natural appetite. Every one verifies the truth of the Scripture narrative, in his own daily history. If our minds were less confused and artificial, we should say at once, 'This *must* be the account of the first trans-'gression in the world. It has a stamp of veracity which 'no intricate analysis of motives ever had, or could possibly 'confer.'

But we shrink from applying this test; because it strikes us that Adam, in his paradisaical state, must have been under a law so different from ours, that to bring our knowledge of ourselves or of others to bear upon the subject, is scarcely reverent or safe. Now if what I have said respecting the creation of man be true, this opinion cannot be a right one: it must darken our minds both respecting the letter of Scripture and respecting its higher theology. The principle that man was made in the image of God, is not a principle which was true for Adam and false for us. It is the principle upon which the race was constituted and can never cease to be constituted. Adam's sin consisted, if we are to accept the Scripture account, in disbelieving that law, in acting as if he were not under it. He would be a God; he was not content to be in the image of God. His offence consisted in giving up that position of dependence, which some would tell us only became his when he fell. His wrong consisted in setting up that claim to be something in himself;—which they would tell us that he was, so long as he continued right. We cannot too often repeat the words which scarcely any one will deny when he hears them formally uttered, and yet which we continually deny in some of our most popular dogmatic statements, 'Adam stood by obedience, and fell by dis-'obedience. He stood by trust in God, and fell by dis-'trusting Him.' The sin of him and of us therefore, is and must be the same. We have a right to justify the truth of the Scripture narrative, by that which we know of our own temptations and our own falls.

But this is not all. If we admit that the law according to which man was created, was a law laid down for him as belonging to a race, we are able to see his transgression in another aspect. He, the individual man, the Adam made out of the dust of the ground, was setting up himself, was making himself his law. So he was breaking that which was a law of kind, a law of fellowship. The history tells us so. The man first obeys the woman, then complains of her as the author of his fault. Strife between two creatures formed for union, bone of each other's bone, is the consequence of both forgetting their relation to God, and seeking to please themselves. The rest of the story is equally significant. We must not allow Milton, much as we may reverence him even as an interpreter of Scripture, (and we *may* find him very useful in that character if we read him aright)—we must not suffer our own later knowledge,—to confuse us respecting the literal narrative in the third of Genesis. It says that the serpent, a subtle beast of the field, tempted Eve. We are not, because we think ourselves wiser than Moses, to put the Devil in place of the serpent, and say that a beast must mean a Spirit. I fully believe that the Devil did tempt Adam; did tempt our Lord; does tempt us. But I believe that the *knowledge* of this spiritual enemy is one of the special blessings which we owe to the revelation of Him who overcame him. Having that knowledge we are bound to use it,—to think that the temptation of our spirit, of our will, is the deepest and most terrible of all, that without it every other would be ineffectual and contemptible. The apostle had a right to say, every Christian ought to understand and repeat his words, '*We wrestle not with flesh and blood, but with principalities and powers, with the rulers of the darkness of this world, with spiritual wickedness in high places.*' And therefore it was no error in our great poet to affirm, that the first man must have been under a spiritual influence, when his spirit or will went wrong. But if we recognise any order in the divine revelations, we shall not be eager to anticipate a discovery which is to come out by degrees, —and which is only safe, only intelligible, when it is associated with truths that were also to come forth, not at once, but in God's due season,—after He had prepared men to receive them. If we will not suffer the sacred historian to tell his own story in his own way, we shall miss some of the precious lessons which he has to communicate,—and not understand better those which he was not appointed to communicate. What he tells us is, that there was an animal nature in Eve, to which the animal nature in an inferior creature could speak. A most necessary fact in the history of man's evil doing; one that enables us to give another passage in the narrative, which is nearly always explained away, its literal force. '*In the* DAY *that thou eatest of this fruit, thou shalt surely die.*'

The commentators in general seem to think that the serpent was right when he told Eve, that she should *not* surely die, that in fact the threat was not accomplished till 900 years after. I apprehend this question wholly depends upon the meaning which we give to the word *death*. We may insist that it shall mean, the moment when the breath goes out of the body. And then we are disposed to say in like manner, that Life means the time during which the breath stays in the body. But this is not the *popular* use of the words. The common people feel that Life and Death are two powers struggling for them and in them; their superstitions show that they feel so. Nor is it the *scientific* use of the words. Every physiologist, if he is not a materialist —I should almost say, if he is one—must attach a meaning to them which is not dependent upon certain moments of time. And most assuredly this is not the sense of the words in any part of *Scripture*. We read indeed in that pathetic chapter which precedes the lesson for this after noon of one patriarch after another, that '*he lived, and begat sons and daughters, and died.*' Then death was fulfilled in him; then it was seen that death had a dominion over him. But if we ask ourselves how this is made manifest at a certain instant, the answer is, 'At that instant the creature 'loses its connexion with surrounding things; it sinks into 'itself; it becomes a mere separate existence.' That is Death. And therefore in the day Adam ate of the fruit, he died. That day he took his place as a creature formed out of the dust of the ground, as a mere Adam, and not as a creature formed in the image of God. That day the man sank into the animal. The sentence did execute itself immediately, and all the results of the sentence would have executed themselves also, if God's order had been dependent upon man's will, if Adam had been able to say, 'God's dominion over me, and relation to me, shall 'cease, because I wish to be independent. My condition 'as a man shall not remain, because I have chosen to be an 'animal.' But this was not to be. The third chapter of Genesis is not only the history of a fall, but of a restoration; not only of death, but of resurrection. '*The man heard the voice of the Lord God walking in the garden in the cool of the day.*' From that voice he tried to shrink. That voice drew from him the confession of his offence. That voice sentenced him to till the ground from which he was taken; which was cursed for his sake; which should bring forth thorns and thistles to him. It told him that he should at length return to the dust from which he was taken. It told him that the serpent should go upon his belly, and eat the dust. It told him that the seed of the woman should bruise the serpent's head.

Each of us, I think, must, at some time or other, have felt the reality of the first words in this narrative. He must have said within himself, 'Such a voice of an unseen 'being have I heard speaking down in the depths of my 'heart, awakening me to a consciousness of His reality 'and His personality, and of my own.' What I would beseech you is, not to stifle these witnesses to the truth of Scripture by some crude ill-defined thought, that the words must have some different signification from that which our human experience gives to them. They may mean *much more* than that, but assuredly they do mean that; and the more you follow out that meaning, the less will you wish to change the letter of them for some other, which would be far less expressive and simple.

But the words which follow are still more hardly treated, because we will not let the actual facts of the world's history expound them. It has often been supposed that the sentence, '*Cursed be the ground for thy sake*,' is in direct opposition to that famous passage in the Georgics, beginning

Pater ipse colendi
Haud facilem esse viam voluit,

in which the poet represents the hardness of the soil as a blessing, because it calls forth the zeal and skill of the husbandman; a passage which commends itself to our consciences, as no less true than beautiful. But the more you study the words in Genesis, the more you will see that they contain the very root of Virgil's assertion. The ground is cursed *for man's sake;* thorns and thistles it is to bring forth to him on purpose that he may not yield to that slavish self-indulgent nature into which he has fallen; on purpose that he may be led to seek help in tilling the earth and subduing it, and in ruling the inferior creatures, from Him who has sent him into the world, under that law and with that blessing. For man's sake too the serpent is accursed; the intercourse between him and the inferior creatures is not broken, but they are humbled, prevented from making themselves intelligible to him; he has to be reminded continually that with all their strength and subtlety they are animals still, not voluntary spiritual creatures. His own nature too is under a curse, still a curse *for his sake.* For he is not to confess it as his master; if he does he is under a law of death; he is to live by faith in God, that faith being sustained by the hope of a helper and deliverer to come from his own seed.

If this is the history of the first man and the first transgression, are we to call the expulsion from Paradise,—a mere outward Paradise of trees and flowers,—a hard sentence? If it was a punishment, was it not a blessing? If we feel that we are reading a Divine history, a history of God's manifestations of Himself, we shall surely say that it was a movement onwards; for the Divine order has not been interrupted because a man has refused obedience to it;—it is only made more evident by that violation. It is seen to stand, not in the will of a creature, but on some deeper, safer ground, which would be more and more clearly revealed. And since God's order is not destroyed, His purpose that man should be in His own likeness, cannot be destroyed. Man has set up a self-will, has fallen under the dominion of the nature which God had given him. This very act is a step in his education,—a means by which God will teach him more fully what he is, what he is not, what he was meant to be, and what he was not meant to be; how he may thwart the purposes of his Creator, how he may conspire with them.

And now comes in that illustration which, I said, the earlier record, contained in the lesson of this morning, might receive from the later one in the lesson of this afternoon. I have all along spoken of man as created to be one of a kind or species; as yet we have only heard of one man and one woman. Yet the existence of a kind was implied in their existence; their transgression was a sin against a law which recognised them as belonging to a kind. From this time we begin to hear of the propagation of the species. Men are multiplied upon the earth. They have multiplied under that law of blessing which was given to Eve; they have multiplied with the knowledge of that curse which was declared to Adam. The blessing and the curse, the life and the death, were both upon them. Each man might try to be independent of God; to be independent of his fellows; to be an animal. Then would follow the results which this chapter discloses. Violence would cover the earth. Every man would be every man's enemy. For the law under which they had been created, the law of kind, would be forgotten,—that nature which belonged to each man's self would be alone remembered and wor-

shipped. Is it a hard thing to think that there is 'a cor-
'ruption naturally engendered in the offspring of Adam'—
in each individual of that offspring? Hard, undoubtedly,
because facts are hard. The sad tale does not belong to
one history more than to another. Brutal violence, men
corrupting their ways upon the earth,—this is just what
we hear of everywhere. Scripture had nothing new to
tell us about this. But it had a work of its own. It had
to teach us how these facts are compatible with others,—
apparently quite at variance with them, which ordinary
history and our own experience also make known to us.
It had to show, how this natural corruption could co-exist
with a perpetual witness in man's conscience, with a continual strife in his will, against it. And it does this work.
It shows us that man, yielding to his nature, resists the
law which he is created to obey; that man, given up to
himself, has yet God's Spirit striving with him. It shows
us how man in himself can have no good thing, and yet
how much good he may have; because there is One who
is continually raising him out of himself,—imparting to him
that which in his own nature he has not. And it brings
out another fact,—without which even these would not enable us to bear the oppressive proofs of the world's sin and
of our own. It exhibits God as interested in the state of
the race; as carrying on a perpetual course of discipline for
its reformation and restoration. To hear that the thoughts
of men were only evil continually, that their spirits were
bent downward, following low, grovelling, divided objects,
therefore without sympathy or union, hating each other,—
this would be fearful; and yet the earliest and the latest
stories, those which concern the most savage, and those
which concern the most civilized ages, would force the dark

conviction upon us. But what light is shed upon the darkness, even if it brings the darkness into more horrible relief, when we are told, 'GOD *saw* the thoughts of men that they were only evil continually.' They were not cherishing their foul conceptions, pursuing their mad calculations, unwatched, uncared for. There was an eye looking down into their most inward secrets, penetrating the intents of their hearts. And that was the eye of One who desired to make them right within; who had determined that His earth should be purged of its corruptions,—should fulfil all the ends of His creation.

And why could He not make it fulfil them, by a fiat of His omnipotence? Because, brethren, He had made man in his own image; because He had given him a Will; because He could only restore and regenerate him by restoring and regenerating his Will. Hence we have to read all the Bible through, of floods, famines, pestilences, earthquakes, anarchy, tyranny. It is throughout, the history of an actual government,—throughout, the history of an actual education; a government of voluntary creatures to teach them subjection;—an education of voluntary creatures to make them free. And He who carries on this government and education, is seen, the more He makes Himself known to us, to be not a hard despot, but a loving Ruler; with that heart and sympathy in perfection which He requires in His creatures.

If this be so, do you wonder that it is said, '*It repented God that He had made man, and it grieved Him at His heart?*' Do such expressions startle and scandalize you? I am not surprised that they should. I do not entirely wish it were otherwise. For there is a sense in which we dare not attribute repentance to God. His Will cannot change; let other wills set themselves against His as they may. His must remain the absolutely good Will, which from eternity it was. His order cannot be changed or repented of, let men transgress it as they may. It stands firm and unshaken. No other can be substituted for it. But here is our strange contradiction. We can bear to think of God's will being changed, of its being different at one time or another,—according to the well or ill doings of His creatures. We can bear to think of the Fall changing the whole constitution which God had established, and making a new constitution necessary. But we cannot bear to think of a gracious and merciful Being, having that grief at the sight of wrong, at the folly and wilfulness of His creatures,—at their malice against each other, at their indifference to the beautiful world He has given them to dwell in,—which we should think absolutely essential to the character of every loving ruler or loving parent among ourselves. We know that a father,—not because he wanted the affections of a father, but because he had them,—would repent that he had been the instrument of bringing an utterly godless and heartless child into the world. And yet we suppose that there is to be nothing to which this feeling corresponds, in the eternal Archetype. This can only be, because we do not really believe the words upon which all others in Scripture turn; because we do not think that goodness and truth are realities in God; we take them to be names for certain qualities utterly unlike those which we are to exhibit one to another. If it be so, brethren, our morality has no ground to stand upon; it is merely the sport of accident or the result of sin. If these expressions of Scripture are not true expressions, but are only used in accommodation to our habits and notions, Scripture is not that which it professes to be. It is not a revelation of God. It gives us hints respecting Him which we are not to believe,—which it is rather our business to avoid believing; and that too, when events affecting the history of the world are said to have proceeded from these feelings in the Divine Mind,—events which lose all their character and purpose when they are referred to any other origin.

This has surely happened with the story of the Flood. As it is told in Scripture, it is a most memorable part of the history of man, expounding the course of God's dealings with him. He is grieved that He had made man, because men were living wholly at variance with the law under which they were created. He uses the powers of Nature to destroy those who had made themselves the slaves of Nature. The Laws under which He has established the earth become the instruments of its purification, and of the punishment of those who have misused it. A man is found who is perfect in his generation, who trusts in God and does not follow nature. In him the race is preserved, and every kind of creatures. The waters do not overwhelm him. He is divinely taught, how man may float above these waters and make them his servants. All in this record is orderly, consistent, moral. The righteous government which physical things obey,—which man is intended to understand and sympathise with as well as obey,—is vindicated. God's repentance is reconciled with His divine, unchangeable Will. *We*, in speaking of the Deluge, are not content to dwell upon its moral history, upon its connexion with the being of man. We must build great theories upon it relating to the structure of the globe; theories of which the Bible offers no hint, which interfere with the directness and simplicity of its story,—but ye of which it has to bear the disgrace, if science confutes them.

To-day, then, as on last Sunday, I plead for the Scripture itself, against our crude interpretations of it, both in its history of the Fall and of the Deluge. I ask you not to believe that a man was able to frustrate the purposes of God; not to think that the world was created in Adam, or stood in his obedience; for the Scriptures of the New Testament, illustrating those of the Old, teach us that it stood and stands in the obedience of God's well-beloved Son; the real image of the Father, the real bond of human society and of the whole universe, who was to be manifested in the fulness of time, as that which He had always been; who was to exhibit in the sorrow, tears, death of a man, the full grace and truth of which all men, so far as they had trusted in God, had exhibited some tokens and reflections. I ask you not to think,—because Adam could only transmit to his descendants the nature which he had, and because all who lived according to that nature, were *evil continually in the imagination of their hearts,*—that therefore God forgot the work of His own hands, or ever ceased, or ever has ceased, to seek after them and strive with them. I ask you, lastly, not to doubt that there is a true and holy repentance in God, since otherwise there can be no true and holy repentance in us. For though our repentance be *for* sin, yet it cannot spring *from* sin. The holy Being must be the author of it. And if He is the author of it, it must issue from something which there is in Himself. Oh! be sure that the repentance which He would awaken in us, is in the strictest sense the counterpart of His own. He would have us wish,—not that His order should be changed, not that His war against evil should be less exterminating than it is;—but that our wills should be brought into conformity with His Will; that His punishments should do the work they are sent to do,—for us, and for mankind, and for the earth. He would have us say, 'Grant that it may repent us and grieve us at our hearts, 'that we and our brethren have made ourselves the slaves 'of nature instead of Thy servants; that we have walked 'after the flesh instead of the Spirit; that we have lived 'each as separate individuals warring against each other, 'not as members of a kind redeemed and united in Christ, '—after the downward tendencies of the old Adam, and 'not according to the quickening Spirit of the new. 'Grant us and all Thy children this repentance; that so we 'may pass safely through whatever judgments and chas-'tisements Thou hast ordained for the corrupted earth in 'which we dwell; that we may be fit to behold it and 'offer thanksgiving sacrifices for it, when it comes forth 'from Thy hands purified and renewed!'

SERMON III.

NOAH AND ABRAHAM.

Lincoln's Inn, Quinquagesima Sunday.—March 2. 1851
Lessons for the day, Genesis IX and XIV

GENESIS XII. 1—3.

Now the Lord had said unto Abram, Get thee out of thy country, and from thy kindred, and from thy father's house, unto a land that I will shew thee. And I will make of thee a great nation, and I will bless thee, and make thy name great; and thou shalt be a blessing: And I will bless them that bless thee, and curse him that curseth thee: and in thee shall all families of the earth be blessed.

THE following words opened the lesson for this morning: —'*And God blessed Noah and his sons, and said unto them, Be fruitful, and multiply, and replenish the earth. And the fear of you and the dread of you shall be upon every beast of the earth, and upon every fowl of the air, upon all that moveth upon the earth, and upon all the fishes of the sea; into your hand are they delivered. Every moving thing that liveth shall be meat for you; even as the green herb have I given you all things. But flesh with the life thereof, which is the blood thereof, shall ye not eat. And surely your blood of your lives will I require; at the hand of every beast will I require it, and at the hand of man; at the hand of every man's brother will I require the life of man. Whoso sheddeth man's blood, by man shall his blood be shed: for in the image of God made he man. And you, be ye fruitful, and multiply; bring forth abundantly in the earth, and multiply therein.'* (Gen. ix. 1—7.)

No one, I think, has ever doubted that this is a divine blessing upon the human race. The words are addressed to the representatives of it, who had just escaped from the waters of the flood. Now the two characteristics, which were said to belong to man in his original creation, are said to belong to him here. The beasts, the birds, the fishes, are to fear him; he is made in the image of God. Neither of these titles can by possibility be limited to a time that was past. The dominion is especially assured to Noah and his sons; the law concerning the shedding of man's blood,— a law, surely assuming that evil had existed and was likely to exist,—rests on the other and more glorious distinction. There was a third part of the original charter which is renewed and strengthened. '*Be fruitful, and multiply, and replenish the earth,*' is a command given to those who had seen and experienced the wickedness of the old earth, with as much emphasis, with as large a benediction, as it was given on the day when the heavens and the earth were finished, and all the host of them.

I apprehend that, even if we had not been told of that signal witness *for* God's order and *against* man's transgression, which is contained in the story of the Deluge, we should still have found nothing to surprise us in the blessing of Noah. The worst sinner who perished when the ark floated, had the right of dominion over the birds and the beasts and the fishes; though in consenting to obey his own inclination he had become their slave. He had a right to feel that the blessing, '*increase and multiply,*' was his; only through his uncleanness, and indifference to the duties of a father, he had made it into a curse. He had a right to believe that he had the likeness of God; only he had acquired the likeness of the serpent, which was sentenced to go on his belly, and eat dust. In every case the cause was the same, and the effect was the same. Each man would live in himself and to himself. He could not therefore be, in the real sense of the word, a man. He was wrapped up in his Adam nature. He could claim no fellowship with his kind.

Still, there is something especially appropriate in this language to the inhabitants of a restored earth. One cannot help feeling that, though it is in strictest accordance with all that has gone before, it has yet a wider scope,—a higher promise. Compare it with the simple records of the garden life of Adam, and you perceive that you are entering upon a more advanced stage in human history. I use the words because they are true, and because I think it is honouring God and his word to use them. I know very well that we shall hear of more, and more complicated, sins than we have heard of yet. But as I find a perfectly holy Being blessing the work of His hands; as I find the sacred historian regarding the world as His world, and man as under His government;—I suppose it is not wrong, but right for us to do the same:— and to try,—if we can,—to understand what step it is that we have gained since the oppressors of the earth were destroyed, and it began its life anew.

One change has been often noticed, and has recently been turned into an argument against the old doctrine respecting capital punishment. Noah and his sons are told that, '*Whosoever sheddeth man's blood, by man shall his blood be shed.*' But, by a still older decree, Cain was *not* to be slain for his crime. His mark was to be a warning that no man should lay hands on him. No doubt this is a remarkable contrast, whether it proves the point for the sake of which it is adduced, or not. One sentence contemplates the offender as an individual wrong-doer, who has polluted the earth with his brother's blood, and against whom the earth cries for vengeance. Henceforth it will refuse to yield him its fruits. The other contemplates men, as forming a society. The blood which is shed is the blood of some particular man; but it is a drop out of a common life. Whoso sheds it is guilty of an outrage upon a body politic: ' *Of every man's brother will I require the life of man.*' Every man *is* his brother's keeper. Every man is shedding his own blood when he sheds his brother's blood. The word brother was addressed to a family; Noah and his sons must have interpreted it by their own experience. But the words '*every man's brother*' expanded the principle of the family to a higher power. They declared that the *race* was a family; they intimated that society was to be built up on the recognition of an actual relationship among the different members of it. Henceforth this becomes the great subject of the book.

In the previous records we had an intimation of cities built; of works in wood and iron; of the harp and the lyre. But all this premature civilization is found in the Cain family. It begins, as so much of the world's so-called civilization has begun, with men breaking loose from family bonds, and forsaking the tillage of the earth, through the desire to sink the consciousness of some crime, in intercourse with their fellows, in the works of their hands, in the delights of sense and sound. Such social progress soon terminates in a deeper barbarism, domestic life having been destroyed to make way for it. But no one can fancy, that such an existence as is reported of the Seth family,—that after so many years they begat children, and after so many more they died—though suitable to the time, and though brightened by glimpses of a higher life,—since it is reported of Enoch that he '*walked with God, and was not, for God took him*,'—can be a type of that which is intended for man. If it were,—if this mere long span of years were to be envied as the high privilege of an earlier and happier dispensation,—you would find it hard to understand the records of all the greatest lawgivers, judges, kings, prophets, spoken of in Scripture; hardest of all to understand the story of His birth and death who dwelt on earth less than thirty-three years, and yet whom we hold to be the Priest, and Prophet, and King of the Universe. Our consciences justify the apparent indifference to chronology in Scripture, where the whole history of the patriarchs from Adam to Noah is summed up in fewer lines than those which describe the interview of Joseph with his brethren, or the one night in which the Israelites came out of Egypt.

And this is surely for the reason to which I have so often referred,—'*In the image of God made He man.*' The image of God may be dimly shadowed forth in length of years; it is actually *seen* in the righteousness, grace, truth, which constitute His eternal being. The exhibition of these to us must be the object, one would think, of a Divine revelation,—of a human history. And these, with all the qualities which are in conflict with them, come out through the joys and sorrows, the intercourse and the quarrels, of brothers and sisters, fathers and children, husbands and wives; through the fellowships and conflicts of nations, through laws and polities; through the discovery of the necessary connexion between crime and punishment; through efforts successful or disappointed, to redress wrong and restore right. It would be a strange puzzle, which I think the most ingenious sophistry would find it hard to clear, if a book, claiming the character which the Bible claims, did not deal with this, the ordinary stuff and material of human existence. We should feel that it was like the Shasters of many nations, a book proving that it came from heaven, by its utter alienation from everything that is acted or felt upon earth.

The covenant with Noah is certainly not the introduction, to a sacred book of this kind. It speaks plainly and simply of the fact of the increase of the species, of men spreading themselves abroad into different countries, of the way in which the life of man was to be reverenced, of the kind of honour which was to be bestowed upon animal life. The distinction in this last case is very remarkable; you cannot have overlooked it. It is one indication of the new step which the history has taken. The blood of the animal is not to be eaten, for the blood is the Life. A higher dignity is put upon Life than it had before, whether it dwells in a man, or only in an inferior creature. It is evidently intimated that there is a relation between the one and the other. And yet there is a kind of contempt put upon the animals. The man is not to be afraid to eat them; they belong to him; he must not dream that there is any divinity in them. The intimation that men were likely to have this dream, and therefore to tremble at any invasion of the sanctity of animal existence, is an introduction to long chapters of Egyptian and Hindoo mythology; it shows that we are coming into contact with the opinions of men upon innumerable subjects, physical and moral, and with the acts in which those opinions have been embodied.

Yet there is no allusion to such opinions or acts. The whole comes forth in the form of a covenant between God and His creatures; He is announcing to them the law under which they exist; He is proclaiming to them the relation in which they stand to Him and to each other; the order in which He has formed the universe,—and to which they must conform themselves in whatever lands they may travel, to whatever races they may give birth.

'*And God spake unto Noah, and to his sons with him, saying, And I, behold, I establish my covenant with you, and with your seed after you; and with every living creature that is with you, of the fowl, of the cattle, and of every beast of the earth with you; from all that go out of the ark, to every beast of the earth. And I will establish my covenant with you; neither shall all flesh be cut off any more by the waters of a flood; neither shall there any more be a flood to destroy the earth. And God said, This is the token of the covenant which I make between me and you and every living creature that is with you, for perpetual generations: I do set my bow in the cloud, and it shall be for a token of a covenant between me and the earth. And it shall come to pass, when I bring a cloud over the earth, that the bow shall be seen in the cloud: and I will remember my covenant, which is between me and you and every living creature of all flesh; and the waters shall no more become a flood to destroy all flesh. And the bow shall be in the cloud; and I will look upon it, that I may remember the everlasting covenant between God and every living creature of all flesh that is upon the earth. And God said unto Noah, This is the token of the covenant, which I have established between me and all flesh that is upon the earth.*

By this passage we may, I think, test some of those notions which we deduce from the maxims and habits of the world around us, and then transfer almost unconsciously to the Scripture.

We suppose a covenant to mean a bargain between two parties, whereby each engages to do certain acts; if there be a failure on either side, the other is free. We admit that, where one of the parties is greatly the superior, the covenant may convey something which the humbler one could not obtain by any act or effort of his own. But we are careful to remind ourselves, that in this case more than in any other, the promise will not be fulfilled if the conditions exacted are not performed. How is the case here? God is said to declare to the sons of Noah, that a flood shall no more drown the earth. He gives them the bow in the heavens, as a sign of this purpose. When He brings a cloud upon the earth, He will look upon the rainbow and remember His covenant with all flesh. Where does the hint of a bargain intrude itself here? How is the appearance of the rainbow, or the pledge which it is said to give, made dependent upon any good or evil act of the creature who looks up to it? And yet this is called a COVENANT; it is the first occasion, on which we meet with the phrase; by the use of it here we must in a great measure determine what is the use of it everywhere else. Nor can I conceive a more beautiful guide to our thoughts respecting the relations of God with human beings, a more divine correction of the false way in which we are apt to think of His position and of ours. Would it have been the least help or comfort to the children of Noah as they travelled east and west, north and south, to think that the world was subject to a Being who might regulate it now upon one principle, now upon another, according as they pleased or displeased him? Alas! it was precisely this notion which they *did* adopt;—which was the root of all their distrust, of all their dark idolatries, of their cowardice, of their neglect of the work of tilling the earth and subduing it. They fancied they were under a capricious ruler, not under One who had said that the order of summer and winter, seed-time and harvest, should never cease; under One who had drowned the earth because He was determined to assert and preserve the order which He had formed; under One who had proved that the rains did not come at their own pleasure, but were obedient to His righteous will, and executed His gracious purposes; under One who had promised that they should keep the bounds which He had assigned for them.

And thus we understand in what sense, and in what sense alone, man was a party to this covenant. He might believe or disbelieve the sign, which was said to bear that divine testimony. He might think it was a pledge of God's care of the world, of God's special care of him his chief minister in and over the world. Or he might think it meant nothing at all, that it was an appearance merely, dependent upon no principle, pointing to no design; which had no import to him, nor to any of the creatures whom God had made subject to him.

All his future acts would depend upon this difference,— because they would depend upon the question whether he worshipped a Being in whom he trusted, or one whom he regarded as an enemy. But a Being who is the object of our trust, upon whom we absolutely depend, is not one whom we can ever think of as trafficking with us. We ask Him to reveal to us what He is, and what we are. We ask for pledges and assurances of our relation to Him. These, the Scripture says, He gives us; without these we may have everything to feed our senses, but we are not men; for man lives by faith, and till faith is called forth in him, he is still but an animal with the capacities of a spirit.

The history of Abram, which we have entered upon this afternoon, is the grand illustration of this truth. I have deferred any allusion to it thus far, for I am most anxious, that we should not look upon Abram as an exception in the course of this history, because God is said to have spoken to him, and made him know that he was to go out of his father's house, or because he became the head of a peculiar nation, or because he is called the 'father of the faithful.' Would it not have been the greatest deviation from the idea of this narrative, as it has come out before us thus far, if God were not supposed to speak to men, to make known His will to them, to give them the power of fulfilling it? Would not the anomaly, the exception be, that he should *not* have intercourse with the creature whom He had made in His image? Would not the absence of such intercourse involve the loss of all that is precious to men? Would it not be the sealing and confirming of their own monstrous dream of independence, that in which lay all animal degradation, all destruction of brotherhood? The Scripture, you will find, assumes it to be the normal condition of man, that he should receive communications from God. Whatever good comes forth from him it supposes to be the result of such communications. We hear of them made to the Egyptian Pharaoh, to the Philistine

Abimelech. They are told of something which they are not to do; that teaching, it is not proved but taken for granted, must come from the Lord of the heart and reins. Of Abram we are told nothing, except that he was descended from Shem, till we hear that God said to him, '*Get thee out of thy father's house, and from thy kindred, into a land that I will tell thee of.*' Nothing is said of the time or manner of the communication. We do not want to hear anything of either. Moses expects us to believe that God knew the mind of the Mesopotamian shepherd, as of all other men whom He had formed, and could make that mind aware of His presence. No heap of words could make the awfulness of the discovery greater; the simplest are the best. But it is not merely the revelation of an actual presence. Abram is taught that he is the servant of Him who has declared Himself to him; he is to go where He bids him; he is to become a wanderer, to settle himself in another land; and there he is told that he shall found a family; and that God will make of him a great nation; and that his seed shall possess the land in which he is only to sojourn.

These words, 'great nation,' belong to the new period. We heard no such language in the time before the flood. The inhabitants of the earth were then probably gathered within very narrow limits; at least, the Scripture gives us no hint which can make us think otherwise. It is by the sons of Noah that the earth is said to be overspread. I shall not allude to any of the ethnological speculations which have been raised upon the story of their families. Most of them are very crude; in nearly all of them there is a large element of vague tradition, which we have grafted upon the simple letter, till we can hardly separate the one from the other. But there are one or two passages in the narrative containing, it seems to me, precious and profound ethnological facts, which we are apt to overlook or to misinterpret. The story of the curse pronounced on Canaan by Noah, has exercised our ingenuity to discover what special nations were comprehended in it. Would it not have been better to consider the occasion and nature of the curse, before we investigated the geographical limits of it? And would not that inquiry have led to the truth, so important for understanding the infancy of societies, but equally important for understanding them in their greatest maturity, that wherever the reverence for fathers is lost, there is a people predestined to slavery; servants of servants, sooner or later, will they become. And whatever opinions we may hold respecting the Semitic or Japhetic stocks, we shall not hesitate to think that, in some way or other, the establishment and recognition of the paternal authority would be associated with the blessing, human and divine, which rested upon the tents of the first, and which the other was afterwards to inherit.

Another of these facts is, surely, that the sons of Noah, to whatever lands they might have journeyed, were to be '*divided after their families, after their tongues, in their lands, after their nations.*' This dispersion, and these distinctions, are surely a part of the original divine order; the fulfilment of God's designs for the race which He had made after His own likeness. To overturn that order, to frustrate that design, the wandering tribes met on the plain of Shinar, and said, '*Go to, let us make bricks, and burn them throughly; and let us build a tower that may reach to heaven; and let us make ourselves a name, that we be not scattered abroad upon the earth.*' In other words, let us build a society, not upon faith in the unseen God and His covenant, but upon faith in brick walls. Let this be the bond of our union. Let us provide securities against the divine power, lest it should crush us. The plan, we are told, was confounded: they left off to build the tower. The earth was overspread, though they determined that it should not be. Distinct families and nations were established, in spite of this attempt to reduce all into one indistinguishable mass. But we are told also that a Babel society *was* established by a mighty hunter, in whom all have recognised the beginner of the great Asiatic tyrannies. Polities rose up, based upon a worship of natural powers, feared, not trusted; whose cruel purposes were to be averted by such means as human wit and strength could devise. The rulers of these kingdoms owned no Lord of man after whose image they and their subjects were formed; they bowed to the powers which they thought they discerned in the storm, or in the dark sky; powers to which they attributed their own qualities; with which they had no sympathy; whose dominion was shadowed forth in their own. Such is society according to man's conception and arrangement of it. Society, of which self-will is the king, and animals are the subjects. But this was not God's society; and therefore it was said to Abram: '*I will make of thee a great nation; and in thee shall all the families of the earth be blessed.*'

I have hastily recapitulated the previous history, that you may see how here, as in every case that has come before us, the divine order is maintained, not violated, by what we are wont, awkwardly and irreverently, to call the divine interventions and interferences. The calling out of the Mesopotamian shepherd; the setting apart of his family and his nation as a chosen family and nation; these are often spoken of as necessary for some high religious purpose, but as disturbing the course of human history. But if the early records are what they have appeared to be, this call of Abram is a step in the unfolding of that social order, which is the order intended for human beings, as such; that order which the individualizing tendencies of men were transgressing and revolutionizing. The polity which Abram was to begin was not to be less human, because it was national. The nationality of it was to be the protest against the universal empires,—which were so inhuman, because they were so ungodly.

But was not Abram, as the faithful man, the father of the faithful, heir of a special privilege which separated him from his unfaithful descendants, still more from the unfaithful majority of mankind? Just so far as this,—every unfaithful descendant of Abram, every unfaithful man, was setting up his own separate, selfish nature, was unwilling to stand upon that truth which belonged to the whole race. Every unfaithful man of the race of Abram, every unfaithful man anywhere, would be a God; he would not claim the right of knowing God and being like Him. Therefore all such were tempted to make gods of their own, and to forget the living God. Abram's faith consisted in not doing this; in acknowledging the Lord to be God; in recollecting Him; in living as if He were that guide and protector He declared Himself to be. The promise to him was, '*In thee and thy seed shall* ALL *the families of the earth be blessed.*' He believed the promise. He counted it the highest blessing and glory which could be given him,—not that he should be blessed, but that he should be the channel of blessings to multitudes unknown.

And therefore said our Lord, speaking to those who counted it their highest glory to be Abraham's children,—'*He saw my day and rejoiced.*' The words were most startling to the Jews; for said they, *Thou art not fifty years old, and hast thou seen Abraham?* The depth of meaning which lies in His answer we cannot yet appreciate. It must be considered in the light of a later revelation, which was made not to the father of the faithful, but to the lawgiver of the nation. But thus much we may see in it. He said, 'I am He in whom God made the covenant with
'the old fathers of the human family, when He bade them
'look up to the bow, which was the sign that He would no
'more drown the earth with a flood. I am He in whom
'He formed all men to be brothers, so that he who sheds
'the blood of another, sheds his own. I am that brother
'of whom He will require the life of every man. I am He
'from whom came the life, the faith, the hope, the love of
'all who had strength to believe that God was their
'Creator and Preserver and Deliverer, not their enemy.
'I am He in whom God could look upon them, and in
'whom they could look upon God. And what I was,
'I am; I am still the eternal bond of Peace and fellowship,
'the seed in which all the families of the earth shall be
'blessed;—the destroyer of every Babel tyranny which has
'mocked the divine government, and spread curses among
'mankind.'

SERMON IV.

ABRAHAM AND ISAAC.

(Lincoln's Inn, First Sunday in Lent.—March 9, 1851.)

Lessons for the day, Genesis XIX. and XXII.

GENESIS XXII. 7, 8.

And Isaac spake unto Abraham his father, and said, My father: and he said, Here am I, my son. And he said, Behold the fire and the wood: but where is the lamb for the burnt offering? And Abraham said, My son, God will provide himself a lamb for a burnt offering: so they went both of them together.

THERE was a passage in the chapter from which I preached last Sunday, to which I did not then allude. The story of Abraham's call is scarcely concluded, before we are told that he went down into Egypt in consequence of a famine; that there he persuaded his wife to call herself his sister; that he was intreated well for her sake; that she was saved by God's providence from the effect of her husband's falsehood. Is it desirable to keep such a story as this in the background, or to find some mystical explanation of it which shall show that the untruth of a patriarch is not like the untruth of another man? I apprehend that any one who takes the first course, must hold his own judgment to be higher than that which guided the writer of the book; that any one who takes the second, must set up for himself a most fluctuating standard of right and wrong. I find this narrative here, given with all simplicity; I suppose there is a reason why it should be given. I assume that it was meant to say what it does say. And the natural *primâ facie* view of the subject is that which accords best with the preceding and subsequent narrative. The whole history, instead of suffering from the admission that the first father of the Jewish nation acted just in the way in which another Mesopotamian shepherd, going into a strange country, and seized with a sudden fear of what might befal him, was likely to have acted,—that he displayed cowardice, selfishness, readiness to put his wife in a terrible hazard for his own sake,—the history, I say, instead of being made more difficult and unintelligible by this statement, is brought out by it in its true and proper character. Any notion that we are going to read of a hero, or a race of heroes, is dispelled at the very outset. The dream that this man had in him, in his own nature, something different from other men, that he was not exposed to every ordinary temptation incident to human beings as such,—incident to the place, time, circumstances, in which it was appointed that he should live, —is taken away, not by surmises of ours, but by the express announcements of the sacred historian, intended for other purposes also it may be, but certainly for this one above all others,—that the Jewish people might not fall into any mistakes respecting their ancestor, or fancy him to be a person of another kind from themselves. And so we feel the force of the words, '*In thee, and thy seed, shall* ALL *the families of the earth be blessed.*' Here is a man, not picked out as a model of excellence; not invested with some rare qualities of heart and intellect; one apt to fear; apt to lie; certain to fear, certain to lie, if once he began to speculate according to his own sagacity on the best way of preserving himself. He is made aware of an invisible guide who is near him; of an invisible government which is over him; and which it concerned not him only, but all human beings in all generations, to be acquainted with. Herein lies his greatness, his strength. What he is apart from his Teacher we see in his journey to Egypt; a very poor, paltry earth-worm indeed; one not to be despised by us, because we are earth-worms also; but assuredly worthy of no reverence for any qualities which were his by birth, or which became his merely in virtue of his call. What he was when he was walking in the light, when *that* transfigured him from an earth-worm into a man, his after story will help us to understand.

And thus, my brethren, the same principle which we recognised in the history of Adam in his first estate,—of Adam fallen, of every man before the flood, good or evil, of those who perished in the waters, and of those who were to inaugurate the new economy of the restored universe,— meets us again in this more advanced stage of the history. All these *lived* because they were members of a race formed in God's image. All might claim that image, confessing their dependence upon Him whom they could not see. All might sink into their own individual animal natures, which were under the curse of death. Of that degradation, and of its consequences, God himself, and all true men hearing and echoing his voice, bore testimony; the warning, by its very terms, declared who could raise them out of this death, how they might hold fast this life. In these respects there is no change. Abraham must stand or fall, sink or rise, as all who preceded him stood or fell, sank or rose. He must yield to the invisible Guide, or become the slave of visible things. He must walk by faith or by sight. There is in him no more stock of faith, than there was in Adam a stock of innocence. Faith can as little be a property as innocence. The child depends and trusts before it has gone wrong; it ceases to trust, and so goes wrong. The man trusts from the sense of weakness, the feeling that evil is close to him; so he becomes right. But there must be an object of trust in both cases. And as that object reveals itself more distinctly, the history of the person or the race that receives the revelation advances. Abraham's story is no mere repetition of Adam's or Noah's. A step, a very great step, has been made in discovery, and the discovery has reference to Abraham himself; to Abraham as connected with a surrounding world; to Abraham as the head of a family and a nation. One great truth unites all these aspects of his life together. He is educated to acknowledge a *Righteous* Being,—a Being the direct opposite of that one whom the Babel-builders worshipped, whom they feared as the probable destroyer of their brick walls, whom by all acts they were to propitiate that he might save them. It is not only One who preserves men from the waters, who blesses them, bids them increase and multiply, and restrains them from shedding each other's blood, that is disclosed to the mind and heart of Abraham. It is a person in whom Stedfastness, Fidelity, Truth, dwell absolutely. The shepherd comes to apprehend a character; one different from his own, which he is able partly to understand through that very difference, through the want of fidelity and truth in himself, and yet which he must acknowledge as the image after which he is formed. Let us trace, so far as we are permitted, the process of his discipline and his illumination.

I. The thought may sometimes have struck your own

minds,—it will be suggested to you by many modern books of a certain school,—that the circumstances of Abraham were eminently favourable to the cultivation in him of a pure, simple, monotheistic faith. A man living under the eye of Nature,—on open plains, amidst flocks and herds,— away from the artifices and deceptions of cities, was likely, it may be said, to preserve his devotion unsullied, and to give it that healthy direction which it loses when a knowledge of the world's evil suggests painful questions respecting the origin of evil, and confuses the belief in a perfectly benignant Creator and Guardian.

I have no doubt that the circumstances of Abraham were the best possible to fit him for the work which he had to do, just as I believe that yours and mine are the best, if we use them rightly, to fit us for the work which we have to do. But I would ask you to remember, that there was nothing in the perpetual beholding of natural objects which could preserve him from the worship of those objects. Cities may be very dangerous, but it is not in cities especially that men have learned to bow before the Sun, when he '*comes as a bridegroom out of his chamber,*' or '*to kiss the hand when the Moon is walking in her brightness.*' These are the special temptations of the shepherd,—of the man on the open plain, —of the devout man, who feels his need of something to adore, and who is not constantly led by the power which men exert over him, to bestow his adoration upon them. The recollection perhaps of the North American Indian and his Great Spirit presents itself to you, and you ask whether that is not, at all events, an instance of a God heard in the winds, seen in the clouds, not taking any definite, visible shape? Whether it be so or not, I think you will perceive in a moment, that the difference between the worship of the

North American Indian and that of Abraham, is even wider than that between the worship of the Sabæan and his. For the marked peculiarity of Abraham is, that he does *not* hear God in the winds, or see Him in the clouds,—that he does not associate Him primarily with the things around him, but primarily with himself and with human beings. This man living out of cities, this settler in lands, which neither he nor any one appropriates, is yet regarding the Lord of All in connexion with a family, with a nation, with all the families of the earth. God speaks to him,—tells him where he shall go, and what he shall do; that is the Scriptural statement, which we may reject if we please, but which we must not pretend to explain by cases and examples unlike it in every respect. You cannot, by any considerations of this kind, escape from the acknowledgment of a distinct call from an actual, personal, unseen Being, addressed to the man himself, felt and confessed by him in his inmost heart and conscience. But if you begin from the belief of such a call, the more you reflect upon Abraham's outward position the better. Think, then, if you please, of the simplicity, the regularity, the monotony, of a shepherd's life. Remember that his flocks not only constitute his wealth, but his work; that all exercises of vigilance, courage, patience, are needful for the performance of that work. Remember, further, that in the guidance and discipline of these animals he has the help of others, who are not merely animals,—that he has men-servants and women-servants,—that these form a pastoral family, of which Sarah is the head. Remember that the conduct and ordering of this human society is a part of his needful business, which we should of course think much higher and nobler than the other, and which we are taught to think so by the Book of Genesis. I will not ask you at present to reflect how much the language of Scripture is studded with allusions to the Lord of All as a shepherd; and that these allusions are no accidental appendages or ornaments of the discourse, but are worked into the very tissue of it. Such observations I may often have occasion to make hereafter. I only give a hint of them now, because they illustrate the truth upon which Abraham's education turns. If his work was not the image of a Divine work; if his government over the sheepfold,—and still more in the tent,—was not the image of the Divine government; the narrative would not be the consistent or the profoundly true one that it is.

II. And this we shall find is quite as important a reflection with a view to Abraham's personal character, as it is with a view to his position and office as a patriarch. Take two or three instances. Abraham asks how it is that his seed should possess the land, seeing that he goes childless, and his steward Eliezer is his heir. He is told that one from his loins should be his heir. He believes the word, and it is counted to him for righteousness. Here we are informed of a blessing which came to Abraham himself. He acquired a new and higher standing-ground. The spirit within him confessed a perfectly righteous Being,— one who could fulfil his own promises,— one who was the Lord over the powers of nature, and the powers of man. This faith of his carried him out of himself: it made him partaker of the Righteousness of Him in whom he believed; just as the eye enters into the possession of the objects which it sees. The phrase '*counted to him for Righteousness*' is the fittest we can conceive for expressing such a result as this; for making us feel that he did not actually acquire a certain amount of righteousness which he could call his own, as one acquires fields or houses by purchasing them ; but that he became, in the most real and actual sense, righteous himself, because he confessed and trusted the Righteous God. The expression teaches us also, as every Scripture expression teaches us,—to regard all good as coming from above, and God's judgment of a man as that which determines what he is, because it is the perfectly true judgment. This passage then clearly belongs to Abraham, distinctly, personally. The blessing is his. And yet it is altogether bound up with his hopes of a seed. He becomes righteous in proportion as he looks forward to that which was beyond himself, and as his own life is identified with the life of his family.

Again, the story of Abraham's effort to realize the prediction by taking the handmaid of his wife, brings out another part of that divine and human discipline to which he was subjected. The humiliating and natural result is, a feud between Sara and Hagar. In the discovery that a divine promise was not to be fulfilled by an act of self-will, —with further discovery that God saw the deserted woman, and cared for her and her child, and that he too had a work, and was to be the head of a tribe,—lay a lesson concerning himself and his Divine Guide, which the patriarch could have obtained in no other way. The feeling of the difference between submission to an instinct and obedience to a divine command,—between the child according to the order laid down for man, and the child of nature,—must have enabled him to apprehend distinctions which he could not have arrived at through the most accurate and formal precepts. But here also the individual lesson came through the family.

Once more. The covenant of circumcision, which was made with Abraham after the birth of Ishmael, and the change which took place in his name, brought out with a quite new force, the truths which he had been gradually apprehending before. That covenant, like the covenant with Noah, was one not of bargain, but of blessing. It was an assurance, that he who entered into it was called, chosen, set apart by God. He had not taken up the position himself; his business was simply to acknowledge that it was his, and to act as if it were. But, unlike the former covenant, man was to make the sign; the sign was a perpetual indication to him that he must give up his own natural inclinations if he would be a true man according to God's call and purpose. It was therefore more distinctly human than the other, if it was less universal; it taught Abraham a truth about himself which the rainbow could not teach him. Yet he only acquired this wisdom through an ordinance which concerned every member of his household, and all who were to come after him, as much as it concerned him.

III. But the history is not confined to the tent of Abraham. Lot, who came forth with him out of Mesopotamia, chooses the plains of Jordan, which are well watered,—a very garden of the Lord. He dwells in the cities of the plains, and pitches his tent towards Sodom. We have a view of these cities, first as engaged in one of the predatory wars of the time, in which Abraham with his train of servants takes part to rescue his kinsman; then as destroyed by fire from heaven. I shall not stop to justify the first narration from the suspicions of certain critics, who say that it must be an interpolated fragment, because Abraham is not there the simple shepherd any longer, but the armed warrior. The more the alleged contradictions of the story are considered, the more thoroughly oriental and pastoral it will appear; externally as well as internally coherent. But the destruction of the cities bears so closely upon the whole life of the patriarch, and on the principle of the book, that I must have adverted to it, even if it had not been brought before us in the lesson for this morning.

That which the covenant had told him concerning himself and every man, was about to be fulfilled in Sodom and Gomorrah. The inhabitants of the cities had become the slaves of inclination and nature; they had sunk into beasts, and below beasts. They could not be suffered to go on in that condition. They had chosen the law of death, and in some signal manner that law would execute itself. Abraham is told that it will. The communication comes to him in a different form from any of what we have heard yet. We have heard of God speaking to him, commanding him, and giving him promises. Nothing has been said of any visible appearance, and when nothing is said we have no right to assume it. Here we are told of three persons coming to him as he was sitting by his tent-door in the plain of Mamre, in the heat of the day. The visitants are called angels. But neither here nor elsewhere in Scripture is the angel represented as of another essence, or even of another form, than man. They converse with Abraham; they eat with him. He feels that the invisible world has been opened to him, that he has had communion with the dwellers in it. There is simplicity, quietness, awe, through the whole record of the interview. No great phrases are used to indicate that it was some deviation from order in favour of a particular person; rather, it seems to be assumed, that such intercourse is according to order, however the confusions of man's life may have interrupted it. But after Abraham has been warned of the birth of a son, two of these angels go on their way towards Sodom. Abraham is left in mysterious converse with a Being who is called 'the Lord.' We do not hear that there is any longer a visible presence. He makes known to him what is coming on the cities in which Lot dwells : Abraham's spirit is drawn out into intercession for them. He asks— not that wickedness may continue to exist; but—that if there are ten righteous in the city, it may be spared for their sakes. He asks this because he is certain that the Judge of the earth must do *right*. He believes him to be a righteous Being, not a mere sovereign who does what he likes. On that foundation his intercession is built; the first recorded in Scripture; the model of all the rest. It is man beseeching that right may prevail : that it may prevail among men; by destruction, if that must be ; by the infusion of a new life, if it is possible. It is man asking that the gracious order of God may be victorious, in such way as He knows is best, over the disorder which His rebellious creatures have striven to establish in His universe. The mercy which is prayed for is not an exception from the righteousness, but the fruit of it.

But if this prayer is in accordance with the highest teaching of Scripture, what can we say of the words, '*I will go down now, and see whether the men of Sodom have done altogether according to the cry of it, which is come unto me ; and if not, I will know ;*' with the corresponding narrative of the angels coming to the gate of Lot's house ? Is not this language anthropomorphic ? Is it not inconsistent with the belief of God's omnipresence ? My brethren, are we sure that we know what we mean when we use that word, 'omnipresence'? Are we sure that we are not hiding a want of meaning, a no meaning, under a wide philosophical generalization? If so, we may talk against anthropomorphism as much as we please, but depend upon it we shall drive men to be anthropomorphic, and idolatrous too, by our vagueness and unreality. For those who are men with actual flesh and blood, and not speculators or philosophers, must have an actual object to believe in, or they must give up belief altogether. They can be Theists or Atheists, but they cannot float in a cloudland between the two; confessing God and making Him nothing, under pretence of making Him everything. The more sincerely and faithfully we deal with our own minds, the more I believe we shall discover that the highest knowledge of all does not come at once; and *never* comes in phrases and abstractions. If man is capable of knowing God, it must be because there is that in him, that in every part of his being, which responds to something in God;—all his acts and ways, all his exercises of observation, insight, foresight, rule, must be derived from some source, and that source must be the Creator. I may repeat this maxim to weariness, but I wish you to feel that it is the maxim of Scripture;— and that it would be false to itself if the maxim was not carried into every, even the minutest, detail. We need not be afraid of any opprobrious phrases. If the Scripture revelation leads to idolatry,—if it does not offer an effectual deliverance from idolatry, such a deliverance as no philosophers have been able, after six thousand years, to devise,—cast it aside. But do not be frightened by the word anthropomorphism; for there may be the deepest reason in the nature of things, in the laws of the universe, why God should only be known in and through a Man.

The whole judgment upon the cities of the plain is, in one sense, the condemnation of the sin which men commit when they become worshippers of themselves; in another, the assertion of the truth which lies beneath that enormity. Man seeing only himself sinks to the point where society becomes impossible, — where every man becomes the corrupter and destroyer of every other. Man seeing himself in God, feeling his own relation to God, grows into the perception of a fellowship and sympathy between himself and every being of his own race,—into a perception of the loving care and government which he is to exercise over all creatures of lower races; grows into this perception, because the divine character,—the mind which upholds all things, and keeps all things at one, the mind, in the likeness of which humanity is created,—dawns more and more clearly upon him. And thus the man is prepared for the last and culminating point in the divine education, that in which he learns the meaning and ground of self-sacrifice; how it is possible, how it is implied in our very existence as servants of God, as members of a kind; how it *may* become the most frightful of all contradictions.

IV. The history of this stage of Abraham's discipline, we have heard in the lesson this afternoon. As in all the other steps of it, the life of the family is inseparably involved with the life of the individual; the most awful experience in the personal being of the patriarch, relates to the child of promise,—the child of laughter and joy. The facts are told in the same style as all that have gone before. '*After these things it came to pass that the Lord did tempt Abraham, and said unto him, Abraham: and he said, Behold, here I am. And He said, Take now thy son, thine only son Isaac, whom thou lovest, and get thee to the land of Moriah; and offer him for a burnt-offering upon one of the mountains which I will tell thee of.*' A very easy explanation, critics assure us, is to be found for this narration. It was a process in the mind of the patriarch. The thought occurred to him, 'It would be acceptable to God 'that I should slay my son;' accordingly he determined to do so. Of course we are indebted to any one who reminds us that this process took place in the mind of Abraham; but if we had not received that instruction, we should have been at some loss to know where else it could have taken place. It was precisely because such deep and tremendous thoughts were presented to the mind and spirit of Abraham, that he referred them to God. He knew that an invisible Being had held converse with his spirit. He knew that this was the Being to whom he owed obedience. He knew that He was a righteous Being. But how could he know if that command came from this righteous Being? Might it not come from some darker source? He was certain of this, that the impulse to self-sacrifice,—the feeling that he owed all to God, and was bound to devote all to God,— was not from any dark source. *That* was assuredly from above. He could no more doubt it than he could doubt his own existence. What then had he to do? The Judge of the whole earth would do right, and would not suffer him to do wrong. He would cast himself upon Him; he would make himself ready to do the thing which would be most agonising to him; he would not try, by any act of his, to save the child which God had given him. If the promises to his race were dependent upon him, the Author of those promises could take care of him; if not, he could put the cause into His hands. To argue upon what Abraham did or did not do, should or should not have done, without considering him as a subject of Divine education, is simply to argue about another Abraham, not the one of which the book of Genesis speaks. If we take the whole story just as it stands, we shall believe that God did tempt Abraham,—as He had been all his life tempting him,—in order to call into life that which would else have been dead; in order to teach him truths which he would else have been ignorant of. Of all truths, the most precious for himself and for his race, was to know that the first-born of the body was *not* to be slain for the sin of the soul,—or as any token of devotion to God. And yet if that negative truth could not be brought into union with the positive one, that a man *is* to sacrifice his child, himself, everything that he has, to God, then would there be a perpetual contradiction in the hearts of the best, the wisest, and the most simple; such a contradiction as sometimes would lead to the death of an Iphigenia; sometimes to the rejection of sacrifice altogether, as a mere barbarous impiety. Frightful as the first result is, I believe it is the less terrible alternative. For there is in deed and truth no middle path. The life of the individual, the life of society, must come at last to make self-indulgence, self-seeking, self-will, its foundation, or else Sacrifice. The one was that upon which Sodom stood, and by which it fell; and that which must,—by a fire from heaven, such as appealed to the sense and conscience of the elder world, or by the withering up of powers, energies, hopes,—involve all cities and nations, which yield to it, in a like ruin. The other was the basis which God laid for the commonwealth, of which Abraham was the beginner: for that wider commonwealth which was to comprehend all the families of the earth.

And surely in doing so, He did not intend a departure from His own primary law. He did not intend that a man should be called upon to make a sacrifice, without feeling that in that act he was, in the truest sense, the image of his Maker. Abraham, returning from the slaughter of the kings, found there was a priest in Salem who could bless him in God's name; who was higher than he was, though he was to be father of many nations. Abraham, returning from the offering of the lamb which was caught in the thicket, felt that there must be a higher sacrifice than that which he had intended to offer. To ascertain how it was possible that the Lord of all could make a sacrifice,—the greatest, most transcendent of all,—was the deepest problem with which the souls of righteous men could be exercised. But if it was hard to conceive the possibility; it was harder still to think that anything which was right in man could be other than a reflex of something in God. It was monstrous, and horrible to believe, that the best offerings of man could be meant to change the will of his Maker,—instead of being the fulfilment of it.

They had this story to guide them in their meditations. Abraham and Isaac went both of them together; Abraham prepared the wood and the fire. He said that God himself would provide the lamb for the burnt-offering. The experiences of a nation's sins and degeneracies, deeper anguish still in the hearts of individual men, helped to expound that riddle. At last the full light dawned upon the mind of one who had found himself sinking in deep mire, where no ground was. '*Sacrifice and offering thou wouldest* not; but a body hast thou prepared me. Lo, I come, (in the volume of the book it is written of me,) to do Thy will, O God; yea, thy law is within my heart. I am content to do it.' A filial sacrifice was seen to be the only foundation on which the hearts of men, the societies of earth, the kingdom of heaven, could rest.

SERMON V.

ESAU AND JACOB.

(Lincoln's Inn, Second Sunday in Lent, March 16, 1851.)

Lessons for the day, Gen. XXVII. and XXXIV.

GENESIS XXVIII. 10—17.

And Jacob went out from Beer-sheba, and went toward Haran. And he lighted upon a certain place, and tarried there all night, because the sun was set; and he took of the stones of that place, and put them for his pillows, and lay down in that place to sleep. And he dreamed, and behold a ladder set up on the earth, and the top of it reached to heaven : and behold the angels of God ascending and descending on it. And, behold, the Lord stood above it, and said, I am the Lord God of Abraham thy father, and the God of Isaac: the land whereon thou liest, to thee will I give it, and to thy seed; and thy seed shall be as the dust of the earth, and thou shalt spread abroad to the west, and to the east, and to the north, and to the outh: and in thee and in thy seed shall all the families of the earth be blessed. And, behold, I am with thee, and will keep thee in all places whither thou goest, and will bring thee again into this land; for I will not leave thee, until I have done that which I have spoken to thee of. And Jacob awaked out of his sleep, and he said, Surely the Lord is in this place; and I knew it not. And he was afraid, and said, How dreadful is this place! this is none other but the house of God, and this is the gate of heaven.

I HOPE the selection of the lessons for to-day will have shown you that the Church, at least, does not wish us to regard the lives of the Patriarchs as the lives of grand and heroic men. The specimens of the history of Isaac and

Jacob are taken from the two most humiliating passages of it. In the first we have an old patriarch, sending forth his elder son to fetch the venison which he loves, and cheated by his younger son at the instigation of his wife. The second belongs to another generation; Jacob is surrounded by his own children; the one daughter of his race is defiled; two of his sons take a crafty and brutal vengeance upon the offender and his whole people.

Do not imagine that I wish to pass over such records as these, which I believe have been brought before us honestly, manfully, deliberately. It would be entirely contrary to the purpose which I announced at the commencement of this series of sermons if I turned away your thoughts from the difficult passages of the book of Genesis, to fix them upon those passages in which all perceive some value, and from which some moral may readily be extracted. Still less do I wish to select the idyllic or poetical passages of the story, that you may forget how much there is in it of prosaic reality. But I apprehend that your minds are more likely to be perplexed by the words I have just read to you, when they are taken in connexion with the narratives between which they are interposed, than by those narratives in themselves. You could hardly help feeling that there was something brave and truthful in an historian, who exhibited the ancestor of his own tribe in a less advantageous light than the ancestor of a rival and opposing tribe. You might be disposed to think he must have been under some higher and diviner guidance than his own, when he laid bare the fury and meanness of the men after whose names his countrymen were called. But you are puzzled when you reflect that the cunning Jacob obtained a blessing, of which his more frank and noble brother was deprived; that he received divine communications to which the other was a stranger; that his seed,—that seed which exhibited the most detestable passions of savages,—were the inheritors of the highest promise ever bestowed upon men. This association of what is high with what is low, of spiritual glories with the most earthly propensities, suggests doubts to your minds which you might be glad to quell, but cannot. Must not morality suffer, you ask, when He whom we proclaim to be a God of Righteousness favours the man whom our consciences pronounce to be base, condemns him in whom we are compelled to feel sympathy? In order to defend the history, are you not obliged to set up a certain sacerdotal theory about human character which interferes with all ordinary obligations, and makes common men feel that the so-called religious standard is utterly at variance with the faith and probity which are required in their dealings with each other? I am certain that these thoughts are stirring in a number of minds: it is because they ought to be met fairly that I have taken my text from the brighter rather than from the darker part of Jacob's biography. But I have chosen it also, because I regard it as in no sense less belonging to the realities of this book, than the story of Jacob's imposture, or of the massacre at Shechem; because it seems to me no beautiful episode, but a part of the regular narrative, connected with all that has gone before it and with all that follows; because I cannot think of Jacob's vision as indicating that a communion with the invisible was vouchsafed to the infancy of our race, and is denied to it in its manhood, but only as the first step in a series of manifestations, each more perfect, more substantial, more permanent than the last.

I spoke last Sunday of the temptation of Abraham to slay his son, as the last great step in his education. The discipline which had raised him to a higher personal standard, which had enabled him to be truly a man, had been discipline through and for his family. His relations with his wife, his nephew, his children, had shown him what was petty and grovelling in himself,—had been the means of awakening the faith, hope, patience, which lifted him above himself, and made him act as the servant of God. That crisis when his love for his new-given child and his faith in the promise were brought into apparent conflict with a more awful duty, was really the reconciliation of his human feelings with their divine original; the moment when he knew that he was made in the likeness of His Creator. The solemn transaction with the sons of Heth respecting the burial-place of Sarah, and his directions respecting the marriage of Isaac, are the only other memorable records concerning him. And why are they memorable? Simply because they concern the great common-places of humanity; because they have to do with those events in which one man has the same interest as another. Readers are sure when they lay down the book of Genesis that they have perused a very marvellous narrative. Learned critics supply them with a phrase, and tell them that they have not been occupied with history in the strict sense, but with mythical stories which contain moral or spiritual lessons of more or less value. Alas for men who spend all their lives in their studies, and have never yet discovered that birth, marriage, death, burial, belong to the facts, and not to the legends of mankind! The marvel of the history, as I tried to show you last Sunday, lies in the *absence* of the peculiar, the grotesque; in the homeliness of all the details; in the inherent littleness of the personages who are the subjects of it. But the feeling of the reader is right and natural, though the explanation of the critic is forced and artificial. That *is* a strange history which teaches us to look upon the familiar as most wonderful; upon the every-day order of existence as a divine order; which connects God not with exceptional acts, but with the habitual course and current of existence. The Bible is unlike other books, precisely on this ground. It is more offensive than other books, precisely on this ground. We can tolerate a *religion*, any religion; but a *history* which exhibits God as an actual personal Being, without whom the vulgarest affairs of men are unintelligible and anomalous, interferes with the different schemes we have made for ourselves;—we are glad, by any outrage upon the letter of the story, to persuade ourselves that it belongs to a region of cloud-land, with which we have nothing to do.

The story of Isaac's first meeting with his wife has so much of simple quiet beauty, that we expect to find their after life in some degree corresponding to it. We are disappointed to hear merely of a man who is rich in flocks and herds, whose chief controversies with his neighbours have respect to the digging of wells, who repeats the falsehood of his father respecting his wife, whose story seems not only free from romantic incidents as that of the elder patriarch was, but whose character wants the marked individuality of his. He is the heir of the covenant. This is his one distinction, the only one of which he is conscious himself, or which he can transmit to his descendants. He lives in tents, away from the cities of the plain, expecting that at some distant day his seed will become a great nation through which the families of the earth shall be blessed

This belief mingles with all his care of his flocks and his herds, with the digging of his wells, with his love for his wife. Whenever he loses this recollection, the coarse Adam nature is all that we discern; the man sinks into the creature made out of the dust of the ground. Upon him and upon Rebecca both, the desire of offspring, the expectation of a birth, the actual occurrence of it, confer a blessing which they could gain in no other way. Their faith and hope are called forth. They feel at once their connexion with God. The mother is taught that two nations are in her womb; the elder shall serve the younger. A mysterious feeling of her relation to the future, of generations to be blessed through her, raises her above the sordidness and selfishness of her earthly nature. The glory of being a mother illuminates her whole existence. The children are born. She has the sense of a prophecy hanging over them. She wonders how it may be fulfilled. They grow up with just the opposition of characters, that may be seen among members of the same family in a patriarchal tent, or in an English home of the nineteenth century. The one has the strong impulses of the hunter: the other dwells near the hearth, caring for all plain, quiet occupations. As we might expect,—courage, frankness, a sense of dominion, belong to the first; thoughtfulness, timidity, subtlety, to the other. The one realizes half the blessing of man. He has the feeling that he can govern the earth and subdue it. The other half,—that he is made in the image of an invisible Being,—seldom presents itself in his dreams or aspirations. To the feeble man, conscious of personal insignificance, the thought of the unseen and the future, the vague dim promise of the covenant, appears as something actual; all the more true because it is not what his hands can grasp, or what they are required to mould. The moment comes which brings the thoughts of their hearts forth into act. Jacob makes his brother's hunger an occasion for bargaining with him for his birthright. Esau says, '*What profit shall this birthright do to me?*'

Neither one nor the other knew what good it would do. The vision of something to be realized now or hereafter dawned upon Jacob, a vision probably mixed with many sensual and selfish expectations; still of a good not tangible, a good which must come to him as a gift from God. The absence of all want, all discontent with the present and the visible, is the feeling which exhibits itself in the acts and utterances of Esau. There is one desire common to both. The father's last blessing is a very sacred thing, to which great advantages must be attached. Each would have this. Esau feels that he has a claim to it. Rebecca will fulfil the prophecy, and win it for her younger son if she can. She has a strange notion that it is God's prophecy; and therefore must come to pass; and therefore that she must do something to make it come to pass. Jacob's faith is of the same kind with hers. He enters into the plot and carries it through. The old man finds that he has been deceived. The blessing once given cannot be recalled. But Esau's bitter cry brings the assurance that his dwelling too shall be in the fatness of the earth.

Esau has apparently been robbed of the treasure that he desired most. But has he really lost anything? Was there any occasion for his exceeding bitter cry? All that he had ever thought to win comes to him in the richest abundance. Instead of the dreary pastoral life, he has the rich free hunter's life. A society soon forms itself around him. He becomes the chief of a tribe,—a tribe which rises, it would appear, speedily to consequence among the people of the desert,—which acquires possessions and government. His frankness and courage are thought to deserve a reward. He has it. Just the one he would have chosen for himself, just the one which qualities such as his can win.

And what did Jacob, who so meanly bought the birthright and earned the blessing, gain by these acts? First of all, he has to leave his father's tent; then, with no share of his brother's courage and recklessness of danger, to make a lonely journey through a desert; then to come among kinsfolk who cheat him as he has cheated; then to exhibit himself in the pitiful condition of a suppliant before Esau, and to receive his forgiveness; then to be the witness of his daughter's shame and of the crimes of those who were to be the heads of the chosen race; to see them making themselves hateful in the eyes of their neighbours, and plotting against one another.

Was his blessing nothing then? Had he been deceiving himself all the while as well as others? No surely. The blessing came to him even as soon as he had begun his wanderings. '*For he lighted upon a certain place, and tarried there all night, because the sun was set. And he took of the stones of that place and put them for his pillows, and lay down in that place to sleep. And he dreamed, and behold a ladder set up on the earth, and the top of it reached to Heaven, and behold the angels of God ascending and descending upon it.*' This gift appertained to his birthright; this was the privilege of the covenant. He was permitted to learn that the visible world is not all with which he has to do; that there is an unseen world, of which he is also a citizen; that the Creator of the visible and invisible is connected with the lowest, poorest, most insignificant of His creatures; that there is a way from Heaven to earth, and from earth to Heaven; that a man may know what that way is. Strange discovery to burst at once upon the mind of a herdsman, whose wit might indeed have been sharpened by the exercises of craft, but in whom mere fancy was as little likely to be awakened as in the dullest ploughman of our own day! Amazing discovery! And yet the very one for which his mind had been preparing, the very object to which his faith with all its dimness and confusion had been pointing, the one thing which could elevate a heart that had never been able to dream of victories over nature or the outer world. The poor plain shepherd had here his high gift; the first great step in his divine education; the assurance which raised him to the feelings and dignity of a man. He knew that though he was to be chief of no hunting tribe, there might yet come forth from him a blessing to the whole earth.

This assurance was given to him in a dream. I shall have more to say upon that point presently, and of the effects which the dream left upon him when he awoke. I will only observe now, that however he arrived at the conviction, he was convinced that the God of Abraham and of Isaac was with him, and would be with him in all his journeyings, and in the land to which he was going; and that the same Being who was with him would be with his seed after him. Suppose this to be a fact, and not a mere fiction, or an impression upon his mind, what follows? Then all that befell him in his after years,—his marriage with Leah and Rachel, his service with Laban, his flight, his reconciliation with his brother, the birth of his sons, the loss of her whom he loved best, the separation from Joseph, his descent into Egypt,—would be parts of a divine discipline; different acts of His government who had said, that He would not leave him till he did the thing which He had promised. Every day of that evil pilgrimage of which he spoke afterwards, brought him some new experience divinely directed to the purpose of curing the sin which was most especially his; some punishment aimed at that evil which was darkening his soul and confusing the light that fell upon it from above. This was a blessing indeed, the highest that can be vouchsafed to a creature; not to be left to itself, not to be allowed to go on weaving its webs of falsehood; to be reminded at every turn, ' See what that tortuous act of yours has done ' for you, see by what an inevitable, eternal law it has ' brought forth its appointed fruit; see how certainly those ' who sow the wind, be they who they may, must reap the ' whirlwind.' I say this was a blessing quite unspeakable. And it corresponded to the faith which Jacob had cherished,—as the gifts and rewards which Esau obtained corresponded to his character. But how does this kind of reward, great as I admit it to be, interfere with our belief of God's righteousness? How does it afford any warrant for the peculiar morality which priests are said, and too truly said, to have encouraged and admired, greatly to the detriment of themselves and of those whom they have influenced? If your idea of God's justice is, that He is to find a man with a ready-made virtue, and to bestow prizes upon it, you are indeed at war, not with this passage of Scripture, but with the whole of it. You are at war equally with the witness of your own hearts and consciences, as to what you want and as to the blessings which you should wish your Creator to bestow. Surely it is an infinitely grander, more moral, more rational and more comforting doctrine,—that all good in man is but the reflection of His good; and that He brings those who without Him have no goodness, to a perception of that which is in Him,—that it may become theirs.

As to the second point, I acknowledge without hesitation, that men whose thoughts are turned by whatever means to the invisible world,—and who have a confused apprehension that they are to find their home in it,—are tempted to a kind of dissimulation which active energetic hunters like Esau seldom practise. They feel as if they had a peculiar secret, a lore of their own, which cannot be explained to other men. They have a notion that the blessings which they dream of are of so transcendent a character, that a little double dealing in pursuit of them *must* be pardonable, *may* be commendable. I admit that this early instance in the world's history is a very distinct warning that habits of this kind would be characteristic of a certain class of men; and that class the one of which the pretensions would be the greatest, and which would practically, though secretly, exercise the greatest influence over the world. The warning is there. Thank God for it! I cannot conceive any so useful or so solemn. If Christian priests, like Shylock the Jew, have made use of Jacob's example as a justification of their own craft,—on their heads be the sin and the blasphemy. God is teaching them in that story, of his willingness to deliver them from their most terrible danger, from the foe that is nearest to them. If they will turn medicines into poison,—if they will pretend that a tendency which the devil has implanted in them, is part of the faith which they have received from God,—they must and will meet with the reward of so horrible a contradiction. The God of Truth will not reveal Himself to them. He will answer them according to the idols which they have cherished in their hearts. Every day they will make Him more in the likeness of their own insincerity and untruth. I say, *which the devil has planted in them.* For I do hold that this tendency to falsehood,—which lies so near a true and precious faith, and must either destroy it or be destroyed by it,—is more essentially and radically *devilish* than those habits of mind to which Esau was prone. They were fleshly, worldly tendencies. The priestly or spiritual man is not free from these, God knoweth. Woe to him if he fancies he is not open to the assaults of the very lowest of them! But he has, in some more direct way than the majority of men, to contend with spiritual wickedness. Dunstan was not wrong in saying, that he had more conscious and perilous struggles with the Evil one than the men of the court. But he should have known, that the Evil one was assailing him then chiefly when the thought of lying for God suggested itself to him; that he was in the grasp of the fiend when he dallied with that suggestion; that he was conquered by him when he yielded to it. And let none say, —that in Jacob's case, or his, or any other,—the sin consists in pursuing a glorious and righteous end by unrighteous means. If the true end was clearly before the inward eye, the way to it would be clear also. It is because our eye is not single; because there are perplexed, contradictory images floating before it,—Self mixing with God, the knowledge of a righteous and true Being confounded with the attainment of some personal gratification; that we prefer an irregular and tangled course to a straight one. If the disciples of Loyola had fully settled in their minds what end God had set before them as the prize of their high calling, there would have been no crooked arts in their policy. So far as they proposed to themselves the reconciliation of the members of Christ's Church, His glory and the diffusion of His Gospel, as their ends; so far their instruments were trust, obedience, self-sacrifice, all that is noblest in man. It was because the paltry object of supporting a Church-system,—of binding men together under a visible head, of spreading their own order over the world, mingled in frightful confusion with this holy purpose,— that faith was turned into the admission and tolerance of falsehood, obedience into slavery, self-sacrifice into the cringing of court-parasites or the ministration to all popular delusions and diseases, in the pulpit or at the confessional. And so it must always be. A really right end involves right means. Therefore our faith must be in a present and living God, not in any scheme of ours; then He will purge our eyes to know Him as the God of Truth, and to feel that the ground upon which we stand is dreadful, because He is there.

And thus I am led to the subject from which I have been too long detained by my desire to show you the truthfulness of this book; viz. the connexion between the vision of Jacob and his history, and the history of mankind. It was a vision, a dream of the night. We are told so expressly. This was the method which the Guide and Teacher of men judged fittest for them in their infancy. In this way He apprised them, as no doubt many peasants in our own time have been apprised, that there was another world about them than that which the visible sun illuminated. But the all-important part of the narrative is that which concludes it. When Jacob *waked* out of his sleep, he said, '*How dreadful is this place!*

Surely this is none other than the house of God! Surely this is none other than the gate of heaven.' The dream had come in a night and was gone in a night. The ladder was seen no more. But that which had been revealed, was a permanent reality, was a fact to accompany him through all his after existence. He might lose it amid the sights of the earthly world. All mere efforts of memory to recollect it might be unavailing. New visions might be needful to recal the former to his mind; new sorrows and fears might be needful to drive him back into the unseen world, and to make him seek for the mysterious help that had been promised him. Still that which had been discovered to him could not pass away. He would know inwardly, that the clouds which concealed it from him were drawn up from his own earthly nature. And though there was something, doubtless, in the place where he had slept which seemed to him specially dreadful, and which he may have felt always to be so; yet the words of the vision itself told him that God would be with him *whithersoever* he went. So that by degrees he will have learnt that every place was dreadful for the same reason; that it was not only between Beersheba and Haran that the angels were ascending and descending; that anywhere the same glorious pageant might be presented to his inward eye.

Now the great question we have to ask ourselves is, ' Was this a *fact* for Jacob the Mesopotamian shepherd, ' and is it a *phantasm* for all ages to come? Or was it a ' truth which Jacob was to learn just as he was to learn the ' truth of birth, the truth of marriage, the truth of death, ' that it might be declared to his seed after him; and that ' they might be acquainted with it as he was,. only in ' a fuller and deeper sense?' If we take the Bible for our guide, we must adopt the latter conclusion, and not the former. The mere ladder set upon earth and reaching to Heaven, we hear of no more. It was a part of a dream. It had all the quality and character of a dream. But that which it expressed, comes out clearer and clearer in every subsequent revelation. When Jacob in a later time of his life wrestled with a Man till the break of day,—when Moses heard the Voice speaking out of the bush,—when Isaiah in the year that king Uzziah died saw the Lord also sitting upon a throne, high and lifted up and his train filling the temple; each felt that he had learnt something which was to be the staff of his future life; that which was to be a strength to the patriarch in every personal and family sorrow; that which would prepare the lawgiver to found and sustain a nation; that which would enable the prophet when the fire had touched his lips, to say, '*Here am I, send me.*' That which each saw was not a repetition of that which his predecessor had seen. The teaching was progressive. Only each was sure that the world into which he had been brought was not a shadow-world; that he had been made aware of the substance, apart from which all things we converse with are but shadows. And when our Lord said to the true Israelite whom He had seen and known whilst he was praying beneath the fig-tree, '*Hereafter ye shall see Heaven opened, and the angels of God ascending and descending upon the Son of Man*;' surely He gave him to understand that this Son of Man was that ladder between earth and Heaven, between the Father above and His children upon earth,—which explained and reconciled all previous visions, and shewed how angels and men could meet and hold converse with each other.

JACOB; REALITY OF HIS DREAMS.

In the first book of the Bible we hear of Jacob in a lonely place between Beer-sheba and Haran seeing a ladder set upon earth and reaching to Heaven. In the last book of the Bible we are told that St. John in the Isle of Patmos saw the Son of Man walking in the midst of the golden candlesticks, and holding the seven stars in his right hand.

I have hinted a little at what is intermediate between these two Visions; I would dare to ask you now, whether the higher and most perfect revelation is not that which belongs to us, whether St. John was not permitted to declare to us the law and mystery of our personal and social existence; that which can alone interpret to us its order and harmony; that too which tells us the meaning of our strifes and discords? Oh! brethren, we talk much of the future, of that which is to come; we know not how or where. Why do we think so little of that which is, of that in the midst of which we are living and moving and having our being? The future will be to us but a very vague and dim shadow, till we inquire what are the grounds of our present life. But if we have courage to do that, Jacob's history may supply us with another lesson. He was taught to say, '*Verily God is here, and I knew it not. This is none other than the house of God. This is none other than the gate of Heaven.*' Then he was enabled to look on into a far distant future; to feel that he should be interested in that which happened long after he left the earth; that he should live because his God was not the God of the dead, but of the living; that the blessings to his distant seed would be blessings to him. Here was the real difference between him and Esau. *He* had no feeling of a present, of a living *God;*

therefore he was content with a mere present *possession*, with plenty of corn and wine and fatness of the earth. In time, no doubt, he and his posterity would feel their need of Beings to worship, of beings to protect them. They would form their gods out of the visible things in which they lived. Earth would become the archetype of Heaven, and therefore all their belief in Heaven would be something to make them more afraid of the earth, less able to till it and subdue it, less able to redeem it from the weeds and the beasts that possessed it. This is the last and highest result of the tribe of hunters, of those who seemed as if they held the earth in fee and had an undisputed right to the property of it. The poor wanderer in the desert, the plain man,—whose ignorance and cowardice, and meanness, were purged away by God's discipline, who lived in a land which was not his own, and died an exile,— left a family out of which there grew a nation, which was itself to give birth to a universal church; which was to possess and conquer and civilize a world. If we begin from the invisible, if we confess Him whom we cannot see to be the ground and root of all that we do see, if we unite ourselves to a present King and Father, if we believe that every place we walk in is a dreadful and a joyful place because He is there, that we ourselves are dreadful beings because our bodies are temples in which he has promised to dwell,—a mighty and glorious future lies before us in the blessings of which we shall be sharers along with the distant seed that will then be inheriting the earth; because heaven and earth are made one in Christ; and the spirit and the fire which have come forth from Him will quicken and renew the whole visible universe. Shall we take up this position, or shall we spend our time in considering how much of the fatness of the earth, of its oil and wine, we can appropriate to ourselves,—not caring how much we shut out from ourselves the good things which eye hath not seen or ear heard,—not caring if the earth remains for ever an habitation of unclean beasts and evil spirits?

SERMON VI.

THE DREAMS OF JOSEPH.

(Lincoln's Inn, Third Sunday in Lent. March 23, 1851.)
Lessons for the day, Genesis xxxix. and xlii.

GENESIS XLII. 8, 9

And Joseph knew his brethren, but they knew not him. And Joseph remembered the dreams which he dreamed of them.

MANY persons, in our day, have come to the conclusion that the Bible contains a number of records respecting the early life of the world, which may be very instructive to us if we only interpret them according to our more advanced knowledge, and do not hold ourselves bound by the scriptural explanations of them. It is not denied that these explanations have a worth of their own. 'They tell
' us how men looked at the marvels of their own life, and
' of the world, when those marvels were just beginning to
' be noticed: how naturally and readily they referred them
' to some supernatural source. It is our privilege, we are
' told, to have rid ourselves of the theocratic element out of
' personal and social life; we see, or may see, all miracles,
' prophecies, presentiments, brought under ordinary human
' principles and laws: but we are not to be the less

thankful for the light which history, sacred or profane, 'throws upon the condition of those who were still re-'cognising the prints of divine footsteps in the earth about 'them,—or in the more startling experiences of their own 'minds.

I may have many opportunities of considering other applications of this doctrine. I shall speak to-day of one which the history of Joseph brings specially under our notice. He had dreams of his own greatness, the Scripture says, which were fulfilled. He foretold a coming famine in Egypt, and provided against it. He referred his own dreams, and his power of interpreting Pharaoh's, to God. 'A very natural conclusion for *him* to arrive at,' our philosophers will say. 'If we take the history of his 'after life as it stands, what were his early dreams but the 'acting out of that law which an eminent teacher of our 'day has expressed in the words : " Our wishes are a fore-'feeling of our capabilities,"—what was there in his 'judgment of the condition of Egypt, and in his arrange-'ments with respect to it, which differed from what we 'should call, in our times, a rude political discernment or 'intuition?'

I hope, through God's grace, to consider these questions fairly; I am thankful that they have been started. I believe much is to be learned from them which will help us in our understanding of Scripture, and will increase our love for it.

The formula that 'our wishes are fore-feelings of our capabilities,' is, I believe, one of much beauty and worth. Many difficult passages in the biographies of great men are explained by it. Perhaps all of us may have learnt from what has occurred to ourselves, that it is not *only* applicable to great men. In looking back to the castles of earliest boyhood, we may see that they were not wholly built of air,—that part of the materials of which they were composed were derived from a deep quarry in ourselves,—that in the form of their architecture were shadowed out the tendencies, the professions, the schemes, of after years. Many may smile sadly, when they think, how little the achievements of the man have corresponded to the expectations of the child or of the youth. But they cannot help feeling that those expectations had a certain appropriateness to their characters and their powers; that they might have been fulfilled, not according to the original design, but in some better way. I do not think that such retrospects can be without interest, or need be without profit, to any one. However shifting the scenery of a man's life may have been,—however various and contradictory the purposes which he has formed and which he has relinquished,—he will be able in most cases, if he looks for it, to trace some predominant thought or wish which has connected them together; which explains their diversities; which has never quite deserted him at any time. Some dream there has been,—it may have belonged to the day or the night, it may have been part of a lively consciousness, or of an almost passive impression,—which has said; ' This or that ' thou mayest do. To this or that, thou art destined.' As new outward circumstances draw us hither and thither,— as new desires or faculties are called forth in us,—this first intimation seems to be lost or banished. But it appears again in another form. The new circumstances, the new faculties, look as if they might themselves be imparted for the sake of this primary half-forgotten aim. If we could pursue it, we think it might point and concentrate a number of vague floating desires; it might cure us of much mawkishness and restlessness; it might quicken resolutions and hopes that are languid and drooping. Then come bitter disappointments from without and from within; cross-blasts seeming to drive the new-fledged purpose downward to earth; a number of mocking voices declaring how vain it is; wild experiments to realize it terminating in shame: terrible discoveries that we were weakest just where we thought we were strongest; that the lesson which we fancied we were sent to teach the world, was one which we had scarcely begun to learn ourselves. It is well if any man escapes out of this state of mind without settling down into the conclusion,—'Let 'us eat and drink, for to-morrow we die: let the stream of 'the world carry us where it will; we will struggle with 'it no more. All things come at last alike to all. He 'who has most of determination suffers most, when he 'finds that he must become the victim of influences which 'he cannot control.' But even he who *does* sink into this wretchedness will have moments in which flashes of strange light come to him,—showing him capabilities of good in him which might have brought those dreams of childhood to fruition.

> 'And even as life returns upon the drowned,
> Life's joy rekindling brings a throng of pains,
> Keen pangs of love, awakening as a babe
> Turbulent with an outcry in the heart.
> And fears, self-will'd, that shun the eye of hope,
> And hope, that scarce can know itself from fear,
> Sense of past youth, and manhood come in vain,
> And genius given and knowledge won in vain.'

All such dark experiences attest the truth of the wise man's saying. And if there should come out of this death a better and a higher birth; if the man should consecrate himself at the eleventh hour to the noblest service and the highest objects; he will find that that service and those objects were in very deed foreshown and forefelt in his childish aspirations. They told him what he was meant to be, and what at length he is making a serious effort to become.

I have not concealed the great merit of this philosophical generalisation from the actual experiences of life, or the evidence which it furnishes that the person who made it had himself entered livingly into these experiences, and was no mere generaliser. But now, I would ask you, 'If this is true, do we not want some other truth to sustain it? ' Can any one think that his presentiments have this signifi- ' cance, and not ask himself, Whence came they? How can ' I interpret them? Who can interpret them for me?' It seems to me cowardly and ignominious not to propose this question manfully to ourselves. How persons can boast of their deep penetration into the laws of humanity who will not do it, I cannot understand. It is no idle curiosity which forces it upon us. The practice and the suffering of life make an answer to it necessary. Perhaps you have found one. Perhaps you can talk about the 'destinies,' or the 'eternities,' or the 'mysterious abysses,' from which these thoughts and wishes and presentiments come to us. Very good words, if you can make any use of them; still better if they are only expressions of an ignorance which wishes to be enlightened, indications of a vagueness which longs for clearness and reality. Very bad words, if they are resorted to as substitutes for reality,—as fine high-sounding expressions for cheating others and cheating yourselves into the belief that you have found something which you have not found, or have ascertained that nothing is to be found. But good or bad, they have all been tried before. If any phrases have been used up in the past history of the world, these have been emphatically so. If there are any to which a man should *not* resort, as to the ultimate results of modern wisdom, they are these. All the heathen world were trying to make out who put the strange thoughts into their minds which were working there; who connected these thoughts by such strange links one with another; who bound the different fragments of their lives together;—by what wonderful art those fragments could become a whole. They tried 'the eternities,' 'the destinies,' 'the mysterious abysses.' It would not do. Something more actual, living, personal, was needful. They must have actual beings who could teach them; who could impart light and knowledge to them; who could see the past, the present, and the future in one. They tried to conceive of such Beings. They could but shape their conceptions from the things and the persons which lay around them. Looking for a ground of their thoughts and experiences, their thoughts and experiences became the ground of those to whom they referred them. They could not bring their lives into unity. For that which should have united them was itself divided. Do you think, that it would be well that we should go over this wearisome experience again? Do you think that the way of showing the advancement of our knowledge, is to take up a position which must compel us to repeat all the different experiments that men have made, while they were searching for some firm ground upon which they might stand, some fixed order to regulate their spiritual movements and their outward acts? But if you would not do that, I believe you must go back with me to Jacob's tent, and must learn how a Hebrew boy behaved himself in Potiphar's house, in an Egyptian prison, at the court of Pharaoh. You must learn over again the first elements of human history, that you may find a principle upon which you can safely and consistently act in this day;—a principle which will fill up the hollow that was left in the deep maxim of our own 19th century sage, and can raise it from an intellectual generalization into a practical truth.

The heads of the Jewish tribes, as we become better acquainted with them, are just what we should have supposed they would have been from the lesson of last Sunday; full of all rude and savage impulses, impatient of home subjection, not yet tamed by the sterner discipline of law Just the inclinations and tendencies which we saw in Esau are in them. At the same time they have inherited much of their father's craft; they will compass their ends by force or cunning, or both. It is no Arcadian picture; the simple life of shepherds, as the book of Genesis represents it, is infected with vices which we think the most foreign from simplicity. And yet the vices are those specially belonging to such a state of society; the complications and refinements of cities are not there; you cannot attribute the evils which spring up in the patriarchs to contact with the surrounding world. They are all children of the covenant; that covenant has told them that they have a nature in them which they are not to obey; that covenant has told them that One whom they cannot see has taken them into His service. They may remember it or forget it; to forget it is to follow their inclinations and impulses; to remember it is to believe in God; to believe that He is present with them, guiding them, protecting them. The

Scripture did not represent Esau or Jacob as arriving by any efforts of thought or reasoning at one conclusion or the other. The first did what his nature prompted him to do; became a hunter; acquired dominion. The other followed his inclination too; suffered for it; became a wanderer; then God revealed Himself to him, and made him know that He was with him, and would be with him whithersoever he might go. Jacob became aware of a fact; a fact which his brother had not cared to know; a fact for himself and his seed after him. The Scripture says God discovered that fact to him. The Being who had made man in His own image, told this man that he was made in His image: taught him that he was not meant, like the serpent, to go on his belly and eat dust. That is the only explanation given; the only one that could be given if the history was consistent with itself. It assumes that man lives because he is related to God; that when he denies that relation he chooses death. It assumes that God is continually teaching men of their relation to Him, and that they are continually flying from His voice.

Joseph's story is in strict accordance with these principles. He grows up in his father's tent; a child favoured by his father, therefore hated by his brethren. He has dreams of greatness; his brothers' sheaves are to bow down before him, the sun and the moon are to pay him obeisance. In his vanity he tells the dreams, and is hated the more. His brothers plot against his life; throw him into a pit; sell him to a company of Ishmaelites. Not a word is said of what has been taking place in himself, during all this time. There is no description of his anguish, or of any thoughts of comfort that came to him. We are merely told that God was with him,—that he found favour with

Potiphar, an Egyptian,—that he became the steward of his house. It is the next part of the story, which we read this morning, that reveals what has been passing within him; what has been the effect of the pit, his banishment, his slavery. The words to his master's wife, '*Can I do this great wickedness, and sin against God?*' tell us that the child of the covenant believes the covenant. Away from the tents in which he has been brought up,—without any outward tokens to remind him of any lessons he has received there, in an hour of tremendous temptation,—he confesses a righteous Ruler, whom he is to obey; he trusts in Him, and does obey Him; he goes to prison for it. His dream is not very likely to be fulfilled; the sheaves are not bowing down to him; the sun and the moon are not doing him any obeisance. But he hears of other dreams. Two servants of Pharaoh are troubled with the thoughts that have come into their minds. They long for a diviner. Joseph tells them that dreams belong to God. He has been learning a wonderful lesson. Other men's thoughts and dreams come from God as well as his. The child of the covenant is not a witness for his own privileges, for his own relation to God. In him and in his seed all the families of the earth are to be blessed. He is to be a witness to all, of the source from which thoughts, intimations, prophecies, come. He believes God who has sent the dream can give the interpretation. He declares the riddle to them, and, as he said, it comes to pass. At the next stage of the history he is brought before Pharaoh, who has also dreamed dreams. They concern not himself, but the land he governs. He has consulted diviners, who cannot tell him what they mean. Joseph believes that God hath sent these dreams for a purpose: that He cares for the land of Egypt; that He wishes Pharaoh to know what is coming upon it; that He wishes him to provide for the future. The Hebrew boy becomes the first man in Egypt; the dispenser of corn to that land, and other lands. His brethren come to buy, and bow before him. He knows them, and they know not him. Then he remembers the dreams which he had dreamed of them.

I wish to fix your minds upon this part of the narrative; the other portions of it may come before us in the lessons for next Sunday. We all fancy that we understand the story of Joseph and his brethren; though perhaps there are depths in it, even as a domestic record, which we have none of us penetrated. But those passages of it which respect his own dream,—and the dreams of the servants of the king, and of the king himself,—are often regarded as merely ornamental, half mythical, additions which we are glad to pass over. I believe we do so at a very serious loss to ourselves,—at a very great risk of falling into the superstitions which we are most careful to avoid. You acknowledge the fact of dreams; you acknowledge that people have been puzzled by them in past ages, and probably are now. You acknowledge that people have been made the victims of the most wretched impostures through their eagerness to find a way out of the perplexities, which the thoughts on their bed have caused them. Where is the escape from this danger? Do you think we find it, when we are taught that the scenery of dreams is borrowed from the external world,—from the places and circumstances with which we are familiar when we are awake? But when you have proved all that, you have left the great riddle unsolved,—the real cause of human anxieties just where it was. *I* bring all this scenery about me in my dreams; but *how* do I bring it? What are the *thoughts* which invest themselves with that scenery? Who am I, the dreamer? Till you have found a reply to these questions, you may produce endless theories of dreams and apparitions, but you have not taken one step to relieve the heart of its confusion, or to prevent it from seeking all unlawful, mischievous aids to quiet itself. Joseph met it with this answer, '*Dreams belong to God.*' ' However ' your thoughts came to you, do not seek by tricks and ' magic to make their meaning clearer to you. There is ' an unseen teacher of your spirit, to whom you may refer ' these and all your perplexities. There is a righteous ' and true Being, whom you may consult about them. ' No doubt there is a purpose in all He does; be sure ' that His purposes with you, His human creatures, are ' specially wonderful. And He means you to discern ' them. He does not intend your lives to be dark ' enigmas to you.'

All this, you say, belongs to an early stage of history. I grant you that it does. It professes to belong to that stage. But if dreams are, there should be some words to tell us that they are under a law; that they do not come by accident; that they have a connexion with the mysteries of our being; that they may have to do with the future as well as the past. Other deeper truths may be told us as we proceed; but these cannot be indifferent to us. Men in the early times may have been more troubled by their dreams than we are; and therefore it was fitting that the help needful to secure deliverance from the trouble should be given especially to them. But they *do* affect us, whether we are frank enough to confess it or not. We know that though our dreams may never have told us anything about that which is to come, they have told us secrets of our own experience; they have shown us how near dark fierce thoughts, which we fancied at a great distance, were lying to us. The confusion which is in them, reminds many how confused and incoherent their waking existence is. They bring past, present, and future so strangely together; they force us all to feel, if we do not reflect, that there must be some conditions of our minds which are different from the conditions of space and time. There is something in them, then, which needs to be interpreted. I think the interpretation for us and for the old world lies in the belief,—that we are under a living and Divine Teacher who does not wish us to walk in darkness.

But you care so much more for the thoughts of the day, than of the night; they are so much more practically important. True; and so much more wonderful. When shall we know how wonderful they are? Oh, brethren, if you have ever been really lost in the mazes of your own thoughts; if they have been so tormenting to you that you would have fled from them, had it been possible, to utter vacancy, almost idiotcy; if you have found them interfere with all manly action, and the maddest course of action seemed better than the indulgence of them; if you have, any of you, been in a state approaching to this,—and how many noble spirits at certain periods of their history have not only approached it, but realized it!—oh how would you welcome the words, '*The interpretation of these belongs to God.*' And when we have listened to all magicians and diviners, calling themselves philosophers or priests, and have tried their medicines for stifling thought and doubt, their systems of opinion, their rules of conduct, and have exclaimed, 'Miserable comforters are ye all,' we must a last, in despair of them and of ourselves, grasp, if it be with ever so feeble a hand, at this truth. If we do, how shall we have to rejoice and give thanks for having been cast into deep pits and mire, where no ground is; for then is a man able to hear a voice which says to him, '*When thou walkest through the waters I will be with thee, through the rivers, they shall not overflow thee. Lo, I am with thee always.*'

There are crises, however, in a man's life, when he is neither troubled with the dreams of the night nor of the day; when he is called to act, and to act at once; when there is no time for weighing motives and balancing arguments; when life and death hang upon the decision of a moment. To such a crisis had Joseph come when he spoke the words, '*Shall I do this great wickedness, and sin against God?*' The belief of a living, present God was then all in all to him. And at such a season it is all in all to every man, into whatever age he is born. Let no one, indeed, who is exposed to a fierce and sudden temptation, refuse any help that is afforded him by the lowest, most grovelling considerations. If the fear of punishment,—the shame of detection, the loss of credit, suggest itself to him as an argument for resistance, let him welcome it,—or any external impediment to crime, as an angel from heaven. The subtle suggestion, 'If thou hast no truer reason than this for being righteous, thou hadst better sin,' has caused the fall of thousands. No one bears more clearly the image and superscription of the tempter. But though this is true, let us all beware of trusting to any one of these motives, or fancying that it will stand us in any stead. In some foreign land,—where the traditions of childhood and home are no longer about you, where the laws of society are looser, where opinions you have held tenaciously are discredited,—there be sure that nothing will avail but the belief of a present Helper and Deliverer; of One who cares more for us than we care for ourselves; who may bring us into prison, but who will not suffer any who trust in Him and not in themselves, to fall from Him.

Thus far then we have not found that we shall gain much, by casting, as the phrase is, the theocratic element out of our lives, or, to speak plain English, by ceasing to believe in a living God who guides us and rules us. Alas, brethren, we have been casting away this belief more and more! In our religious talk about feelings and systems, in our philosophical cant about theocratic elements and abysses and eternities,—this practical faith has vanished more and more from us. And therefore I believe we are in the greatest danger of dreamers, and diviners, and magicians, who will arise among us to practise impostures, probably under the name of science. We are in danger of falling into hopeless mazes of speculation, seeming ever to advance, really returning to the point from which we set out. Finally, we are in danger, when any great trial of our moral strength comes, of sinking ignominiously, because we have nothing better to rely upon than calculations of consequences, or religious terrors, or a sense of honour; all which the gusts of passion may scatter to the winds. And lastly, I believe we are unable, through this unbelief, to realize that coherency and harmony in our lives which we trace in the life of the young Hebrew, amidst all the changes of his fortune. 'His days were linked each to 'each in natural piety.' The wishes of his infancy foreshadowed the events of his manhood. Every step of his discipline was a step in the formation of his character. It was so because he referred all dreams, instincts, events, to God; because he did not think about his own character, or how he was to bring his dreams to pass; but left himself and his history in God's hands. It will be so with us in the midst of all our complications if they drive us to the same course; if they lead us to think that because the path is too tangled for us to find it, we must trust Him to guide our steps. It will *not* be so, if we undertake to build up a character or make a scheme of life for ourselves; or if we choose any of the flickering lights of human systems, or of human teachers, to follow. The sparks which we have kindled, or which they have kindled, will not lead us through the darkness. We shall cry to one and to another, ' *Give us of your oil, for our lamps are gone out.*' And this because we have not gone to Him who is ready not to sell but to give, that we might get oil for ourselves; who is as willing to take the government and education of us, as He was to guide the Hebrew boy and the lord of Egypt.

But I must not forget, that while the dream of Joseph belonged specially to his own personal history, the dreams of Pharaoh were of a nation's abundance and famine. I do not wish to pass by the suggestion, that Joseph's interpretations and prophecy, and all the arrangements which are said to have been consequent upon them, were only the effect of ordinary sagacity and foresight; such as a politician in our day may exercise without any dream or interpretation or prophecy at all. I have said already, that both this view of the history, and that which we have just been considering, have, as it seems to me, a real worth. That worth consists in the witness which they bear against the inclination of divines to separate the narrative of Scripture, and the actors in it, from common life and experience; to represent them as exceptions, and not as rules; and so to outrage the conscience of Christendom, which has always received the Bible as a book of laws and examples for human beings. If any statements, even those which infringe most upon the divine authority of Scripture, warn us of this evil method into which we have unquestionably fallen,—and set us upon asking how we may return to an older and more honest one,—I cannot but bless God for them, and think that He has permitted them for the instruction of His church. That the way which the modern school takes to avoid the error, in the former instance, is not the right one, I have argued from our *individual* experience; that the way which it takes in this case, is not the right one, I could argue as confidently from our *national* experience. The first cry was, 'If we could 'but quite expel the theocratic element from our own 'lives, how clear and free they would be!' But the steps we have taken in this direction, did not seem to have made them at all freer and clearer; did not hold out any promise of their becoming so. 'If we could but get the theocratic 'element out of *politics*,' it is said, 'what insight and fore- 'sight our statesmen would possess; how ready they would 'be for all emergencies; how little they would be embar- 'rassed by any antiquarian maxims!' Do you find that we are making progress towards *this* consummation? Do you find that as the idea of God having any concern in the politics of the world has been more and more banished from our minds, our politics have become more consistent, more harmonious, more hopeful? Do you find that the trammels of old party-maxims can be cast off, or that if they are cast off, the freedom is a safe one? Do you find that there is no weary repetition of old phrases; no weary recapitulation of old experiments; no tendency to disappointment and despair even in the youngest, in whom hope is wont to be most alive? May it not be possible, brethren, that, in this case as in the other, we have sought to fill up the chasm which separates Scripture from the daily life of mankind, in the method which is just the reverse of the true one? Instead of talking about Joseph's political sagacity and foresight,—for which he certainly gave himself no credit,—might it not be better if we talked less of our own; if we inquired whence these qualities must come, supposing they be worth anything? And might not that consideration lead us to think, as Joseph thought, that man is made in the image of God; that God exercises providence, and that the creature who bears His image is intended to exercise providence; that the past, present, and future, are open to Him; that therefore,—in a measure according to the circumstances and exigencies in which He places Him,—He would have His creature study and interpret the past, the present, the future? May it not then be that, instead of the theocratic element having been too strong, at any time, in the politics of the world, it has always been far too weak; and that to this weakness we owe very much of the vagueness and imbecility of politicians, as well as very much of the unfair dealings and dangerous pretensions of priests? Yes, brethren, of *priests;* for the priest, who is sent into the world to testify that God is the King of the earth, may set up himself to be the king of it; he may secularize the Universe, that he may be the one spiritual person in it. If he does so, he will assuredly become, in the most radical and dreadful sense, secular himself. And if you acknowledge his falsehood, if you submit to be secularized by him,—if you say that your civil transactions have nothing to do with God,—he will establish his power over you; not a divine, godly power, but a very earthly, sensual, devilish power. Believe priests to be perpetual witnesses in their words, lives, sacraments, that you all of you stand in a direct relation to God; that you all of you are in covenant with Him; that every work of yours is a vocation from Him; that no part of your civil transactions is indifferent to Him, or can be excluded from His cognisance. Believe this, that politicians may possess manly strength and freedom, true insight and foresight; that they may recognise the past as connected with the present, and the present as the seed of the future. The Bible in its first book, and through after pages of it, is teaching you this political lesson; this is the lesson which we find opening upon us in the family-records of the book of Genesis; this is the lesson which the Code will more fully unfold; this is the deepest secret of the prophetical lore. Cast it away, and every new experience of the world, instead of giving you fresh light, will only be a fresh riddle: every new power you acquire in the world of sense will make you inwardly feebler; every new society you establish will only reproduce the weakness and rottenness of the old. Confess it, embrace it, act upon it, and every experience may be welcomed as part of the divine teaching, to correct past errors, to prepare blessings for the time to come; every discovery, every machine that gives you a victory over matter, will be a fulfilment of the divine promise and covenant; every colony that you send forth will raise up a race of men to till, subdue, enlighten, and civilize the earth.

And do not fancy that, in using this language, I am speaking as a Jew, not as a Christian; as a reader of the history of Joseph, not as a reader of the Sermon on the Mount, and the Epistles of St. Paul. The Sermon on the Mount brings into clear light and manifestation that divine and fatherly kingdom, of which Joseph saw the first glimpse when he became the teacher of Pharaoh, and the preserver of Egypt. It invites men to be like their Father in Heaven. It was spoken by One having authority, who showed forth that image in which man was created; who fulfilled the office of Prophet, because He was the Son of Him to whom the past, the present, and the future, are known; who exhibited the office of a King, because He was the Son of the King eternal, immortal, invisible; who created man to rule over the works of His hands. And the Epistles of St. Paul declare how He ascended on high, how He sent His Spirit to dwell among men; to endue them with gifts of wisdom and foresight; to fit them for all offices of obedience and government. The Gospel does indeed disclose to us a society consisting of all kindreds and nations; but it confirms the witness of the old dispensation,—that every special kindred and nation is grounded on the name and stands in the might of Him, who raised up a prisoner to inform princes of His will, and to teach senators wisdom.

SERMON VII.

JOSEPH AND HIS BRETHREN.

(Lincoln's Inn, Fourth Sunday in Lent, March 30, 1851.)
Lessons for the day, Genesis XLIII. and XLV.

GENESIS XLV. 7, 8.

God sent me before you to preserve you a posterity in the earth, and to save your lives by a great deliverance. So now it was not you that sent me hither, but God: and he hath made me a father to Pharaoh, and lord of all his house, and a ruler throughout all the land of Egypt.

WE finish this afternoon our yearly readings in the book of Genesis. I do not think we could find any words which exhibit its character more perfectly than those which I have taken for my text. They belong expressly to the life of Joseph. But Joseph,—contemplated in that aspect in which I purposely omitted to speak of him last Sunday, —is himself the most perfect embodiment of patriarchal history; the point of transition from it to the subsequent national history.

I. '*GOD sent me before you to preserve you a posterity in the earth.*' The brethren of Joseph were standing before him. To them he seemed to owe all that had been wretched in his past years; the unexpected change he might naturally attribute to his own faith, continency, wisdom, or to a new and opposite set of circumstances

But that natural conclusion was an impossible one to a child of the covenant who believed it to be true. He must refer the whole series of events, those which were linked to the sins of others, those which looked like the result of his own virtues, to God. How he could do this, and yet regard the wrong doings of his brothers as very heinous and needing punishment,—how he could do it, and yet feel that faith, obedience, moral strength, are the conditions of all greatness and victory for man,—we may consider presently. I wish you only to observe now that he did take this course; that he did refer the whole order and purpose of his existence, all that had been adverse to it, all that had been prosperous in it, to God. And you will not fancy, that his words implied a lazy acknowledgment of some ultimate cause to which it is convenient that all agencies, influences, operations, should be traced, lest we should be overwhelmed with their multitude. No such philosophical necessity had ever occurred to the mind of the Hebrew shepherd. When he was alone, when he was amidst his brethren, when they contrived his death, when they made him a slave, when he grew to be trusted and tempted, when he was in prison, when he was telling dreams, a living present Guide and Teacher had revealed Himself to him, as the One whom it was his privilege to know, and of whom his life was to testify in all its conditions of poverty or greatness. To think, 'Any part of this 'web of life has been woven by another than Him,—my 'brothers were able to throw me into a pit, I was able 'to win these honours without Him,'—would have been an utter inconceivable horror; simply the loss of the treasure which had been imparted to him in his father's tent, and compared with which all more recent treasures, except so far as they were the expansion and multiplication of this, had no worth at all.

I am sorry to use so many words for the purpose of impressing you with what may well seem so plain a truth. But it is because of its plainness that we forget it. In a complicated state of society, much of our time is spent in trying to unravel its complications; if not, we lose ourselves in them. In either case, it is very hard indeed to preserve or to acquire the habit of honestly and simply confessing an actual personal Being, as the source of the order we find in our own existence and in the universe. Phrases importing that we do, are very familiar to us; far too familiar. They are so ready for use, and are so much used, that their stamp is worn off, and they become merely conventional. For this reason it is so profitable to go back into this early morning of the world's day; not that we may talk about its clearness and freshness; not that we may fancy the earth was another earth than it is now, less subject to the damps and dreariness of night; not that we may fancy it was illuminated by some different sun; but that we may convince ourselves that it has a sun now which will warm us, and show us our way if we walk in the light of it. And this is the more necessary; because a very serious doubt, which must be settled, arises some time or other in all our minds, how, when so much of what we see and feel around us is evil, we dare attribute the universe and all its scheme and order to God. Must we not, in some sense, dispute his absolute goodness, or else let in, at some corner of our minds, the idea of a rival creator,—an Ahriman as well as an Ormuzd? In a number of different phases we shall have hereafter to face this question, and to see what help the Scripture gives us in solving it, when it has become most intricate and apparently hopeless. But now,—before the deeper puzzles of the conscience and heart have been brought out, while crimes are broad, coarse, palpable, and there is no casuistry among those who escape from them,—we have to inquire, how Joseph was able with such simple boldness to speak of God as having ordained a series of events, the actors in which,— no one felt more keenly than himself,—had been heartless, cruel, and false.

The answer, you will perceive, is precisely that to which all our previous examination of this book has led us. He recognised with infinite wonder an order in the whole story of his life; that order he was certain was God's. He knew that violence and disorder had been at work in it. What temptation had he to think of *them* as God's? Imputing to Him a distinct purpose of good and blessedness, what a strange perverseness it would have been to think that anything which had marred the good and blessedness, anything which had striven to defeat the purpose, was His? It was no distinction which the schools were to elaborate; it was the great eternal distinction, deeper than that between day and night, light and darkness, which a heart cultivated, purged, made simple by God's discipline, confessed, nay, found it impossible to deny. And just that which Joseph discovered in his own particular experience, Moses has been setting forth for the Universe. The order which God created is very good. The order which He preserves and upholds is very good. There was no flaw in it before man fell, there is no flaw in it since man fell. That fall had actually no power to subvert it, or derange it. That fall was precisely the refusal of a man to recognise his own glorious place *in* this order; an effort to make for himself an independent place *out* of it. He wants to be something in himself; he will not act and live as one made in the image of God. The history goes on, the disbelief and disorder multiply. But the eternal order goes on asserting itself,—calmly, uninterruptedly. God treats man according to the law which He laid down for him on the Creation-day. He speaks to him, unveils Himself to him, shows him that he can only live while he confesses a relation to Him. Do you find a few acknowledging this truth, the majority setting it at nought? But you find also that the few are leading simple, orderly, human lives; that the others are out of order, are inhuman. You must use that language; any other carries contradiction on the face, and in the heart of it. But how are these inhuman, disorderly creatures regarded by their Creator? Have they succeeded in establishing that place for themselves outside His universe which they seem to covet? No! they are within the circle of it, they are under His discipline and education. He is teaching them by their own disorders; by all that they are doing to set at nought His government, and to canonize their own self-will. He claims them as belonging to Him. They may resist the claim, they may choose a way of their own. They may try to shut themselves up in their separate Adam nature. But they cannot do it. The divine order is hemming them in, forcing them in their most inconsistent acts to acknowledge its presence, and to pay it homage. They are husbands, children, brothers, fathers. They cannot live in themselves, to themselves. They must act as if they belonged to a society. They will try to construct that society upon the basis of selfishness and self-will. They will throw aside the family bonds, and set up a mere wild, desert independence, or combine under some mighty hunter, or build cities where they are knit together by a desire to get a greater number of material enjoyments than they could procure separately. But in the desert the feeling of tribe is still present; their ready submission to the tyrant shows that they are meant for government; the cities must acknowledge a law; when it is utterly cast aside, and absolute self-indulgence reigns, fire comes down from heaven to assert its reality. And meantime the world is not left to these wild experiments to frame an order from disorders. God brings out Abraham, and teaches him what it is to be a husband and a father. The mystery of these relations discovers itself to him by slow degrees,—through his own errors, through the delay in the fulfilment of God's promises, through the witness which the covenant bears that he lives for the sake of a race unborn. So the ground is laid for a divine and human society. There is to be no hasty building upon that ground; the children of the covenant are to be for the present shepherds merely; every inclination they may feel to connect themselves with tribes apparently more advanced and organized, is disappointed. Yet they are not to be stationary. The twelve sons of Jacob bring forth a set of experiences, altogether different from any which we could hear of in Abraham's tent. The brotherly relation is elucidated through these experiences; as the fatherly and filial had been in the birth, circumcision, and sacrifice of Isaac. The sins of brothers form the subject of the narrative; through these sins we come to understand the true form of the character from which they are departures.

II. This is the second principle which the words of Joseph expound to us: '*God hath sent me before you to preserve you a posterity in the earth, and to save your lives by a great deliverance.'*

He starts with assuring them that GOD has been the orderer and director of his history, and that He has had a purpose in it. What purpose? The modern answer I think would be, 'To save His saint, and show the difference between him and his ungodly brethren.' A very proper answer that may be, but you see it is not Joseph's. He does not speak of a difference between himself and his brethren. He speaks of them as members of one family. He thinks that the special work to which he has been appointed,—that to which all his troubles and all his prosperity have been subservient,—is to preserve for them a posterity on the earth. What! to preserve a posterity for Reuben, and Simeon, and Levi, for those who had exhibited so much lawlessness, recklessness, instability, and whose seed,—as their father foresaw on his death-bed, —would resemble them in many of their worst features? Yes, for this very end. Joseph had no notion that his preservation meant anything, that it would be any lesson for the times to come, except so far as it served for the establishment and propagation of the covenant-family. He could not separate himself from it even in thought. He could not dream of any blessings for himself which were not blessings for it. The sin of his brothers had been that they would not feel themselves part of a family, that they would not act as if they belonged to it. What must his righteousness be but to take the opposite course? Wherein was he better than they if he did not recognise the sacredness of the bond which they had set at nought; if he had projects, or schemes of life, or hope for the future, apart from them?

Children feel that this is the sense and purport of the

story. They read it with intense interest, because they do not give it that narrow character which it receives from our mature religious selfishness. And therefore they are not perplexed by the question, 'But how was he not afraid to 'confound good with evil by putting himself on the level 'of his brothers, though they were not righteous men and 'he was?' They have an instinct to see that Joseph took the best of all methods to show the difference between good and evil, and that he could not have shown it if he had *not* put himself on the level of his brethren. He had indeed a power to which they were strangers, and he was bound to use it. Feeling himself to be God's servant, he could become God's instrument for educating them into an apprehension of their wrong-doing,—and into a perception of the blessings which they might claim. His roughness to them, his questions respecting their state and kindred,— the imprisonment of Simeon, the demand to see Benjamin, his unexpected kindness, the putting his cup into the youngest brother's sack,—were all steps in a discipline which he knew that One better than he was carrying on through his means. The effects of it must have made him wonder. To see how words apparently in nowise connected with their past history should have struck a chord in them which had never vibrated before, and led them to say, '*We are verily guilty concerning our brother;*' to see how such filial and brotherly love could be awakened in those who had conspired against him, that they should be ready to give up their own lives for Benjamin; this must have stirred deep and awful thoughts in him as it does in us. What a mysterious influence is this for one man to exert over another! That he should be able to call forth a Conscience in these rough shepherds! That he should open springs in hearts hitherto ice-bound! In Joseph's mind, these observations will not have taken so formal a shape; they will have been woven into his own personal feelings and sympathies; his absorbing belief in a present God will have turned them into acts of thanksgiving to Him, rather than into reflections upon man. Still, in one way or another,—we may be sure that he and we, at a distance of four thousand years, must have our deepest thoughts upon these things in common. For to us also the beauty of the history is in this,—that we see how truly a man may be the image of God in the practical teaching and discipline of those who are brought under His influence; how, if we indeed seek for His guidance and inspiration,— wondering at the latent harmonies there are in human spirits, trembling at their frightful discords, knowing our own incapacity to bring out the one, too conscious how often by a rude and ignorant meddling with instruments so subtle we have produced the other,—He will enable them to respond to a touch which is in truth His and not ours.

Joseph's story in this respect expands the principle which we have traced throughout the book of Genesis, and presents it in a higher form. A fuller revelation has been made of the method in which God was educating him; that revelation enables him to educate his brothers. But as the power of educating has been acquired through suffering, it can only be exercised through sympathy,—a sympathy the more perfect because it never sinks for a moment into indulgence, because it is mixed with sternness and punishment. His delay to own and embrace his brothers is of course the bitterest mortification to himself, the heaviest cross he could bear. There was a fear lest his father should die before he could meet him; the famine might sweep them all away before they were reconciled. Such thoughts must have come into his mind, but he could not give heed to them; his work must be done; for the sake of his family he was sent there; he must act for it, whether he puts his brothers to torture or himself.

III. And so he was indeed '*saving their lives by a great deliverance.*' He was providing against the immediate destruction which the famine was threatening them with; he was providing against the more thorough and permanent destruction which their own selfishness and crimes were working out. He understood this to be the purpose of God in His ways to them; a clear line of light was visible, running through all their deeds of darkness; it shone the brighter for that darkness; it directed him to the point whither all was tending; it showed him the direction of his own steps. God's intention was to save life, not to destroy it; there were all around powers and principles of destruction interfering with that intention and thwarting it; somehow it would accomplish itself; somehow death would be shown to be less mighty than life,—evil than good; his business was to act in the faith that it was so; to walk on manfully when he could not the least see how it was so or could be so; to trust himself implicitly to the God of his fathers, certain that He was righteous and true, whatever else was unrighteous and false; to be confident that if he did this in one place or another, in a prison or as chief man in Egypt, he should be a fellow-worker with the Creator of heaven and earth, a counter-worker of all that had marred His creation. So now '*it was not you that sent me hither, but God.*' 'That is my 'calm, deliberate conviction, wrought into me by years of 'trial, confirmed into a settled uniform certainty by those

vicissitudes in my lot, which at first sight would seem to
' be very unsettling. You have been my teachers, divine
' messengers and helpers to me on my way, fitting me
· to know what my task on earth is, fitting me to fulfil it.
' I owe you gratitude, not blame, for my own part, and
' that gratitude I have expressed by being in my turn your
' teacher; by showing you what a blessing God has put
' on your family; what it is to make divisions in that
' family; how we may in very deed act as if we had the
' covenant, and were brothers.' His speech was far nobler
and simpler than this; but these thoughts were all implied
in it. And there were still other words which he spoke
that are necessary to the understanding of his life, and of
the divine purpose as exhibited in it and in the whole book
of Genesis.

IV. '*He hath made me a father to Pharaoh, and lord of
all his house, and ruler over the land of Egypt.*' You might
have fancied that these words would have been uttered
first. The dignity seemed so much the greater to be
lord over a great kingdom, than to preserve a little
Palestine family. But it could not be greater in the mind
of Joseph; his human affections made the support of that
little family, a dearer object to him than Pharaoh and all
Egypt. And his affections did not give out a false note,
they responded to God's own teaching and inspiration;
the support of that family was not only a higher and
nearer duty to himself, it was a mightier service to
mankind. He was maintaining, so he believed, a seed in
which all families of the earth were to be blessed; a witness
for the divine order upon earth; a witness against all
contradictions and subversions of that order. But though
this obligation was first, it did not exclude the other.

His glory in Egypt had not been sought for by himself, it had been thrust upon him. God, who had sent him to save his own family by a great deliverance, had surely just as much proposed that he should be a father to Pharaoh and a lord of his land. So Joseph judged; on that faith he acted.

I would earnestly entreat you to consider what his course of action was. The commentators on the book of Genesis at the time of the Reformation,—when preaching in pulpits was more regarded and had more influence than it has now,—were wont to speak of the patriarchs as great preachers. So I believe that they were,—very great preachers; yet the specimens of their preaching, which I find in the only book that can have preserved any reports of it, do not answer to our common notions. Joseph did not go to Pharaoh saying, 'We Hebrews have 'a religion which is much better than the religion of you 'Egyptians. Cast off your own; embrace ours.' He said nothing at all about a religion. You might suppose,— from one part of the policy which he sanctioned and established,—that he had forgotten it; for he confirmed the previous privileges of the Egyptian priests, and did not insist that their land should be given up to Pharaoh. Joseph did not understand that he was sent into Egypt to bear witness of a religion, but of the living God, who had called him out, and made a covenant with him and with his fathers. That God he believed had chosen a family to declare His name,—to set Him forth as the Righteous Being,—the ground of the order of the world,— the only Deliverer of it from its disorders. Joseph's sermon to Pharaoh was therefore a simple declaration that this Righteous Being was the Lord over Egypt,—

that He could set it in order. And his sermon to the Egyptians was the proof which his administration gave that he had spoken truth. He showed them that there was an order in the disposition of seasons; in seed-time, and harvest; an order which sudden prosperity, followed by famines, did not interrupt; of which those startling changes were themselves signs. He showed that plenty and famine were themselves sent to cultivate self-discipline and providence in men; that men were therefore themselves the subjects of a higher order. He used the experience of their wants and sufferings as a means of leading them to acquiesce in an arrangement, or, rather, to propose it, which made them for the first time conscious that they were under a government which was caring for them, and watching over them; a government not arbitrary, not seeking its own ends, but confessing obligations to its subjects, while it demanded obedience from them. He organized a community,—he made the king feel that he stood in an actual living relation to his subjects, and his subjects in an actual relation to him and to each other. Scripture represents this as a divine work, for which a man must have a divine vocation. But it does not represent Joseph as moulding Egypt according to a Jewish type. There is little in his institutions, which corresponds to the after-organization of the Jewish nation. Being God's servant, he was to take the materials which he found lying about him, to show that there was an order in them, however they might have fallen into disorder; not to bring in some scheme or notion of his own. Kings, priests, proprietors, were already there. He was not to alter that fact; nor to say that these were not the elements of a human society, but to prove that they were;

not to tell Egyptians that God had not been working among them, till a Hebrew boy came there, but to show them that He had; that they ought to have owned His working in all the common business of their lives; to believe that He was working among them for good, and not for evil.

'But a child of the covenant ought to testify against 'false worship.' And was not this a testimony against false worship,—the greatest that could be borne? Do you mean by *false* worship idolatrous worship? Did not Joseph declare that an *unseen* Being was the King and Lord of their society and of outward nature? Do you mean by *false* worship *devil* worship,—the worship of malevolent powers, who were plotting mischief against the land, and those who dwelt in it? Joseph declared by his words and acts that a *Righteous* Being, one perfectly gracious, who was doing good and only good to those who dwelt in it, ruled over their society and over nature. It is most important to remark, that this was the first form of the Jewish protest. When the family became a nation, it was to speak out boldly against idolatry and devil worship,— to maintain a perpetual and dreadful fight against them. But we shall mistake the nature of that fight altogether, if we suppose it was a struggle for a Jewish religion against other religions. The story of Joseph in Egypt is written to confute such a falsehood. Before any law had been given,—before any word had been spoken about idolatry, as such,—the Hebrew youth is uttering that very truth concerning God which Moses and Joshua and David were to utter in quite other methods. He was declaring Him to be the true and merciful King of the whole earth; he was claiming his right as a child of the covenant, to exhibit

Him in that character, and to organize a society which was not in the covenant, upon that conviction.

If there is anything in these statements, brethren, which jars with previous notions and theories of yours, once and again I say, ' *To the law and to the testimony; if we speak not according to this word, there is no light in us.*' If I have in any way tortured the Scriptures, if I have departed from their literal meaning, I would beseech you not to heed what I have said. The effort to follow them strictly, has removed a great many crude and artificial notions from my mind. I think it would have that effect upon yours. I never can believe that the Bible has less power of making itself intelligible than other books; I have always found that it threw much more light upon others, than it received from them. Its commentators are often of exceeding value when we use it to expound them; otherwise they are very difficult. But it is especially when we ask its help in unravelling the tangled skein of our own personal and social life, that its meaning comes out to us strong and clear. We see then, that it is not telling us about itself or teaching us to make it an object of our worship; that it tells us of a living Lord who was with Joseph, and who is with us. It is telling us what the will and purpose of that living Being is towards us and towards the universe. It is telling us what His method is in dealing with the creatures whom He has formed in His image. It is telling us how He forms them into societies, and deals with them as belonging to a society; how it is their continual tendency to act as if they were selfish creatures having no relation to each other. It tells us how in so doing they sink into worshippers of the visible, and forget the invisible. It tells us how a family is called out to show forth the true divine law of society, and to strive against the false and destructive perversion of it. It tells us how the members of the chosen family are just as prone to that perversion as any other men,—and exhibit it in a new and more pernicious form,—pretending that God has set them up against His other creatures, not as blessings to them. It tells us how He is true, though all men should be liars; how His chosen seed, in spite of its own pride and sin, does its work, and will at last accomplish it altogether.

The book of Genesis forms a very complete introduction to the history of that seed; not anticipating the subsequent developments, but in a specially simple family-history embodying the principles which must hereafter be seen in the nation and in the church. Some writers are fond of speaking of the characters and facts which it brings before us, as types of those which we are to read of in the New Testament. Joseph especially they look upon as a type of the Son of Man. I have not used this language, because I am afraid it is apt to beget a feeling that the Bible is not so much a real book containing a history of actual men, as a repository of ingenious analogies. I know no feeling against which, in these days, we have more need to struggle than that. But the great truth which is implied in this typical view of Scripture, I have endeavoured to illustrate in each discourse. Because I regard Abraham, Jacob, and Joseph, as actual men, men made in the image of God, I must regard them as showing forth some aspect of His character and life whom I recognise as the express Image of God's person; some grace answering to the full grace which was in Him. The whole story of Joseph would seem to me a mere strange episode,—an exhibition of virtues for which there was no ground, an awakening of hopes never to be fulfilled,—if I did not think that in the fulness of the time He was manifested whose goings forth had been of old, from everlasting, whose life had been in all ages the Light of men; that He was separated from His brethren through their sin; that He was sent before them to preserve life and to build up a family on earth and in heaven; so that God, and not Caiaphas or Pontius Pilate, was the author of His death and His resurrection; by which death and resurrection He has proved Himself to be the Head of His Church, the Brother of every man, the Ruler and Deliverer of the Nations.

SERMON VIII.

THE MISSION OF MOSES.

(Lincoln's Inn, Fifth Sunday in Lent, April 6, 1851.)
Lessons for the day, Exodus III. and V.

EXODUS v. 22, 23.

And Moses returned unto the Lord, and said, Lord, wherefore hast thou so evil entreated this people? why is it that thou hast sent me? For since I came to Pharaoh to speak in thy name, he hath done evil to this people; neither hast thou delivered thy people at all.

No one doubts that the History in the book of Exodus is the history of a deliverance. The most superficial reader would say, that the subject of it is the redemption of a people out of slavery. The Church has adopted this view of it so completely, that we do not break the ordinary course of our reading on Palm Sunday and Easter Day. The chapters respecting the plagues which were sent to Pharaoh, respecting the Passover, and the passage of the Red Sea, are our lessons on the Passion and the Resurrection. The Law of Redemption (so the Church teaches) is asserted in the Old Testament facts; is evolved and fulfilled in the facts of the New. We are not taught to look upon one as belonging to an earthly, the other to a spiritual economy; the one as merely a figure of the other. The Jewish Redemption is nothing except as it has a spiritual foundation.

The Christian Redemption is nothing if its results do not affect the earth. Neither is figurative; both are substantial

At the close of the book of Genesis we found the records of the Hebrew family becoming interwoven with those of the Egyptian monarchy. There was no confusion between them. The family remained a family surrounded with all its patriarchal traditions, marked out by the sign of a divine covenant. The kingdom of the Pharaohs was already existing. Joseph subverted nothing which he found. He merely taught kings, priests, and people, that they were different parts of an order established by God; that there were relations between them, and obligations due from each to the other. He never for a moment forgot his own peculiar position. Only by remembering it, could he help a people which did not share it with him. If he had ceased to look upon himself as a chosen witness for the unseen God, he would have lost his power of serving the king and nation of Egypt.

This is the connexion between the inhabitants of Goshen and the natives of Egypt, when the curtain falls upon the first act of this divine drama. Before it rises again, they are changed. Another Pharaoh, perhaps another dynasty, is ruling. The stranger race is multiplied, it has become dangerous and suspected. They are still no part of the Egyptian nation, but are distinguished from it by race, occupation, the covenant. It is reasonable to suppose that they are also distinguished by want of organization; by ignorance of the arts in which Egypt was beginning to excel; by greater grossness and barbarism. The patriarchal family had grown into a horde; it must have lost its domestic character, yet it was attached to no polity. The low habits which the sacred historian attributed to the sons of Jacob would assuredly be perpetuated and diffused among their descendants,—settled in a rich country, with a considerable command of material enjoyments, still practising pasturage,—though surrounded by men who had made much progress in tillage.

A people in this state was ripe for slavery. It only required a monarch with some ordinary notions of policy, and some ambition of making himself illustrious by great works, to conceive the plan of using such a set of ready-made tools to build tombs or treasure-houses. The Scripture narrative brings a monarch of the kind before us, with magicians as his advisers. It scarcely requires the commonest and oldest information we possess respecting Egyptian wisdom, though the latest may be very serviceable, to explain what kind of advisers these must have been. They must have possessed a knowledge of nature beyond that of their countrymen, who had sufficient experience of the utility of such knowledge to reverence teachers endued with any rare portion of it. The magicians must have considered this knowledge as divine; and have come more and more to regard the different powers of nature and the different objects in which these powers were exhibited, as themselves divine. They will have been politicians as well as naturalists, ready to employ their lore and the mastery which it gave them over the things of the earth, to uphold the authority of the monarch, or to promote his plans. They will therefore have fallen into a scheme of trick and dissimulation, which would have been ineffectual and impossible, if there had not been some truths lying at the root of it; and some real assurance in their own minds both of those truths and of their own capacities. It is this mixture of faith with insincerity,—of actual knowledge with the assumption of knowledge, of genuine power with the desire to make the power felt and worshipped, a readiness therefore to abuse it to low grovelling purposes,—which we have to recognise in the impostures of all subsequent ages, and to which we are here introduced in one of its primitive manifestations. It was most natural for a politic monarch to wish that a body of strangers, who were doing little good in a certain portion of his land, should be made slaves, and so become agents in carrying out what seemed to him magnificent projects. It was most natural that a body of politic priests,—disliking these strangers, for the traditions and customs which separated them from their influence,—should readily cooperate with him in that plan, or should be the first suggesters of it. It was equally natural that his Egyptian subjects should sympathise with the design, and should feel that they were raised in the degradation of another race. But it was impossible that king, priests, and people, should effect this seemingly sage and national purpose, without forging new chains for themselves, without losing some perceptions of a moral order in the world and a moral Ruler of it, which had been implied in their government and worship, and which Joseph's arrangements had drawn out; it was impossible but that with the loss of this feeling, they should sink further and further into natural and animal worship.

These remarks I believe are quite needful for the understanding of the life of Moses, upon which we entered this morning. That life is encompassed, in the *Antiquities* of Josephus, with a multitude of incidents, all tending to glorify the great Lawgiver of the nation, and to show what feats he was able to accomplish for his Egyptian masters while he was content to be the leader of their armies. The Scripture narrative may be summed up in a few lines. Very simple lines indeed,—belonging no doubt to a remarkable story, but one which cannot be called eventful or glorious, seeing that in the course of eighty years only five or six events are recorded, and the majority of those not tending to the exaltation, but to the humiliation of him who is the hero of them. Moses is saved by his mother's love from the sentence of exposure which had been pronounced upon the Hebrew children; Pharaoh's daughter pities the child, draws him out of the Nile, brings him up as her son. He learns the wisdom of the Egyptians; he feels for the misery of his own people; he kills an Egyptian who was oppressing one of them. He tries to convince two Hebrews that they are brethren, and finds that his own countrymen are likely to ruin him for wishing to make them free. He flies into the land of Midian, helps the daughters of a priest who have come to a well to draw water,—dwells with the man, becomes his son-in-law, begets two sons; for forty years keeps the flock of Jethro in the desert.

This is all we hear of the deliverer and leader of the Hebrew people, before the event which was recorded in the first lesson for this morning. Our previous studies in the book of Genesis will have prepared us to think that a revelation of God is not an interruption of a Scripture narrative; not an exception from that which it lays down as the law of man's life,—but a part of the divine order, without which human life would be irregular and confused. And we were not left without signs and tokens to guide our thoughts respecting the

THE PURPOSE OF VISIONS. 159

nature of such revelations. What was said of the ladder which Jacob saw in his vision, and of his own impressions when he awoke, would lead us to expect that no discovery of this kind could be merely momentary, or for a momentary purpose. It must be merely the removal of some cloud which concealed an actual abiding presence from the man to whom the vision was granted,—that he might know the ground upon which he was at all times standing. In Jacob's case we saw that the vision was not to the outward eye. It came to him in a dream, as if for the very purpose of declaring that it was not an appearance to the senses which made the place whereon he had slept dreadful. In Jacob's case we found that the blessing was one which he could not limit to himself. The words which were spoken to him concerned his seed. The God who was near him when he knew it not, would be as near to them as He was to him.

Moses had passed many more years in the world than Jacob; knew much of which he was ignorant; had experienced a kind of sorrow which had never reached him. He had passed through the sore trial, of feeling himself the member of an utterly degraded race, which he had dreamed of helping, and could not help; in the very sufferings of which he was not allowed to share. He had had an early inward intimation, that he might unite and deliver this people. The intimation had come to nothing. They were more crushed than ever; he was bound to a strange country, connected with a family which belonged to no tribe of Israel. Did the covenant of his fathers mean anything? Was it true that an actual living Being had called them out from all the families of the earth? Was it true that He had promised to be with them and to protect them? All appearances contradicted such a belief. But if it were true, if that promise were ever fulfilled, what was the truth or the promise to him? The flock he was keeping was not the flock of any Palestine shepherd. He might call himself an Egyptian, a Midianite, an Ethiopian, as well as a Hebrew.

Yes. And this education in an Egyptian court, in the family of a Midianitish priest, in an Ethiopian desert, was just the one which was to prepare him for understanding the vocation of a Hebrew in the world; was just the one which was to fulfil all his early wishes and anticipations; just the one which was to make him fit for a deliverer and lawgiver of his people. It required that he should be far from kinsmen and from country,—from every external association with the covenant of his fathers,—that he might hear and understand the words, I AM THAT I AM; that he might believe the assurance, *I Am hath sent thee.*

Before Moses heard these words, he had turned aside to see a great sight. A bush was burning and was not consumed. Apart from the meaning which he may then or afterwards have discerned in that sign, there is something, I apprehend, in the method of this revelation which must have been very instructive to him, and may be to us. It is an outward sign, something appealing to curiosity and wonder, which first seizes the attention of a man, whether he be a shepherd on a lonely plain or the dweller in a city, and which compels him to ask himself, 'What is this? whence comes it?' He may turn aside to see the great sight merely as a sight. The impression it makes may be upon his senses, or through his senses upon his imagination. But if his mind has been much exercised with inward conflicts before,—if he has been seeking for something not to gratify his eyes, but to be a rest and home for his own being, if his thoughts concerning himself have been connected with thoughts of other men, if he has been labouring under a weight which is resting upon himself and upon them,—then the visible object will not be that which takes possession of him or holds him captive. It will be but the *sign* to him of something behind and beneath. He will ask for that which is signified by the burning bush. Its terror, and its wonder, will be not in itself, but in that.

'*And when the Lord saw that he turned aside to see, God called unto him out of the midst of the bush, and said, Moses, Moses. And he said, Here am I.*' This form of speech we have already met with in the Scripture; we shall meet with it often again. I can conceive none which so perfectly indicates and expresses the revelation of the unseen Lord to the conscience of His creature, and its acknowledgment of the Divine Presence in the acknowledgment of itself. A man says, '*Here am I,*' when he feels that there is One higher than himself holding converse with him. He knows that he is, because he believes that God is. But the voice said, '*Draw not nigh hither; for the place whereon thou standest is holy ground.*' Then came to a waking man in broad daylight that assurance of an invisible Being near to him, before whom he must bow down, which came to Jacob when he was asleep. It was the discovery to him of an actual person; of the God of his fathers, of Him who had spoken to them. He was not a name, then; not a tradition, not a dream of the past. He lived now as He lived then; He who had been with men in past ages, was actually with him at that hour. '*And He said, I am the* GOD *of thy father, the God of Abraham, and of Isaac, and of Jacob. And Moses hid his face; for he was afraid to look upon God.*' The visible appearance was nothing; the burning bush had no awe in it. That had only led him to turn aside and see. The awe was in that he could not see; but which was so intensely real; '*he was afraid to look upon* GOD.'

And yet the same revelation which awakened this fear gave the assurance, '*I have surely seen the affliction of my people which are in Egypt, and have heard their cry by reason of their taskmasters; for I know their sorrows; and I am come down to deliver them.*' I do not apprehend that such a communication will have made the fear of Moses less. There is something infinitely awful in the belief of One who knows what we are feeling and thinking, and what hundreds of other beings are feeling and thinking. If we actually had this belief, if we realized it as Moses must have done at that moment, we too should hide our faces. The sense of that penetrating eye would be for a time overwhelming. But, '*I have known their sorrows, I have heard their cry;*' here is the pressure from beneath which supports the pressure from above; this imparted to Moses the trust and hope which were stronger than his fear, though they did not destroy it. And the declaration, '*I am come to deliver them,*' gave the interpretation to all those dim anticipations and vague dreams which he had cherished, that he was to be the deliverer. Another and a mightier than he was interested in this work; HE would undertake it, HE would carry it through. The promise made hundreds of years before to Abraham would yet be accomplished; '*I will bring them up out of that land, unto a good land and a large, unto a land flowing with milk and honey, unto the place of the Canaanites, and the Amorites, and the Perizzites, and the Hivites, and the Jebusites.*' All this is possible, all this must be. This broken race of slaves has not been multiplying for nothing during all these years; it will yet do what it was called out to do. Mighty tribes will fall before it, the good land shall be ours.

You say this was a powerful impression upon the mind of a shepherd. So say I too. The question is, how you are to account for that impression, whence it came. Given the impression, I want to know the impresser. I can only speak about it as the Bible does. I believe it was God who gave him the impression. I do not find it very wise to conclude that Moses made it upon himself. He had the impression before, that he was to set his people free. He could make nothing of it. The wish was there; not the power to fulfil the wish. That came when the living and eternal God made him know that He was, and that He was a deliverer. The words, '*I have seen the oppression wherewith the Egyptians oppress them,*' are immediately followed by these, '*Come now, therefore, and I will send* THEE *unto Pharaoh, that* THOU *mayest bring forth the children of Israel out of Egypt.*' The man begins to understand that he is made in God's image, and that he can only be what is righteous, and do what is beneficial, when the righteous and wise Lord moulds his character and directs his acts.

Yet this inspiration is not sufficient. For when the creature is brought into communion with the Creator, a feeling of superhuman power alternates with a sense of weakness and helplessness such as was never realized before: '*And Moses said unto God, Who am I, that I should go unto Pharaoh, and that I should bring forth the children of Israel out of Egypt?*' This is the first of a series of utterances, betokening the consciousness of a vocation, and reluctance to enter upon it, which I believe have attested the truth of this narrative to thoughtful and earnest men who knew their own hearts, more than all arguments on behalf of it. They have perhaps felt strongly and often the temptation to say, 'This is only what we 'have ourselves experienced; it is not the account of a 'revelation at all;' but when they have tried to explain fairly to themselves what they *have* experienced, they have been much more disposed to confess with silence and awe, ' Moses has delivered the simple fact; we were perverting ' it by notions and theories of ours. God was with us, ' and we knew it not.' No! brethren, it was not a discourse which passed in the mind of a man, where none was present but himself. There would have been no discourse; the whole would be a fiction; your lives and mine would be a fiction, if it had been so. Moses knew that One was sending him who had a right to send him and whom he ought to obey. He felt in himself an utter incapacity for the work which was laid upon him; he had a desire to shrink from it, and to bury himself in the earth, rather than undertake it. And with this cowardice he had the courage to speak it out; he believed that the Being who was holding converse with him desired truth in his inward parts, and would bear no prevarication. He could tell all that was in him, because he was sure that there was One near who understood him, and could set him right; of all assurances the most helpful to a man who craves to be right himself; the most indispensable to one who has a great task to fulfil for his brethren. Such a conviction does not make him fanatical; he knows himself to be full of fanaticism, as well as of timidity; he could have no hope of being cured of either tendency if he could not lay open his heart to a Being who knew the secrets of it, who could make him calm and bold; careful of obeying his own impulses; equally careful not to be scared by appearances or possible consequences from going on in a straight line to the end which is set before him.

But the great revelation of all, that for which I said Moses had been prepared by so marvellous a discipline, was still to come. '*And Moses said unto God, Behold, when I come unto the children of Israel, and shall say unto them, The God of your fathers hath sent me unto you, and they shall say unto me, What is his Name? what shall I say unto them?*' It was an awful question; asked with deep awe: 'The Egyptians have their Ammon, their hidden God. 'They have other names for each power and object they 'worship. God of our fathers, by what name shall I dare 'to speak of *Thee?*' The answer came forth: '*And God said unto Moses,* I AM THAT I AM: *and he said unto him, Thus shalt thou say to them,* I AM *hath sent me unto you.*' Oh! that I could persuade you, brethren, and persuade the teachers of our land, not to try to make words of such deep and tremendous significance as these more intelligible by translating them into the dry philosophical formula of 'the 'self-existing Being.' Oh! that we could believe that the Scripture form of speech is the right form; that in it we have a living, life-giving substitute for our dead phrases; that when we cling to them we are in infinite danger of merging the person in a vague generality, the substance in a phantom. We should indeed be able and most ready to point out the connexion between Scripture forms of speech and all others; we should not suffer ourselves to be deceived by a mere repetition of the divine words; or give ourselves credit for entering into truths because we can quote glibly the texts which express them. But when we are most feeling the bondage of customary religious phrases and technicalities of theology,—such sentences as these offer themselves to us as the greatest helps to our emancipation; as hints how language may be a ladder set upon earth and reaching to heaven,—how the peasant who knows no logic and can comprehend no abstractions, may rise to true and practical apprehensions of God, from which our logic and our abstractions are excluding us.

But further, I would beseech you to remember that Moses was called to be the deliverer and founder of a Nation. The more we read of that nation, the more we shall feel that it could not have for its basis any abstraction or logical formula. It stood upon no conception of the unity of God, it stood upon no denial of the Egyptian faith, or any other; it stood upon no scheme of making the speculations of priests or hierophants the property of the people. Either it stood upon this Name, or both it and all that has grown out of it are mockeries and lies from first to last; roots, branches, flowers, fruit, all are rotten, and all must be swept away. 'The Lord God of the 'Hebrews, the God of our nation, the God of Abraham, 'Isaac, and Jacob, the God of our family, has established 'and upholds the order of human existence and of all 'nature,' this is the truth which Moses learnt at the bush; the only one which could encounter the tyranny of Pharaoh, or the tricks of the magician; the only one which could bring the Jews or any people out of slavery into manly freedom and true obedience.

We hear much from a certain school in our days of the intense nationality of the Mosaic Economy; especially we are reminded again and again that the God whom the Jews worshipped was the Lord God of the Hebrews. So far from suppressing this fact, I shall delight to bring it before you, to present it in all the aspects in which the Scripture presents it. I believe that there ceases to be any reality in the story if we explain away this fundamental characteristic of it; that the Jews, instead of having done more for the world than any other people, would have done nothing for it, if they had not believed that the Lord was *their* God. But while you give all possible prominence to this assertion, while you remember that in the very passage of which I have been speaking Moses is told to say to the people, ' *The Lord God of your fathers, the God of Abraham, and Isaac, and Jacob, hath sent me to you: this is my name for ever, and this is my memorial unto all generations,*' do not let the remembrance of that other pass from your minds. Do not suppose that the deep hollow in the heart of the lonely shepherd could have been filled by the thought, all cheering and wonderful as that was, of one who cared for his fathers and chose them. Abraham in his intercession had said, ' *Shall not the Judge of the whole earth do* RIGHT?' His own discipline, the discovery of his own wrong, had led him to perceive a righteousness lying at the root of the universe. Faith in God's Righteousness was the source of his own righteousness. And now that Moses is going forth to encounter the unrighteousness of the world in its high places,—now that the chosen people are called to this higher stage of their history, now that they are not only to witness for good in the earth but to fight with evil —

that Name is proclaimed which tells them that their calling is to struggle for that which IS against that which is NOT; for the Absolute and Eternal Truth against every thing that is counterfeit and false. And this truth is living, present, personal. He himself is the Lord of hosts, claiming the subjection and allegiance of every power upon earth; putting down every power which tries to be independent of Him, and to set up its own self-will. The vision of such a Power, working at every moment near to every man, is appalling. And yet upon it rests all the security of the words, '*I have seen the affliction of my people, and heard their cry, and know their sorrows.*' It was no partial sympathy, though particular men, actual creatures, were, as they needs must be, the objects of it. In all acts towards them, the sympathy of the divine nature with the sufferer, the hatred of the divine nature for the oppressor, would be gradually unfolding itself. Love would be seen to be the eternal twin of Truth; not a feeble creature of time pleading for the infraction of the laws upon which heaven and earth rest, seeking exemption for one and another from its universal obligations.

I have alluded already to those struggles in the mind of Moses himself, which are so strikingly brought out in the fourth chapter of Exodus, when he found that he was not eloquent, neither heretofore nor since the Lord had spoken to him; when he exclaimed, '*Oh my Lord, send, I pray thee, by the hand of him whom thou wilt send.*' I would not willingly destroy the force of such passages by any elaborate comment upon them. You cannot fail to perceive, I think, how perfectly they are in harmony with that view of the Divine Education, which forced itself upon us so strongly in the Book of Genesis. Throughout we see the divine Will treating men as voluntary, spiritual creatures; not crushing, but calling forth into lively consciousness, the will that is in them; allowing it to feel itself, to assert its own freedom; then teaching it slowly, gradually, wherein that freedom consists; what destroys it. But this discipline becomes now more distinct than before, because we have reached a time when we are to see how men are trained to be leaders and shepherds of a people; and how those processes which are to go on in the heart of a whole society are first transacted and experienced in their own hearts. One remark I would make in reference to this subject, which may not be without use hereafter. Moses, we are told in the fourth chapter, was assured of the reality of his commission by certain outward signs, which signs it was promised that he should be able to exhibit before Pharaoh. It was *after* he received this evidence that these doubts and internal conflicts occurred which made him wish to give up his task altogether. There was no charm then in these miracles. They *had* a deep meaning and purpose; they had *not* the power,— they were not *meant* to have the power,—of overcoming the resistance of the human spirit to the will of its Creator.

But that resistance was overcome. Moses went to the heads of the Hebrew tribes, and told them that the Lord God of their fathers was caring for them, and about to deliver them. They bowed their heads and worshipped. He knew that he had come in the right Name; he had not to prove his commission; their sufferings interpreted it. Through suffering God had revealed Himself to their fathers, through suffering He spoke to them. He had now encouragement for the other part of his task. He went in unto Pharaoh and said " *Thus saith the Lord God of Israel.*

Let my people go, that they may hold a feast unto me in the wilderness. And Pharaoh said, Who is the Lord, that I should obey his voice to let Israel go? I know not the Lord, neither will I let Israel go.' We may think that this would be of course the language of a heathen king, of one who was not in the covenant. The Scripture does not teach us so. We are told that the Lord spoke to Laban and to Abimelech, and that they understood His voice. When Joseph told Pharaoh who was reigning in his day, that the Lord had sent him his dream, and had interpreted it, he believed the message and acted accordingly. It is never assumed in any part of Scripture that God is not declaring Himself to heathens, or that heathens may not own Him. We shall find precisely the opposite doctrine in the Old Testament as in the New. When then this Pharaoh said, '*Who is the Lord, that I should obey his voice?*' we are to understand that he had brought himself into a condition of ignorance and darkness, which did not belong to him in consequence of his position, or of any natural disadvantages. He had come to regard *himself* as the Lord, his will as the will which all things were to obey; therefore he said inevitably, '*Who is* THE *Lord?*' He had lost the sense of a righteous government and order in the world; he had come to believe in tricks and lies; he had come to think men were the mere creatures and slaves of natural agencies. Had God no voice for such a man, or for the priests and the people whom he represented, and whose feelings were the counterparts of his? We shall find that He had. But it must be another voice than that which said, '*I am the Lord. Let my people go.*' It must utter itself in plagues of fire and darkness and blood.

Pharaoh said that the people were idle, and therefore

that they desired to cease from their works. He commanded the taskmasters to increase their burdens; they were to make bricks without straw. The officers of the children of Israel saw that they were in evil case. They thought that those who professed to be their deliverers had proved their worst enemies. And Moses and Aaron felt the same. Had they not deceived themselves after all? Was not the whole of that strange vision in the desert a mockery? Was not Moses born to be the plague of his nation, and his own? And Moses said, '*Wherefore is it that thou hast so evil intreated this people? why is it that thou hast sent me? for since I came to Pharaoh to speak in thy name, he hath done evil to this people; neither hast thou delivered thy people at all.*'

It was the hardest, bitterest of all experiences, yet for a man who had a mighty work to do,—and who must be assured that he was merely the instrument in doing it, not the author of it,—the most necessary. And such, even such a discipline,—only deeper and more dreadful, because He was not merely the deliverer of a nation, but of mankind, not merely *a* man, but *the* Man, not merely the servant, but the Son,—did He pass through,—who trod the winepress alone, when of the people there was none with Him; who knew the sorrows and oppressions of His creatures by actual experience of them; who in the hour of redemption felt the most unutterable desertion; and who yet could say, (and the Jews understood what He meant, for they took up stones to stone Him,) '*Before Abraham was*, I AM.' *

* Part of the Gospel for the day.

SERMON IX.

THE MIRACLES OF MOSES, AND THE HARDENING OF PHARAOH.

(Lincoln's Inn, Palm Sunday, April 13, 1851.)
Lessons for the day, Exodus IX. and X.

EXODUS x. 20.

But the Lord hardened Pharaoh's heart, so that he would not let the children of Israel go.

THREE questions arise out of the chapters which we read this morning and this evening, each of which has exercised the skill of commentators, and, what is far more important, the hearts of earnest practical readers. The first concerns the nature and purpose of the miracles which Moses wrought in Egypt; the second, the powers which the magicians are said to have put forth in rivalry of his; the third, the hardening of Pharaoh's heart, which is attributed in my text, and in many other passages, to '*the Lord.*'

As the last subject bears the most seriously upon our own lives and upon our views of the character of God, I wish to keep it most prominently before me, and to devote most of this discourse to it. But I cannot omit the other topics. They too are, in a moral point of view, deserving of the greatest attention. The right consideration of them will, I believe, be very helpful to the right consideration of the deeper enigma.

I. A free-thinking traveller in Egypt, who wrote about twenty years ago, said that he had seen himself all the plagues, which Moses speaks of as miraculously inflicted upon the land. Allowing for the exaggeration of a man who wished to utter a startling sentence, there is little in this statement to which a literal believer in the Mosaic narrative need object. The sacred historian never intimates that there had not been plagues of locusts, or of hail, or of flies, or of darkness before, or that there might not be again. More than once he suggests a comparison between the one which he is describing and others of a like kind. In what sense then, it may be asked, did they deserve the name of portents or miracles? I answer, these names, or some equivalent names, would have been given to them by the Egyptians themselves, or by any people to whom they occurred, without any reference to the purpose with which Moses connects them, or to the Being who he says was the sender of them. That which presents itself to the senses of men as something strange, unusual, fearful, they will call a portent: that which awakens their wonder, and for which they cannot account, they will describe as a miracle. The scientific man is as much bound to admit the existence of portentous facts as the most vulgar man; only he says that he can account for a great many of those by which the other is staggered. Those which he cannot account for he still believes are referable to some law; they are not mere accidents or irregularities.

The business of the magician or enchanter, was to deal with portents of this kind. He was to produce them if they were wanted, for the service of himself or of his masters. If they came without his summons, he was to explain their origin, and to suggest any measures that were desirable in consequence of them. His power had two supports. First, the *certainty* in men's minds that all phænomena must have some cause, with the witness of the conscience that the cause had something to do with them. Secondly, the *uncertainty* whether the cause might not be a malevolent being, whether his indignation might not proceed from some delight in injuring them, from a mere capricious pleasure in exercising power, from some honour or service refused to himself for which he required compensation or propitiation. The office of the soothsayer could not have been so honoured as it was, if there had not been an inward testimony in the heart to the worth and reality of the function which he assumed. It could not have become the false thing that it became, if there had not been an ignorance of a moral standard by which his explanations could be tested.

Now consider what was the foundation of the message which Moses brought to the king of Egypt. He said, 'The I AM,' the perfectly true Being, had sent him. He said this Being cared for a set of slaves upon whom Pharaoh and the Egyptians were trampling. He said that the Lord God commanded Pharaoh to let this people go. First of all he gave signs and tokens, such as the magicians were wont to give of their skill and potency, claiming the power of producing these signs, not for himself, but for the invisible Being who commanded Pharaoh to do what was right. Then all the powers of nature to which the Egyptians did homage, to which the magicians taught them to do homage, began to be ministers of destruction to them. One terrible visitation

followed another. 'All these,' said Moses, 'have a moral
'end, all come from a righteous Ruler. These powers of
'nature are His. They have broken loose upon you, not
'in wild disobedience, but as the regular orderly ministers
'of His purposes. They come from no capricious decree.
'They obey a law. God's order has been violated by
'you; He is asserting it. Man, His chief and highest
'creature, has been put down. He is determined to raise
'him up, and to show that these natural agents are his
'servants, not his masters. Again, a man has forgotten
'that he only reigns because he is made in the image of
'God. Pharaoh has presumed to reign for himself, to set
'himself up as an independent self-willed ruler. These
'natural agents, these plagues of fire and darkness, are
'sent to mock his supremacy, to make him feel his
'weakness, to show him that he can only be a master
'when he confesses himself to be a subject.'

I cannot conceive any sublimer witness than this for an order of the universe, and for that order which had been from the beginning, which was proclaimed on the Creation-day, when God said, '*Let us make man in our image, after our likeness;*' which was proclaimed in the Flood, in the Call of Abraham, in the lessons which the Hebrew prisoner gave to the king. Throughout it is a *moral* order, a *human* order; not interfering with the order of nature,—vindicating it, interpreting it, but still rising above it. The order of the family we found was more precious and sacred than the order of seed-time and harvest; yet God by bringing out the one into clearness brought out also the other. Now we are to learn that the political order,—the relation of kings to subjects, of the highest to the meanest,—is more sacred than the laws of light and darkness, than those which regulate the flight of insects or the inundation of rivers. Yet in recognising the one, we learn to recognise the other. In feeling that there is a connexion and correspondency between them,—and that Right and Justice which lie at the foundation of man's being do at last determine the movements of all involuntary creatures,—we come to feel that they are the legitimate subjects of human investigation, and that it is for the glory of God that we should understand them.

The simplest and most patient study of that portion of the book of Exodus, which refers to these Egyptian plagues, will, I think, lead us most to this conclusion, that Moses is in these acts of his life, as in all others, the witness for a divine eternal law, and the witness *against* every kind of king-craft or priest-craft which breaks this law; or substitutes any devices of man's power or wit in place of it,— or represents it as tolerating the oppression of any one of the creatures who are the subjects of it. How a man can be an assertor of such a law if he does not begin with the confession and assertion of an absolute LAWGIVER,—of One who commands right because He IS right in Himself, in His own inward essence,—I cannot understand. Moses protested against the deceits and impostures of the magicians, precisely because he protested for the living and eternal Lord. If he did not go in to Pharaoh with the real faith that he came from Him, he had no faith to withstand them. He might disbelieve them, contradict them, ridicule them; but he could not strike at the root of their falsehood, —for he could not sever the truth which was latent in their falsehood from it. He could not justify the knowledge that there was in them by a higher knowledge. He could not expose the immorality of the ends to which they turned their power over nature by showing that such a power had a moral end. You think you escape from miracles by getting rid of this story of Moses. No; you make everything miraculous; you leave the world at the mercy of fortune-tellers and soothsayers; you teach men to look upon everything which they see as a portent, and to trust to the most dishonest expounder of it.

For there will be, there must be, a mixture of some observations that have been the result of experience,—of some traditional or distorted science, of some anticipations of truths which may hereafter be brought to light,—in every scheme of jugglery, whensoever or by whomsoever produced. No man, thanks be to the God of Truth, can invent or concoct a pure, naked, absolute lie. We all know this now. Everybody repeats it. But then we repeat it lazily, indifferently, with a shameful tolerance for lies, and a shameful indifference whether the truth is ever severed from them. And so it will be and must be more and more,— till we lose all capacity of discerning what is genuine from what is counterfeit, if we do not believe that the genuine proceeds from an actual God, and the counterfeit from an actual Devil; if we do not believe that God wills us to know the truth, and that the Devil is seeking to make us dwell in a lie,—till we become naturalized to it, and unable to breathe in any other atmosphere. I hold it then to be a special token of honesty and veracity, that Moses records the success of the magicians in several of their experiments. We might fairly have discredited the story as partial and unlikely if there had been no such admission. Certainly it would have been no guide to us in walking amidst the impostures of later times, in confronting them, and not being entangled in them, if we had been told that all which the deceivers attempted came to nought. We do not find it so. Even the most flagrant chicanery is not always disappointed; and in nine cases out of ten, fact and fraud are curiously dovetailed into each other. If you will not do homage to the one, you will not detect the other.

II. But supposing the contrast between Moses and the magicians did set forth the opposition between good and evil, the true and the false, is not that distinction lost when we are told that *the Lord hardened Pharaoh's heart?* Do not these words distinctly describe God as the author of something in man which is pronounced to be utterly wrong? Is He not said to have foreseen Pharaoh's sin, and not only to have foreseen, but to have produced it? After pleading for the literal interpretation of Scripture, must we not take refuge in some figurative, unnatural sense of this language, in order to avoid the worse alternative of finding in it a positive denial of God's goodness?

I apprehend the literal meaning is here, as in other cases, the safe one, provided we take all possible means to ascertain what the letter must have signified to the mind of the writer, what it would signify to us, if we interpreted it according to the context of his language and thoughts, not according to some theory of ours. Let us reflect then upon the previous statements of the historian. 'The Lord,' he said, '*had seen the affliction of His people, and heard their cry, and knew their sorrows.*' He determined to deliver them. He commanded Pharaoh, their oppressor, to let them go. What is the effect of that command upon Pharaoh? It irritates and provokes him. Is there anything very strange in that? Is it not just what you would expect that it would do? But then, if it were so, I should say, in any common case, He who sent the command produced the irritation and provocation. That would be the obvious, natural way of stating the fact, why must I depart from it in this instance? Is it merely because I believe the command to have been a right and a good one? Would that be a reason, if I was speaking of any human father or mother, for not saying, 'The precept so jarred against the feelings of the 'child to whom it was given, that it provoked him to the 'very utmost?' You do not object to it then on this ground. But if not on this, upon what other? Is it not that you think God so infinitely *powerful* that He could have made Pharaoh do just what He liked, and therefore that a form of speech which would be appropriate in the case of an ordinary parent, is *not* appropriate in His? If you take that ground, keep to it. Do not mix it up with the other ground of *goodness*. It is a question of *power*. And on that question I join issue with you. I say that the Bible, not in this passage, but throughout, exhibits God's operation upon the will of the creature whom He has made in His image, as something quite distinct from that operation by which He compels the obedience of involuntary creatures. He treats the first always as creatures capable of resisting Him; yes, and as creatures whom no *mere* power can ever bring into submission to Him.

But 'hardening the heart!' That is so much stronger a phrase than merely 'irritating and provoking.' Assuredly it is. The one may merely point to a temporary excitement; the other indicates a continual process. But if you have admitted the possibility and even propriety of one form of language, let us see whether it does not naturally, inevitably pass into the other. Moses says that God not only sent the command to Pharaoh, but that He sent one punishment after another to him for resisting that command.

It does not surprise you to be told, that some of these punishments shook the heart of the king for a moment, but that presently he relapsed into his previous determination, and that after each new act of remorse and each new effort to throw it off, he became harder and more obstinate. You know enough of yourselves and of your fellow-men, to feel that such a statement is reasonable, nay, that it has a great air of probability. Must you not say then that the punishment itself hardens the heart? And if you have the same strong conviction which Moses had, that the punishment was the deliberate act of a Person, can you help saying that *He* hardened the heart?

You still do not like to say it. I feel thankful that you do not. Your reluctance is a witness for that very truth which Moses is here trying to teach you. He wants you to feel that the will of God was altogether a good will; and that therefore Pharaoh's will,—which was a bad will, a proud self-will,—strove against it, and was lashed into greater fury by meeting with that which was contrary to itself. It is good to shrink from any phrase, yes, though it be a phrase of Scripture, which seems to impugn the absolute entire goodness of God. It is well to determine that we will not suffer such a phrase, let it come with what authority it will, to impugn the very ground on which we give it that authority; that we will not let God's book set us at war with God Himself. But when we have adopted this true and manly resolution, we shall, I believe, find that these words of Scripture are most necessary to us,—for the very purpose of making us understand the awful contradiction which there may be between the will of a man and the will of his Creator; how that contradiction may be aggravated by what seemed to be means for its cure; how

GOODNESS HARDENS. 181

it may be effectually cured. The subject is a very profound and awful one. But it is one which we must face in the actual work of life, and which we therefore should not refuse to face when it presents itself to us on the page of Scripture. I find the startling words respecting Pharaoh justifiable, because I do not find that I can describe facts of every-day occurrence in ourselves, if I may not have recourse to them.

Great and severe troubles come upon us. We say that God has sent them. We actually think so. Friends who look on, observe that God is trying us, doubtless for our benefit. They complain afterwards, that we are not better than we were before, not gentler, more resigned, more humble. Our sufferings have only embittered us. They wonder at it. God has shown us His great power. We have said it was His. Should it not have changed the whole course and habit of our lives? At all events, how can it have stiffened and made rigid that which it seemed sent to soften?

There is another instance of hardening, brethren, which seems more terrible than this, and yet with which we are quite as familiar. We speak of prayers, sermons, sacraments, as God's ordinances. The language is scriptural; our consciences approve it. But do not our consciences and Scripture agree in testifying that the appointed feasts, the Sabbaths, the solemn assemblies, Lents, Passion-weeks, Easter-days, may harden the hearts not of those only who neglect them, but of those who observe them? May we not become duller, more inobservant of the facts of which these seasons speak, less concerned about the meaning of the facts year after year? Does not the very repetition of the names and sounds seem to produce this effect?

This, you say, is an opposite case to that of Pharaoh. He is said to have been hardened by strange and unexpected events; I am speaking of the hardness which comes from routine. I admit the difference. I only wish you to see in how many instances, most unlike each other, the same strange, tremendous truth is brought home to us; that messages which we attribute to the Lord of all,—messages of terror and of mercy, rare and sudden, or often repeated, —may make us less disposed to obey Him, less in the state of mind in which He would have us be, than we were before. But if you desire an exact parallel to the story in the book of Exodus, then consider how frequently we have all been called to notice within the last thirty years,— within the last three,—that thrones may be shaken to their foundations, and that those who sit upon them, whether they call themselves civil rulers or ecclesiastical, may come out of the whirlwind which they confess that the Lord has sent, not more gracious to their subjects, not more just in their dealings with other nations, but in all respects more pitiless, more defying, more determined to assert the dominion as theirs which God has so solemnly by His judgments declared to be His. What can we say, but that the Lord hath hardened their hearts?

But how then does it ever come to pass that the hearts of any are *softened?* How is it that individuals, yes, and that kings and nations, have come out of the fires with their dross burnt out and the gold shining clear and bright? Is this the Lord's work, or is it their own? Surely they would all confess, 'It is not our own work. We were ' proud, self-willed, choosing a way that was not good. ' He has chastened and subdued us. Are we then to say, as some delight to say, 'It is mere *sovereignty.* He decrees 'that this man should be gracious, and that obstinate?' How can we say that, if all the evidence we have considered, whether drawn from the words and facts of the Bible, or from our own lives, has gone to prove that no mere act of divine sovereignty, no mere decree, *can* affect the heart or will of any human being? '*For this cause,*' it is said, '*have I raised thee up, for to shew in thee my* POWER.' The demonstration that the Creator was mightier than the creature; that the king must give way before the King of kings, was decisive. The Will and Order of God were proved to be the Will and Order which must and should prevail, let what would stand in their way. Just what was wanting, was the consent of the creature's will to the divine Will. *That,* this mighty demonstration could not bring about. It is the very purpose of the divine historian to show us that it could not. There needs a demonstration of the Love of the Almighty Lord, a recognition of *that* by the spirit of the man, in order that it may humble itself and repent in dust and ashes. When once it perceives this Love as the essence of the divine Mind,— as the spring of all its purposes, as directed towards it and the whole universe, as manifested and expressed in those punishments which grieve it most,—then the softening begins, and not till then. Up to that moment the severe lesson and the gracious one,—the famine and the plenty, the locusts and the east wind which drives them away,— are equally lost, are equally hardening. Not but that they serve, one and all, very great and glorious purposes. They declare what God is doing and means to do. They are His proclamations of war against oppression and falsehood, they are actually missiles and engines against the oppressor and the liar. But while they are only thought to proceed from a great Lord,—and not from a Father who desires that we should be like to Him, that we should hate oppression and lying as He hates them, that we should be gracious and true as He is, that we should be fellow-workers with Him to carry out His plans for the extirpation of evil and the establishment of righteousness and peace on the earth,—they will stir up the discords of our hearts, not bring out their sweeter music.

My brethren, it is very needful that we should fully recognise this distinction; it may save us from much despair, both of ourselves and of our fellow-men. We shall give up wondering and complaining that circumstances which are thought eminently favourable have not produced the effects which we looked for from them; we shall let go our displeasure that the trying discipline has not made our own characters or the characters of those we care for, what we think it ought to have made them. We shall learn not to worship circumstances or discipline, but to seek for Him who ordains them; to ask what He is, and what He would wish to do with us. And to these questions we can find an answer. If we have trusted that Passion-weeks would of themselves work a reformation in us, we shall have been as sorely disappointed as if we expected it from personal sorrows or national judgments. But Passion-week *will* tell us, whence the help is to come which it cannot bring. It may tell us, indeed, that the mere sight of the Lamb of God in His outward form could not soften the hearts of Jewish priests or Roman soldiers. It may tell us that the hearts of those who saw Him hanging on the cross were hardened by that spectacle, so that they cried, '*He saved others, himself He cannot save.*' It may tell us that the sop at the Paschal feast,—the last token of friendship and tenderness from the Master and Lord, hardened the heart of the Son of Perdition, so that Satan entered into him, and he went out a conscious traitor. It tells us that even the eleven had their hearts hardened; so that at the Last Supper they were disputing which of them should be the greatest; so that they could not watch with Christ one hour during the agony; so that they all forsook Him and fled. But it tells us of a Love deeper than all this mockery, betrayal, desertion; of a Love brought out through them and by means of them. It tells us that in the agony and death of Christ the will of the Son yielded itself absolutely, unreservedly, to the Will of the Father; and that the whole of that perfectly loving Will shone forth in the acts and sufferings of a Man. It tells us, that with this sacrifice God is well-pleased; that this sacrifice is an eternal bond between the Creator and creature, which sin and death and hell cannot break. It tells that we may give up ourselves to God, and that His own Spirit,—the Spirit in which Christ offered up Himself,—will come down to consume the sacrifice. It tells us that,—whatever reluctance we may feel in ourselves, or see in our brethren,—there is a mysterious power which can make us willing; it tells that however hard our hearts may be,—and whatever new hardness they may have contracted from God's own discipline and our refusal to understand it,—the divine Spirit of grace and discipline can subdue even all things to Himself. It teaches us to find something beneath all Pharaoh's hardness and our own,—something far beyond our faculties to understand or measure in the words, 'And I, if I be lifted up, will draw all men unto me.'

SERMON X.

THE PASSOVER.

(Lincoln's Inn, Easter Sunday, April 20, 1851.)

Lessons for the day, Exod. XII. and XIV.

EXODUS XIV. 13, 14.

And Moses said unto the people, Fear ye not, stand still, and see the salvation of the Lord, which he will shew to you to-day: for the Egyptians whom ye have seen to-day, ye shall see them again no more for ever. The Lord shall fight for you, and ye shall hold your peace.

THE feast of the Passover may have suggested very different thoughts to Israelites eating at the same table, partaking together of the lamb and of the bitter herbs. We may imagine two persons coming to it during the period of Persian or Roman ascendancy; both well instructed in the history of their country; neither of them indifferent to the events which they were commemorating,—patriots, and religious men. One may have fixed his mind on the destruction of the Egyptian firstborn,—upon the change in Pharaoh's mind from defiance to cowardice, upon his subsequent relapse,—upon the overthrow of his hosts in the Red Sea. Such reflections were naturally suggested by the narrative; they could not be passed over by any reader of it: a deep moral surely lay in them. Yet one who was occupied chiefly with them would be likely to contract a vehement and ferocious habit of feeling; along with some hatred of oppression there would be in his mind a peculiar hatred for Egyptians; he would contemplate the Lord of all exclusively, or mainly, as an Avenger.

The other Israelite might consider that the service was instituted to remind his countrymen of their own exemption; to tell them that the destroying angel passed by the houses upon which he saw the mark of blood; to awaken their wonder that the Red Sea should have been made the instrument of their protection instead of their overthrow. In such feelings you will be disposed to recognise a more genial temper, one sensitive to present mercies; willing to forget, in gratitude for them, any darker events that were associated with them. But you may reasonably suspect that a leaven,—a very large leaven,—of self-congratulation and self-exaltation will have defiled this keeper of the feast. He will have been apt to look upon Israelites as possessing in themselves, for their own sake, some claim to the divine kindness and favour which other nations had not. If practical experience and a recollection of the Scripture history prevented him from seeing, in the people at large, any distinguishing merits, he may have discovered them in certain individuals for whose interest the Lord was so solicitous that He tolerated the rest, or permitted the faults of the one as a foil to the excellences of the other. Gradually he must have become by this process of meditation more exclusive, than even the man who started from a consideration of the divine vengeance. It will have been more necessary for him to dwell upon the curse of the surrounding people and of his own, that he might understand the blessings and security of those who had a right to feed upon the paschal Lamb. And he will have lost the sense which the other had of the divine Justice, of God as a punisher of wrong-doing. The vision of a capricious being favouring one race or portion of a race, will have been all that he could take in; such a being will have become his God.

But is it not possible to conceive a third Israelite coming to Jerusalem from some distant heathen land, with a fervent desire to participate in the great national solemnity and thanksgiving, yet possessed by a spirit unlike either of these? In the country where he was sojourning he will have heard continually, of great avenging deities ruling the powers of nature, inflicting plagues and torments on men, —to be conciliated and propitiated by hecatombs of oxen, or by the more precious sacrifice of children. He will have felt that those who confessed these deities had hold of a truth; that to deprive them of it would have been to make them think that wrong was safe and would go unpunished. But he will have felt also how continually wrong *was* safe and *did* go unpunished through this very belief,—through the confusion of the people as to the nature of the evils which provoked the divine displeasure; through the tendency of the priest to represent the chief of these evils as offences against themselves, as omissions of some services which *they* had prescribed, and through their willingness to overlook or forgive positive injuries to individuals and to society if such services were performed. He will have seen how really the people hated the gods whom they worshipped in this character; how much it was the whole aim and scope of their religion to provide escapes from them:

yet how much their own minds were fashioned by their belief,—how every day the lust of vengeance became their absorbing passion, how the relaxation of that vengeance must be purchased of *them*—just as the relaxation of the divine vengeance was purchased by base hypocritical submission, by flattery, by presents.

Such a Jew will, moreover, have been familiar with the notion of divinities who patronised particular soils and races; who for the sake of these favourites would manifest themselves in the hour of battle, would put on human shapes, would suspend the laws of nature; who could be invoked as helpers and protectors in every emergency. He will have seen that this faith proved itself to have a foundation,—by the strength which it imparted to those who possessed it, by the courage with which they could struggle to the death for their hearths and homes, by the confidence with which they could go forth into other regions to spread the name of their tribe and of the God who watched over it. But he will have seen that the belief in a divine protector was gradually absorbed into a belief of the excellence and glory of the particular people whom he protected,—into a feeling that they were a law to themselves and might hold down all other people by their might; he will have seen that when they reached this period of declension they will have begun to lose their national unity and strength; that visible men will have seized the power which they had ascribed to gods; that those who had exulted in their intellectual superiority, or in their reverence for an unseen law, will have become slaves of brutal instincts, or a mortal tyrant.

A man who had contemplated the heathen divinities under both these aspects,—or rather who, without any effort of contemplation, had been forced by all the ceremonial of heathen worship and the speech and practices of the people around him, to feel that these were the habitual prevailing impressions respecting them,—will have turned to the records of his own country's history with a strange wonder. He will have perceived in them that which corresponded to each form of belief with which he had become familiar. He would remember how each of those forms had at different times held possession of his own mind; he may have been conscious of a half-righteous, half-restless struggle with both. He may for a time have fancied that Judaism was but a peculiar type of national or tribe-religion. But he will have been struck with this amazing difference,—that writers of the Jewish books, when they speak of God as a judge and an avenger, seem for that very reason to fly TO Him; that the one desire and object of their life is not to be delivered from Him, but to know Him better. He will have perceived that under the pressure of calamity, under the consciousness of moral evil, they betook themselves directly to Him,—asking no counsel of any one how they might avoid the punishment of their sin, but asking Him to rid them of the sin itself. He will have perceived that whenever the Lord is spoken of as caring for the Israelite, it is because He is said to be a God who cares for the oppressed and the feeble. He could not but see that the crimes and wrong-doings of Israelites were punished as severely as those of other people; nay, that the history was one continual record of these punishments. Thus the idea of a God of order and right will have risen up before him, as a refuge from the divisions and contradictions of the world. To have such a God for their God, he will have regarded as the great glory of the chosen people. He will have come then to the Passover, not first or chiefly to celebrate the destruction of Egyptians or the deliverance of Israelites, but first and chiefly to praise God the perfectly righteous Being, to acknowledge Him to be the Lord. And this will have been no cold, distant work, undertaken without reference to his own personal feelings and hopes. To find a solid rock beneath his feet instead of shifting sand, a just God and a Saviour,—instead of chance, or fate, or self-will,—directing the movements of the universe, what a salvation, what a new life to a man must this be! And this personal life, how closely must it have been intertwined with his national life! None could estimate the favour shown to his land, more than he who believed that the God of Truth, the God of the whole earth, had taught his countrymen that He was their King; and who knew what kings the people of the earth had made for themselves in place of Him. On the other hand, no one could less wish than he, to suppress the evidence that this King had come forth crushing and trampling down whatever earthly power opposed itself to His. He would never be disposed to lose sight of the Avenger in the Redeemer, because he would feel that one office was as needful as the other, for the establishment of a righteous and merciful order on the earth.

If you have gone along with me in the previous lectures on the books of Genesis and Exodus, you will not doubt, I think, that the man who celebrated the Jewish festival in this spirit was a true countryman of the patriarchs and of Moses. We have seen throughout that the history is one of God's dealings with man; that no attempt whatever is made to magnify one class of men at the expense of another; that Abraham, Isaac, Jacob, and their descendants are presented to us as average specimens of humanity; often seeming to sink below the ordinary level; that they rise above it only when they acknowledge God as their guide, teacher, deliverer, and as the guide, teacher, deliverer of others as well as themselves; that till Moses knew Him in that character,—till he learnt, while apart from all tribe-associations, in the deserts of Midian, as the son-in-law of a Midianitish priest, to know the God of Abraham as the I AM,—he was not fit to be a deliverer of his people; that he went in to Pharaoh in the strength of His Name, to witness for God as the God of truth and order, against the tricks and sleights of the magicians,—as the Lord of those powers of nature to which the kings and priests and people of Egypt were doing homage; that the acts which hardened Pharaoh's heart were acts done on the behalf of oppressed slaves,—testimonies that God cared for them, and that the rulers of the earth in hurting them were rebelling against Him. This is the plain sense of the record, which one part of it gives out as much as another, and which connects the different parts of it together. One does not get it by straining texts or groping for hidden meanings. It lies there for the wayfaring man. The wayfaring man when the Bible has been opened to him has found this meaning there, whether scholars or divines have found it or not.

And surely we do not lose the thread which has accompanied us hitherto in the chapters which we have been reading to-day. The text which I have taken seems to me to embody the spirit of the whole passage: '*Fear ye not, stand still, and see the salvation of the Lord, which He will shew to you to-day. The Lord shall fight for you, and ye shall hold your peace.*' It was not the children of Israel who brought themselves out of Egypt. They were a set of poor crouching slaves. It was not Moses who brought them out. He had once aspired to that honour, but shame and exile had followed his efforts. After forty years he had learnt that he was not eloquent neither before nor since God had spoken to him. He found that the Israelites looked upon him as a disturber who had increased their burdens, and that all the signs and wonders he wrought before Pharaoh made him more obstinate. It was the Lord who brought them out. It was the Lord who slew the Egyptians and preserved them. This was what the Passover told them on the night they left Egypt; what it was to tell all future generations. The unseen Lord had done this act of vengeance; the unseen Lord had done this act of deliverance. The same Mind, the same Will, was directing both events. The same purpose of righteousness, the same purpose of mercy, must be traced in that punishment which caused that great cry throughout the land of Egypt from the king on the throne to the captive in the dungeon: and in the act by which the children of Israel were led with a high hand into the wilderness. The Lord was fighting for them. They were simply to follow where they were led, to accept the deliverance which He gave them, and to remember whence it came. The blood which they marked upon their door-posts was set there in obedience to a command. The lamb which they sacrificed was offered in obedience to a command. They were to eat it with bitter herbs in obedience to a command. All these were witnesses of a Presence with them, of an unseen Being who was doing the work while they were holding their peace. The cloud that followed them by day, the fire that was with them by night, were testimonies of the same Presence. The Lord God was in the midst of them; the shout of an unseen King was amongst them.

In the lesson which we have read this afternoon, we have this principle brought out into clearer manifestation. People in our day have wished to get rid of what they call the supernatural interference with the course of the Red Sea, and to account for the phænomenon which Moses records by the fluxes and refluxes of the tide. If they only mean, and I believe this feeling is latent in their explanation, that God is a God of order, who does not recklessly trample upon His own laws, I believe there is no one who has taught them that lesson like Moses; I believe it is the one which he was especially commissioned to teach. There is nothing, that I know of, in the story which interferes with the existence of natural laws, nothing which would induce us to doubt that the Red Sea is subject to laws like all other seas What the history does call upon us to own is, that all creatures, and therefore the chief creatures on this earth, are subject to a moral Ruler; to a God who governs all things according to a moral law; who invites man to confess that law as the guide of his acts; who will proclaim it and enforce it in spite of all disobedience on the part of the only being who can disobey it, or is disposed to disobey it. That the story declares. And if there had been no such declaration,—I believe, as I said in the case of the plagues and of the miracles which confuted the magicians,— you would have no natural science; you would have merely a cowardly slavery to nature, man creeping and crawling before her, not daring to investigate her secrets,—because he would no longer regard himself as the minister and image of her Creator.

I grant you that the destruction of the Egyptian first-born and of Pharaoh's host in the Red Sea, are startling and awful events, as the perishing of any number of human beings by any hurricane, pestilence, shipwreck, must be. Why do you think these more so than others? Is it because you have arrived at some knowledge of the future condition of these particular sufferers, which you have not in the other case? How did you arrive at it? The Bible tells you nothing about it. We merely hear that the first-born died, that the hosts of the Egyptians went down into the sea. I know nothing more of them, except that they are not gone out of God's sight because they are gone out of mine, and that the Judge of all the earth will do right. The Bible gives me that assurance. I find it a very soothing and comforting one. I could not bear to look upon the facts which are passing every day before our eyes, if I had not this assurance. The belief that the Egyptians were drowned as much as the Israelites were saved, *'because the mercy of the Lord endureth for ever,'*—can help me to look upon problems which I have no skill to solve, without horror, nay, with confidence and hope. Take away that belief,—give us no hint, no example to guide us in considering the ways of God to His creatures,—and we should sink back into the conclusions which we all feel to be so natural to us, which all men without that help have sunk into. The predominance of evil would lead us to think that it is the everlasting law of the world, instead of the transgression and violation of its law.

It will need but a few remarks to show how the remaining part of the book of Exodus, which we leave this afternoon, and the following book of the Pentateuch, from which the Church takes none of her Sunday lessons, confirm and illustrate the doctrine of the text. After all that has been said, you might still feel staggered at the distinction between Israelites and Egyptians; you might say that it comes out much more markedly in the Mosaic history than I have chosen to suppose; that the notion of referring it to some general principle in the Divine Mind or Economy,—belongs to our century, not to the age in which Moses wrote. Look then at the chapters in the book of Exodus which record the journeyings of the children of Israel in the wilderness, the laws which were given them when the trumpet sounded loud and long, the statutes which were laid down for their special observance when they should come into the promised land. Do you find that the rule which we traced through the book of Genesis has deserted us; that the descendants of the twelve sons of Jacob are represented as more righteous than they were; that there is any one indication in any part of this book, that the Israelites as such, are considered a better, purer, nobler race than the Egyptians? If you have heard the words '*stiff-necked people*' till you have ceased to attach any meaning to them, or have learnt to think of them merely as words of course, can you get rid in like manner of all the events which the historian so minutely records for the purpose of justifying these words, and of humbling the pride of the Jewish people in all time to come? Are not the acts and feelings which are attributed to the Jewish people, precisely what you would expect from a mixed multitude of men, recently slaves, journeying through a desolate and droughty country? Is not their desire for the flesh-pots of Egypt, their dislike of Moses, their crying for water and for food, their readiness to set up a calf and worship it, their dancing and feasting, exactly what you would look for? But would you look to be *told* these things,—just these things,—without any compensating record of high faith and great virtues, by a native historian, by one whose whole heart was Jewish? Must he not have had something higher than this native instinct, this Jewish heart, something which transfigured them, yet without the least extinguishing them? And what was this? Was it not that he felt himself to be the historian of God's acts, the utterer of the law which He had established, the law which He has created man to obey, the law which each Israelite, just as much as each Egyptian, feels something in his heart disposing him to break? And is it not against this fleshly nature in man, this disposition in man to become the servant of it, that the thunders of God are directed? Is it not with this He is warring in whomsoever He finds it, in the race of Shem or the race of Ham, in prince or beggar? And is not this the other lesson which He is teaching us, that men are, and only can be truly men, lifted above the tendencies of their animal nature, when they regard themselves as called by God, as His appointed and elected ministers upon earth? Is Israel said to be a holy nation, a peculiar people, a race of kings and priests to God, while yet Israelites are described by such ignominious names, and those names vindicated by such ignominious facts? What is this, but the truth which we have been learning from the beginning of the Old Testament? That God created men to be members of a kind, portions of a Society:

that as a kind, a Society, He created them to be in His own image; but that the first man, and each man since, has been trying to thwart this purpose, to set himself up as a creature, separate from his kind, separate from God; and that in spite of this inclination God has gone on continually asserting His original purpose and order, gradually unfolding it to men, and by wonderful processes of education leading them to understand it, and submit to it?

Of these processes the most wonderful was surely the institution of Sacrifices, and the whole economy which is connected with them. The ground of the national existence was laid in Sacrifice. The killing of the lamb; the blood-token upon the door, the consecration of all the first-born, were the witnesses that the slaves of Pharaoh were redeemed to be the people of God. The sacrifices which were subsequent to the giving of the law, which presumed a breach of it on the part of individuals or of the whole nation, looked back to this primary institution. Sacrifice was not merely the redress of an evil; it was a return to the rightful, orderly state of each man and of the people. The setting up of a self-will is the disturbance of the order; the sacrifice or giving up of the will is the restoration of it. Therefore, the sacrifices in the book of Leviticus are not like the heathen sacrifices,— schemes to bring about a change in the Divine Mind. They proceed just as much as the law proceeds from that Mind. God declares what they are, and how and why they should be offered. God appoints the persons who shall present them. The priest belongs to a tribe which is chosen to represent the first-born of the nation; to represent, in fact, the whole nation. It is an order which declares the whole people to be called redeemed, sanctified people. It testifies of God's perpetual presence with the nation. It testifies that He is the healer and restorer of the bodies as well as the spirits of His people. It testifies that His highest operations are upon the wills of men; that He seeks to conform them to His perfectly good and gracious Will; that the highest blessedness and freedom of a man or a nation consists in this conformity.

I may have more to say on the subject of the priesthood, if I am permitted to speak to you on the lesson for next Sunday morning, which, though taken from the book of Numbers, bears directly upon that of Leviticus. I have alluded to it this afternoon partly because it is so intimately connected with the doctrine of Sacrifice, and because that doctrine cannot be separated from the Passover; partly because this office rightly understood strikingly illustrates my text. For the priest was in effect to say to the Jew who brought the sacrifice to the door of the tabernacle of the congregation, *The Lord shall fight for you, and you shall hold your peace.* ' You are not come to purchase ' forgiveness of your sin, or deliverance from your sins by ' acts or efforts of yours. Submit yourselves to God, and ' He will work in you forgiveness and deliverance.' And partly I have touched upon this topic because it helps us in tracing the passage from the Jewish Passover and the overthrow of Pharaoh in the Red Sea, to the Christian Passover and all which it implies, assures us of, and foretells.

. A Jew who ate the Paschal Lamb mainly that he might commemorate the destruction of the Egyptian, or the favour shown to Israelites, may not have been absolutely tied to the recollection of those events. He may have hoped that the same power which slew one enemy of the nation might slay another; that Persians, Syrians, or Romans, might feel the terrors of His vengeance. Yet even this hope must have been feeble; for analogies, though great helps to the intellect, are but poor supports to the heart when crushed by actual miseries. He who was mainly absorbed in thanksgiving that one people had been chosen to receive a mercy which had been denied to others, may have often tried to assure himself that the continuance of the race was a witness that promises given to one generation would be fulfilled to another. But how often will the thought have intruded itself to damp all his expectations; 'To whom were 'the promises made? Can they have been intended for 'the wretched godless people I see about me who bear the 'name of Israelites? Is there any sign that they are 'inheriting blessings, the nature of which they do not 'understand? Must there not be an election within the 'election? And is it not a great question,—a question of 'deepest doubt and anxiety,—whether I belong to that election, and therefore whether I have any warrant for 'rejoicing in this feast at all?' But how will it have been with him who counted it his chief blessedness to see God asserting his order through Egyptians and Israelites, and in despite of the unbelief and rebellion of both? Will it have been a great effort of analogical reasoning with him to conclude, that He who is and was and is to come would go on asserting His order till He had put down every enemy of it, till He had completely made manifest His own character and purpose? As he asked himself what were the enemies of God's order, what powers had striven to set it aside, would not the history of Israelites and

Egyptians give the answer; 'The worship of visible things, 'Sensuality, Self-will, Selfishness?' Would he not think that it was God's intention to wage perpetual war with these till He had proved whether they or He were mightier? Must he not have seen again that there were actual physical curses lying side by side with these, which were interfering likewise with the order of human society, and therefore with the constitution of God? Would not Death, the breaker-up of family and national fellowship, present itself to him as the great intruder into Creation, which must be crushed before it could vindicate its true and original meaning? Would he not thus be drawn on to understand,—his own personal experience and miseries at once presenting the riddle and make him welcome the solution,—that the God, the living God, of whose Kingdom from age to age the Passover bore testimony, would not cease His work in the world till all those evils which belong to man as man, to Egyptians and Israelites equally, had been overcome by a victory and deliverance, as signal and as actual as that which took place when the oppressed people came out of the house of bondage, and when their persecutors sank to be seen no more for ever? And if he tried to think of the method of such a deliverance, though his thoughts may often have been baffled, yet some great hints which could not be mistaken will have discovered themselves to his faith and his reason, as he contemplated the troubles of man and the design of God by the light which God himself had thrown upon them. God must be the deliverer, in the least case as in the greatest. Man must be the instrument of deliverance. It must be a deliverance wrought by the First-born of many brethren *for* His brethren; by a High Priest as the representative of a Society. It must be a deliverance wrought by one participating in the evils of those whose chains he broke. It must come through a sacrifice. That sacrifice must be a voluntary one. It could, in no sense, be a sacrifice to overcome or defeat the will of the Creator. It must be a perfect surrender to His Will, one which should manifest it fully, and in perfect absolute reconciliation with the Will of Man.

Thus I conceive, brethren, did God educate His Jewish servants in no forced or unnatural way,—but by a most regular and gradual discipline, to feel that an Easter Day must lie beneath a Paschal feast; and that men of all kindreds and tribes might be called to celebrate a complete conquest and a universal Redemption. And if it has been given to us, brethren, to possess that which they anticipated,—the enjoyment of our possession must depend wholly upon the spirit in which we have claimed it. If we have kept a Passover for ourselves, merely seeking in it some pledge or means of our security, if we have thought of it as a sentence of exclusion upon other men,—we shall have gone empty away; the good which we have sought we shall have missed; we shall not have really partaken of the Paschal Lamb, because we shall not have eaten it with the unleavened bread of sincerity and truth. But if we have desired to give God thanks for His great glory; if, leaving questions about ourselves or other men to Him who alone can take care of us or them, we have blessed Him that He has put down His enemies, Sin, Death, Hell, showing that when they were mightiest He was mightier; that He has perfectly manifested His Love in His perfect

Image, showing that in Him there is Light and no darkness at all; that He has established a complete reconciliation with His creatures; then He will have been indeed with us,—teaching us to hold our peace, and to see the salvation which He has won for us,—enabling us to receive every Easter, though it should come to us amidst ever so many personal or general sorrows, as the sure pledge to each man and to the whole earth of Resurrection and Life.

SERMON XI.

THE REBELLION OF KORAH.

(Lincoln's Inn, First Sunday after Easter.—April 27, 1851.)
Lessons for the day, Numbers xvi. and xxii.

NUMBERS XVI. 3.

And they gathered themselves together against Moses and against Aaron, and said unto them, Ye take too much upon you, seeing all the congregation are holy, every one of them, and the Lord is among them: wherefore then lift ye up yourselves above the congregation of the Lord?

As the story of Balaam, which we have begun this afternoon, is continued in the lessons for next Sunday, I propose to reserve the whole of it for that day. The chapter we read this morning, which records the insurrection of Korah and his company, and their punishment, will furnish ample material for the present sermon.

It has furnished the materials for many sermons, and for at least as many arguments against the Jewish economy and the books which make it known to us. Divines have taken Korah's offence as the type of all intrusions on the part of ordinary people into the office of the priesthood; they have uttered mysterious hints as to the probability that similar crimes would lead to similar results in this world or the next. Objectors have discovered clear evidence in this narrative, that the books of Moses had a sacerdotal origin, and that the whole scheme of the Jewish commonwealth was contrived for sacerdotal purposes. 'What was the crime imputed to 'Korah,' they have asked, 'but the crime which has been 'laid to the supporters of popular freedom, and the 'protestants against exclusive privileges, in all ages? 'What was the miracle of so many men going down 'alive into the pit, but the pattern of all after inventions 'to crush the too rash assertors of human rights by 'a pretended divine intervention?'

There is one observation, very obvious to any thoughtful reader of this story, which has, I think, been overlooked both by those who have quoted it as an authority, and those who have denounced it as an imposture. Dathan and Abiram were sons of Reuben; but Korah, the principal person in the story, the one whose rebellion is first spoken of, was a son of Levi. He belonged to the tribe which was set apart for the service of the Tabernacle. Moses says to him and his company, in answer to the complaint in my text, ' *Ye take too much on you, ye* SONS OF LEVI.' Whatever their sin was, then, it cannot be set down as first of all an instance of *popular* presumption. It is not, as we should say in modern language, the case of laymen complaining of the separation or consecration of a particular order. It is the case of certain members of that order claiming an office, from which they supposed themselves unfairly excluded, affirming that persons belonging to their own class had usurped powers which did not belong to them. It is quite true that these Levites joined with members of another tribe, and that they proclaimed ' ALL *the congregation of the Lord to be holy, every one of them, and the Lord to be among them.'* I do not wish to overlook that point in the case at all. I shall often have occasion to refer to it. But if those who put forth this argument were themselves members of the consecrated tribe,—and if the story was, as it notoriously and professedly was, told as a warning to after times, it must have been meant to point out temptations to which that tribe would be peculiarly liable. I apprehend then that a divine who comments upon this narrative, cannot deduce from it any moral which shall be applicable to his lay hearers, till he has allowed it to bear with the force of its terrors upon himself; he is bound first to ask, 'Of what evil to which *my* position and ' circumstances expose me does it teach me to beware?'

I do not expect this consideration will have any immediate weight upon those, who have been long possessed by the notion that the Old Testament history is an invention of priests. They will at once parry it by the remarks, 'that the tribe of Levi, no doubt, derived its main ' importance in the eyes of the writer from its containing ' within it the family of Aaron; that if the rest of the ' tribe is in any degree depressed by this record, it is for ' the sake of bringing out this family in greater glory ; ' that the secret of priestly power lies in the notion that ' the priest alone may offer sacrifices ; that the terrible ' example which was made of Levites who had ventured to assume this function, was the most effectual protection ' that can be conceived for the sanctity of the priestly ' caste; that it must have derived great additional awful- ' ness from the fact, that the popular champions were ' themselves connected by birth with that caste.'

There are two or three statements mixed together here,

which it is of some importance we should separate. First, it is desirable to ascertain whether Aaron, as a person, is magnified in these books, and whether any inherent sanctity is supposed to dwell in his family. If we adopt the usual belief respecting the author of these books, he had every personal and hereditary temptation to this course. Those who do not hold them to have been written by Moses will suppose them to have proceeded from the members of some sacerdotal college in a later time. They will have had all reasons for attributing heroical and mystical qualities to their first founder. What then do we hear of him? At first he is merely the spokesman of Moses, the person who exhibits the signs which show that *he* has come with a true message. Next we find him permitted to go up into the mountain for a little while, but speedily coming down while Moses tarried in communion with the Lord God of Israel forty days and forty nights. In his absence Aaron does indeed assume the guidance of the people, or rather they put him at their head. For what purpose? That he may make a golden calf, and lead the orgies by which the people expressed their reverence for it. The next fact in his personal history is recorded in the twelfth chapter of this book in these words: '*And Miriam and Aaron spake against Moses because of the Ethiopian woman whom he had married. And they said, Hath the Lord indeed spoken only by Moses, hath He not spoken also by us?.... And the anger of the Lord was kindled against them, and H departed. And the cloud departed from off the tabernacle, and, behold, Miriam became leprous, white as snow, and Aaron looked upon Miriam, and behold she was leprous.*' These are the main facts recorded concerning Aaron, besides those which refer to his consecration as a priest, and to the different offices which were assigned him in that character. Would they not seem rather to warrant an opposite inference, to that which has been deduced from them? Might they not be the basis for a plausible theory, which it would be worth the while of any candidate for neological honours to elaborate, that the legislator was, for the sake of his own dignity, undervaluing his priestly brother,—exhibiting his weaknesses with painful accuracy, showing what a tendency there was in him, not only before but after he had received his consecration, to claim powers for himself which had not been conceded to him?

There would be a difficulty in making out this charge of personal ambition against Moses, because so little is done to make him appear an illustrious hero in any part of the narrative; because *his* weakness, *his* wrath, *his* desire to abandon his work, are brought out as strongly as the errors of his brother; because he is said to have drawn upon himself the heavy sentence of exclusion from the promised land by counting it a hardship that he must strike a rock for a rebellious people. It would be difficult too, to explain, upon this hypothesis, why he should have established his brother in an office which was so soon found to be a rival to his own and a check upon it. But to say that the books of Exodus, Leviticus, and Numbers, are first of all books of LAWS, is to say what all persons, Jews and Christians, who have considered the subject, have said. These books clearly contain the history of the organization of a people. One part of that organization consisted in the appointment of the priest and the assignment of his offices. It follows from this very statement, that this order could not be the paramount one in the

Jewish commonwealth. It was, as an *order*, subject to the law; the priest, as a *person*, was subject to the lawgiver as a person. If you say that a whole book is given up to the laws respecting the priesthood,—and that this is a proof how great the dignity of the function was,—you are certainly right. But remember at the same time that these laws were,—by their very minuteness and accuracy,— restraints upon the discretion and arbitrary power of the priest. He was shackled on the right hand and on the left, if laws are shackles ; he could not impose his own fancies or decrees upon the people except by violating the very title-deed upon which he held his authority ; he was reminded in everything he did that he was a servant of the commonwealth ; that he had certain very great and remarkable functions to discharge, but that he must by no means overstep the limits of those functions ; that the sacredness of them did not in any wise lessen the strength of this obligation, but increased it.

Strictly speaking, the tribe of Levi was not more appointed or called by God, than the tribe of Judah or Reuben. The family of Aaron was not more called by God than any Israelitish family. Each tribe was to occupy its own place in the host, and to look upon that as the place appointed it by God. Each tribe was to subdue and till a certain portion of the promised land, and to look upon that portion as assigned to it by God. Each family had some work to do which God had fixed for it, and not for any other. Each person had some work to do which God had ordained for him, and not for any other man. And the duties and occupations of these tribes, families, persons, having all this divine origin, were all holy; it was wicked to think of them as anything else. But it would have been a most minute and mischievous legislation which attempted to define the tasks that should be performed by each family or person. The Mosaic legislation attempted nothing of the kind; it did what was much better and more effectual; it affirmed a principle of universal and individual application; it established an order which embodied that principle, and showed how all departures from it must necessarily lead to confusion; it enforced its own decrees against that order more solemnly, more tremendously, than against any other part of the society,—that it might bear a testimony as much by its transgressions as by its obedience, to the eternal truth upon which its existence rested.

I have called the priesthood an *Order*. Many people delight to call it a *Caste*. Both phrases are legitimate, but they are not interchangeable. They have a different, I had nearly said an opposite, sense; though the same persons may deserve first one name and then the other. They do not differ in this, that one is, and the other is not, hereditary. That is an accident, which may belong to an order of priests, or may be wanting in a caste of priests. But an order sinks into a caste when it claims a position for itself, and supposes that it has in itself some power of transmitting its privileges, whether by natural birth or by any other kind of succession. A caste rises into an order when it acknowledges God as the only source of its gifts,—God as the present bestower of them, God as the ground of its continuance from generation to generation, God as able to withdraw its privileges at any moment,—God as certain to withdraw them if it acts for its own sake, and not as the instrument of carrying out the purposes of His government. Every caste of priests uses phrases, preserves ceremonies, claims rights, which imply these maxims; for every caste either has been an order, or carries in itself the possibility of becoming one. But there are always clear signs when it has lost the practical belief of these maxims. Then it feels that its great business is to struggle for dominion, to treat all other portions of the commonwealth as secular; then it becomes insolent, ambitious, crafty; then the conflict which it has commenced against other orders is repeated within itself. One part of its officers grasps at the duties of another; strife and revelry become its distinguishing characteristics; these it fosters in its own bosom, these it communicates to the whole body-politic, —these obtain for it the fear of those whom it tries to rule while they are weak, their hatred when they become strong.

The Mosaic history is a continual witness of the tendency which there was in the divinely-appointed order to become a caste; a perpetual record of the ways in which God was counter-working that tendency. The tabernacle said that He was there, in the midst of the people, the I AM, the God of truth. Woe to the man who dared to practise his tricks and deceptions, his schemes for the advancement of himself or his class, in that Presence! The Aaronic family was appointed to offer the sacrifices; it was to show that God Himself was the author of the sacrifices. Woe to it if it tried to persuade the people that it was the inventor of them, or could make them more acceptable! It testified of the holiness of the nation. Woe to it if it desired to set up its own holiness against that of the nation!

But was not this the very thing against which Korah and his company were protesting? Did not they say, 'All the Lord's people are holy, every one of them, and 'the Lord is among them'? Did not they put forth this as their very reason for objecting to the sacrificial privileges of Aaron and his family? Unquestionably. They were the assertors of a popular maxim. But unhappily that popular maxim, — like many others, would have been destructive of the people,—would have been fatal to their moral, political, spiritual freedom. Aaron had carried out the wishes of the multitude by setting up an idol. It has been a temptation, one of the leading temptations of priests in all days, to do this. They submit to be spokesmen of popular prejudices, the agents of popular sensuality; so they become deniers of the invisible God, so they become the tyrants of those of whom they were first the tools. Korah would have asserted for himself, and for the other families of the tribe of Levi, the privilege and right of offering sacrifices. Dathan and Abiram would have claimed that privilege and right for all the tribes. There was a lie in the words. They at once introduced the principle, of which sacrifice is the renunciation, the principle against which the family of Aaron was the permanent protest.

We may deny the ground upon which Jewish society was constituted; we may say that it was a mere fiction to speak of God as a King,—of Him as the distributer of human offices, of Him as making them mutually dependent and serviceable for the good of the whole. We may say manfully, 'There can be no other principle than that of 'mutual strife and rivalry. Men must fight to get the 'best things for themselves, must regard all works and 'duties as prizes to be scrambled for.' But if we admit the maxim which we have traced through the books of Scripture at all, we must not complain because it is consistently carried out; because all men are treated as servants and functionaries of God; because those who are set to make known His government and the method of it to others, are subject to the severest penalty when they become assertors of a competitive, self-seeking principle in their own persons.

Of that penalty I must now say a few words. I have maintained in former sermons that the Bible is to be regarded (all believers in its authority do professedly regard it) as a revelation of laws, not of anomalies. It becomes a guide and an example to us because it unfolds to us unvaried and eternal principles of the divine government,—not because it gives us a set of instances in which those principles were departed from. I hold that this signal judgment upon Korah and his company must be looked upon in the same light, as all the passages of the history which we have considered hitherto. A new society is in process of organization by the Creator and Ruler of the world; a society which is in some way or other to make men understand better their own position and their relation to Him. It answers that purpose if it enables us to judge of some of the startling events which happen in a complicated state of society, by the hints and precedents of this simple one. We read how in the last century the most remarkable thinkers on the continent of Europe, Voltaire and Rousseau for instance, speculated and debated about the causes of the earthquake at Lisbon,—whether it could or could not be reconciled with a theory of Optimism; how a German, who was to prove as celebrated as either of them,* attributed a revolution in his boyish feelings, which affected all his life afterwards, to his reflections on the moral or providential causes of this event. Men want some explanation of this kind then, something besides the interpretation of the physical phenomenon. If they believe the Bible ever so little, they will seek for it, and may be led in their search to very uncharitable as well as very unsatisfactory conclusions. Those who receive the Bible can tell no more about the condition of particular persons who were the subjects of that visitation, than these French or German, these full-grown or childish, speculators. They care much less to know, because Christ has taken off the sharp edge of such inquiries by His words respecting those on whom the tower of Siloam fell,—and because they can calmly leave them in His hands, under whose guidance we all are, and whom we know to be righteous. But it is surely some help and comfort to believe that whenever a natural calamity of this kind occurs,—at least whenever men are the victims of it, there is a moral derangement which needs to be removed, and which God is seeking to remove. If the earthquake of Lisbon swept away hundreds and thousands, of whom we cannot pronounce that they were worse than we are,—at least we may hear in it a voice denouncing those same sins which brought death upon Korah and his company; the ambition and falsehood of priests leading to the unbelief, sensuality, godlessness of a people. It was a handwriting on the wall addressed to all Europe. The attempts of the seers and soothsayers of the age to decypher it, showed that they felt it to be so. And when that natural

---

* See Goethe's *Dichtung und Wahrheit*, Book I. The earthquake happened in his sixth year.

admonition was disregarded, there came in due time a more fearful moral earthquake, of which not one but all kingdoms felt the shock,—itself a more solemn and terrible declaration of what must come to pass when the members of the sacred order seek power, wealth, credit, instead of acting as God's ministers; how the ruin which they have brought upon a land falls most fearfully and heavily upon themselves.

Such lessons as these, I believe, lie in the story of Korah, and show why the omission of it would have been a grievous loss to mankind. When it is compared with those acts of vengeance which are ascribed to Dunstan and other miracle-workers in the Middle Ages,—acts for the assertion of their own power, for the purpose of proving that the priest had the natural and supernatural world at his beck, and that he could break through the laws of both for the sake of extorting wonder and obedience from men,—I can only ask that the two records may be a little more carefully examined, in order to ascertain whether the resemblance between them is not superficial and the opposition radical; whether it was not the special object of the one to vindicate the divine order which the other was subverting; whether the punishment of Korah was not carrying its most direct message to the consciences of those who held themselves to be merely the privileged executors of the divine vengeance upon laymen. I have taken this view of the subject throughout, desiring that we who minister in holy things should remember of what infinite confusion we may be the cause, through our pride and self-exaltation, through our eager assertion of rights and powers, when our business is to confess responsibilities; through our fancy that we are doing God service by lifting up ourselves above civil rulers, by complaining of our ecclesiastical superiors, by feverish and restless efforts to get a position for ourselves which God has not given us, while we are carelessly throwing aside the mighty moral and spiritual influence which He *has* given us,—grasping at shadows, letting go what is substantial, wishing to have our powers acknowledged, not compelling our people to acknowledge them by exerting them on their behalf. I am afraid this restless habit of mind exists in many Levites of this day, who are very loud in their denunciations of Korah, and very quick in finding parallels for him.

But I do not wish to forget that Dathan and Abiram were joined in rebellion with Korah; that the factious ambitious member of the sacred tribe awakened a like factious ambitious spirit in the other tribes. The story is meant for you as well as for us. If what I have said is true, it could not apply to us unless it applied to you. We are sent into the world in this day, as the tribe of Levi was sent into the world under the old dispensation, to bear witness for the consecration and holiness of God's entire family. We become guilty, as they did, when by our words or our acts we lead you to think that you have not received this consecration; that you are not set apart to God; that you and your children and your occupations are not holy in His sight. Our sin in all times has been not that we have proclaimed too loudly and too practically our calling by God; it has been—that with these words on our lips, we have acted as if we had some power of our own, some inherent sanctity, some right to put ourselves in His place. And you have believed us all too readily. In old times men thought the priest was himself a God,— because they did not really confess God to be with them;

in later times they have lost their reverence for the man, and have justified their contempt of him by saying that he was practising a fiction when he represented God as really taking part in the affairs of the world. The unbelief of the modern time was latent in the superstition of the earlier; and has worked itself out as it was certain to do. But it is working out and will work out a new superstition; you know it, you tremble at it,—you feel that the weapons with which you are fighting it are very ineffectual, and lose their edge the moment they come into contact with it. You say that the priest ought to do homage to the laws of the country in which he dwells; and you utter a great truth. But you find that he appeals to some other law higher than yours, and that men recognise the appeal. You then try to persuade him and them, that they are going back to the maxims of an obsolete economy; that all notions of priestly dignity are merely Judaical. The answer is ready. 'No, these notions are emphatically 'Christian. The Jewish priest was circumscribed by local 'and national limits; he was therefore amenable to a local 'and national law; Christ has broken down these limits; 'now the priest can only pay homage to a universal law; 'must assert his place in a universal society.' Another answer is given to you which you can as little trifle with: 'Sacrifice,' it is said, 'is not less precious to the Christian 'than to the Jew; it is infinitely more precious! Every-'thing in the new economy is based upon sacrifice. And 'that sacrifice must be daily, must be habitual. And that 'sacrifice must connect earth with heaven. There must be 'some persons to signify the reality of that connexion, 'some to show that we are not less a society than those 'were who lived before Christ died to make all one. Would 'you depose the living witnesses that such a connexion 'and such a society exists?' You must meet the demands of this kind, for they stir the hearts of hundreds and thousands; to stifle them or crush them is impossible. It is certain that they are breeding discontent in families, insubordination in nations; they will combine with elements of discontent and insubordination from sources the most apparently unlike themselves.

Brethren, it is not by talking against Judaical notions that you will escape these great practical dangers. It is much more by looking manfully into Jewish history, and seeing whether it does not contain truths and principles which,—amidst all changes of circumstances, in the latest stage of growth and development as well as in the earliest, —belong to human beings. It tells us that God is the King of the Nation; the real ground of its orders, of its institutions,—the real teacher of its wise men,—the real author and director of all events that befall it. I hold that whatever else has been changed, that fundamental truth remains; I could not account for any alterations in the outward world, or they would drive me to despair, if I did not believe it. What follows as to the duty of the priest? He comes into a nation. He says he is a witness for something else than mere civil or local or secular government. By all means let him be such a witness. And as a proof that he is, let him do homage to the order which the Eternal Lord has established in a land; let him show that he does not look upon that as merely civil or secular or earthly; let him make the people who are living under it see that, whatever they think, he thinks, and is ready at all times to declare, that their society is no work of human hands, no result of vulgar conventions. Let him say

THE DUTY OF PRIESTS.

further, that God being the author and lawgiver of human society, all its disorders and anomalies are contrary to His will; and that statesmen as well as churchmen, instead of tolerating and excusing them, ought to be labouring day and night for the removal of them,—assured that if they do not, He will bear the most awful protest against the acts of individual men or official men, of civilians or ecclesiastics, against all diseases of long growth or modern introduction, which affect the well-being of His subjects. A man who takes this course may be very disagreeable to the high or the low wrong-doers of a land; he must lay his account with being so. But he will not and cannot be a disturber of the family or national order of a country; he must be bringing the mightiest help to the preservation of both. For instead of looking upon the universal order of the Church as interfering with either of these, he must believe that it stands upon the same divine foundation; that the same Lord who is the Chief Bishop of the universal family, and has endowed it with His Spirit, has called on each nation to be a witness in its own place, within its own limitations, of His Divine authority and Kingship. But since it is the tendency of a mere national organization to become exclusive,—to assert the dignity of birth or the sacredness of property above the dignity and sacredness of humanity,—the business of the priest in each land will be especially to protect it against this danger; continually to proclaim in the ears of kings, princes, nobles, rich men, that the glory which they share with the peasant is their highest glory; to tell them that if they set above this any treasures outward or inward, gifts of money or rank or intellect,—if they do not reckon these merely as lent them for the sake of the whole land,—they will bring upon themselves and upon their country swift destruction. The priest who presents Christ's finished sacrifice for the whole human race,—for rich and poor, high and low,—is entrusted above all men with this commission. Every subordinate minister of the tabernacle is in his position and degree entrusted with it; and therefore it must be for the ruin of both,—they must expect to go down alive into a deeper pit than that which received Korah and his company,—if they show that wealth, honours, distinctions of any kind, are the great objects of their search, that they are fighting for higher places either in man's household or God's; not remembering that '*he who exalteth himself shall be abased, and he who humbleth himself shall be exalted.*'

May the great High Priest,—who came not to be ministered unto, but to minister, and to give His life a ransom for many,—plead for us within the veil, that we may be delivered from the consequences of our contentions and rivalry; that ecclesiastics of all orders, that civil rulers and people, may understand their several functions, their common consecration by Him and to Him; that so we may be all one in Him, a family of kings and priests to His and our Father.

SERMON XII.

THE PROPHECY OF BALAAM.

(Lincoln's Inn, Second Sunday after Easter, May 4, 1851.)
Lessons for the day, Numbers XXIII. XXIV. and XXV.

NUMBERS XXIII. 11, 12.

And Balak said unto Balaam, What hast thou done unto me? I took thee to curse mine enemies, and, behold, thou hast blessed them altogether. And he answered and said, Must I not take heed to speak that which the Lord hath put in my mouth?

THERE are many particulars in this story of Balaam which remind us of the prophets who are spoken of in the Homeric poems and in the tragedies of Greece. He was summoned by Balak in the full faith that whomsoever he cursed was cursed, and whomsoever he blessed was blessed. He was evidently supposed to have that knowledge of things past, present, and future, which is ascribed to Calchas, and which gave him his high repute with the Grecian fleet. He is appealed to, just as that seer was appealed to when a pestilence was raging in the host, or when the ships were weather-bound; just as Tiresias was sent for to explain the calamity which had befallen Thebes, and to clear up the mystery which overhung the house of Œdipus. Balaam gives offence to the king of Moab just as they offended the heroes of the classical tales. However legendary these tales may be, all persons admit that they describe accurately a certain state of society. The prophets must have possessed this credit. Some of them must have been willing to incur the risk of displeasing rulers.

A mere parallel of this kind would be of little worth for its own sake; nor do I conceive that it is wanted for the proof or illustration of the Scriptures. It becomes important in consequence of the questions which are often asked respecting the reality of the knowledge of these prophets, and the source from which they derived it. On this subject very different opinions have been entertained. In old times Heathen seers were often said to be endued with a diabolical sagacity; if they were ever right an evil spirit enabled them to be so. The ordinary opinion in this day would probably be that they were mere deceivers, able to impose upon people somewhat more ill-informed than themselves. The holders of both these opinions are wont to contrast these false prophets with the true Jewish prophet, who received his illumination from God. All infidel schools would of course deny that difference; the most modern one would probably say, that the Hebrew as well as the Gentile prophets were shrewd observers and politicians, who sometimes dishonestly, but often in good faith, proclaimed themselves the receivers of a divine inspiration.

We who acknowledge the Bible as the high and ultimate authority, must desire that our decisions should be revised, corrected, even reversed by it, if we have adopted them from tradition, or fashioned them by our own weak, hasty inductions, without consulting it; those who question or deny its claim, should at least be willing to know what it actually says, lest they should impute statements to it which are not to be found in it, nay, which positively contradict those that are found in it.

Balaam is a heathen prophet; he is certainly not produced as a specially favourable specimen of one. In the New Testament he is represented as the very type of false and evil teachers; that view of his character could not have been confined to St. Peter and St. John; it must have been the one habitually prevailing among their countrymen. It was never doubted among them,—the story perfectly justifies the belief,—that he was inclined to fulfil Balak's wishes, and that he did ultimately fulfil them more effectually than by any words; that he deliberately set before the Israelites that temptation into which we are told, in the lesson for this evening, that they fell. And yet the teaching of Balaam is *not* ascribed to an evil spirit, but to God: he is *not* treated as a mere pretender to powers which were not his; his knowledge and foresight are acknowledged as real. The difference between him and those prophets who were the wise and noble guides of the Jewish nation, and its neglect of whom was one of its greatest sins, must therefore be sought for somewhere else than in the nature or the origin of their respective gifts. It is not only affirmed again and again, that God put words in Balaam's mouth, but that he knew it; and that he had a fear of speaking any words except those, and of not speaking those words. It is taken for granted that this was not a sudden, unwonted communication. He asks counsel of the Lord, and expects guidance from Him. These are not inferences drawn from the story by unnatural torturing, they are the plain obvious facts of it. Those who have most studied the moral of the story for their guidance, and for the instruction of others, have been most compelled to take notice of them;* it is by remembering them that the apparent difficulties of the narrative become the most solemn and practical portions of its lessons.

If this discovery came upon us all at once, I conceive it might be startling, even shocking, to our minds. But the whole previous history has been preparing us for it. It has been the assumption throughout the Scripture narrative, that God is the teacher of men, that they have no teaching of any kind which does not come from Him. And this not in some loose, general way. When we want to escape from the plain honest import of words, we say, ' Oh yes! No doubt that is true *in a certain sense.*' Thanks be to God, there are none of these ' certain senses,' which are in truth most uncertain, in His Bible. The words are pure words. They mean what they say. If God is spoken of as teaching any person whatever,—Jacob or Laban, Joseph or Pharaoh, Moses or Jethro,—we may feel sure that the writer wishes us to understand him simply, not to find some cunning explanation of his language which will empty it of all its significance. He must intend an actual communication,—a communication of intelligence, perception, living power,—to that in a human being which is capable of receiving it. Whenever a man exhibits such intelligence, perception, power, the Scripture does not refer it to some impression made upon his outward senses by the things which surround him, and which appeal to *them.* It supposes that these outward things remain blank and dead to him who has not some power within, which is capable

* See, for example, Butler's celebrated sermon on the Character of Balaam.

of interpreting and quickening them. It supposes that the more a man gives himself up to these things, the more helpless, the more inhuman, he becomes. But it declares also that there is One, even He in whose image he was formed, who does not allow him to remain their victim, who makes him aware of a world which his eyes and taste do not reveal to him, a world closely connected with himself; a world with which he can converse, in which he can live; a world with which he is meant to converse, in which he is meant to live; because there is a spirit in him which is created to govern the sensible world, not to be governed by it.

Now a person deeply and inwardly assured that he is not sent into the world merely to gaze in stupid wonder upon its spectacles and phantoms,—assured that he has that within him which passes show, assured that he is endowed with a power of looking into the heart of things,—such a man is recognised by his fellow-men as a *prophet*. They have found by experience that this character belongs to him. They have found that he divines secrets which are hidden from them; that he can connect the past and present and future, which seem to them lying utterly apart from each other. They cannot doubt that he both sees and foresees; that he has an intuition of the nature and causes of events, and of their results. And beside this, their own hearts own his power and penetration. He can ascertain by undoubted auguries what is passing in them; he can anticipate their conclusions; can awaken in them that which had gone to sleep; can bring into light that which was yet unborn.

In this acknowledgment there is no falsehood. On the contrary, there is homage to truth, the deference of men to one who is higher than themselves; and yet who they feel has sympathies with them; who has glimpses into a real world, a world of which they know little, yet which they are sure they have something to do with. Neither is *he* false in admitting that he has exercised the faculty which they ascribe to him, least of all in saying that the faculty is not his own,—that the light which his eye beholds is not created by the eye, that it comes to him from the Source of light. When the prophet owned that his teacher was One unseen and Divine, he had the most inward assurance that his words were true,—true *because* they were opposed to his natural pride and self-sufficiency.

And how then was Balaam a false prophet? No Jew or Christian says that he was a false prophet because the predictions which he uttered came to nought. We delight to maintain that they were confirmed; that what he spoke of the goodly tents of Israel was fulfilled more perfectly than he dreamed; that the Star which he saw in his vision did actually arise and shine upon Gentiles as well as Hebrews. That test of truth, if it were enough, the prophet Balaam could well endure. But it is *not* enough to satisfy the demands of Scripture or of our consciences. A man may be false, though all his words are true, though he has gifts and endowments of the highest order, though those gifts and endowments proceed, as all proceed, from God, though he refers them to Him, and seems to hold them as His vassal. Let us endeavour to trace out this falsehood, as the Scripture, illustrated and interpreted by sad experience, discovers it to us.

Balaam dwelt by the river of the land of the children of his people, with a consciousness of that power in himself which Balak and the Moabites ascribed to him. How terrible is that consciousness of power! How fearful the thought, 'I possess a secret which is unknown, or only 'dimly known, to these people about me! I see sights 'which they cannot see; I hear words which they cannot 'hear! They believe that he whom I bless is blessed, he 'whom I curse is cursed. What reverence accrues to me 'from that belief! And how well I am entitled to it! 'How I overlook them! How mean the thoughts and 'purposes of these rulers are in comparison of mine! How 'little they know what they are doing! How they tremble 'at every passing breeze! How little they are able to 'foresee the dangers which are actually threatening them!'

Such thoughts as these, brethren, lead to *one* effect most surely. The inward eye becomes more dim; the light that was in the man turns to darkness. Himself takes the place of the God whom he believed in and worshipped. He awakes like Samson after the hair has been shorn, and feels that his strength is departed. But the shadow of it must be preserved. He must persuade himself, and persuade others, that wisdom and power are his still. He resorts to the tricks of the diviner. He imposes upon men with appearances, leading them to fancy that he obtains his insight by some conjuring arts which he can exhibit before them. Speedily the falsehood, which he has been practising on others, returns upon himself. Though he has vaunted of the powers which set him above ordinary men, he begins to covet their possessions; to think that, after all, these are the most real things. And why should not he, the wise man, obtain them, nay, have a larger share of them than others? Henceforth this becomes the only end which he can distinctly propose to himself.

He would be happier if he *could* thoroughly make it his end. But he cannot. He is haunted with the sense of something else truer and deeper, that is immeasurably more worth seeking after. He still is sure that there is an invisible Teacher near him, that all his wisdom has come from Him. At times this truth overmasters him. He has forsaken God through his pride, through a love of power and a craving for earthly goods. But God will not leave him. He comes to him in the dark night; He makes him feel that there is a Presence which cannot be put by. At such a moment, in such a crisis of his life, the messengers of Balak come to Balaam. They know his weakness. They bring with them the rewards of divination, and flatteries as potent as they are.

Moreover they invite him to a work which has many attractions. A curse carries with it a far greater semblance of power than anything else. All who are seeking to make themselves admired and feared, exercise themselves in cursing. It is the shortest road to fame. Yet Balaam resists. God says to him, '*Thou shalt not curse this people, for they are blessed.*' The conviction that this is the Divine Will, is too mighty for all Balak's promises. His messengers return home.

But they come again. Balak was no doubt familiar with the evil side of the prophet. His struggles and repentances he might also have heard of, and have believed that they would be readily overcome, or were feigned to increase the price of surrender. The new bait was before his eyes. He repelled it; but alas! with a fine sentence. He cannot be content to resolve against it in a better strength; he must utter his purpose in words which will sound strong and eloquent in his own ears: '*If Balak would give me his house full of silver and gold, I cannot go beyond the word of the Lord my God, to do less or more.*'

He was playing with the hook when he seemed to himself to be thrusting it away. Perhaps he had mistaken the voice of God before. How could he be sure? He would seek for further guidance. Could any one blame him for doing so? Was it not piety? Yes! that piety which is another name for falsehood, which leads to the very consummate act of falsehood. Oh! how wretched the case would have been if Balaam had been merely carrying on this debate with himself, as we with our refined, atheistic philosophy would say that he was,—as now that he had brought himself into a false state of mind, he probably thought that he was. But neither we nor he can alter the fact. The Scripture here, as in every other case, tears off the mask and shows us the reality. It was not a mere dialogue with himself, a game in which the same hand was moving the pieces on both sides. God was debating the case with him, was educating him, as He educates us all, by permitting him to taste the effects of his own self-will, by making him understand what it was to tamper with truth and try to warp it to his own purpose. '*Go*,' said the Voice: '*but only the word that I shall speak unto thee, that thou shalt speak.*'

Was this merely the echo of the Divine word in a hollow, bewildered conscience? That is not a full explanation of the fact, though it is one which we must not disregard. Balaam *did* go, and was intended to go. He would not have learned the lesson which he was to learn if he had not gone. And yet his going was a wilful act. It was the struggle of one determined to have his own way, claiming the privilege of a man, while he was reducing himself into the condition of an animal, one that must be held in with bit and bridle, because he will not be guided and governed as a spiritual creature. You are puzzled at the language of Scripture about God's permitting Balaam to go, and then being displeased at him for going. You may well be puzzled. For what are so utterly bewildering as the mazes and contradictions of a human will, confessing a Master, struggling to disobey Him? But would you rather that the Bible left this fact unnoticed? Would you rather that it described human actions and events without reference to it? Is that the proof which you demand that it was written *by* God and *for* men? You will not have that sign if you ask for it ever so much. Not here alone, but everywhere, you will be met with these contradictions; man striving with God, God dealing with him as a voluntary creature, such as He had made him to be, not crushing his will by an act of omnipotence, but teaching it to feel its own impotency and madness.

And this surely is the sense of the next part of the story. How '*the dumb ass rebuked the madness of the prophet,*' I know not, nor care to know. But I believe that whatever sounds it uttered, they did convey exactly that meaning to the mind of the prophet which it is said that they conveyed. He felt that the instinct of a brute was made the instrument of teaching him; that what he could not learn by gracious inward discipline, was brought home to him by rough, humiliating, outward discipline. I feel too deeply the essential veracity of the story, to be troubled with minute questions about its details. I would not force them upon any one's belief merely by uttering the coarse sentence, that 'they are in the Bible, and therefore must be received.' The heart and conscience are too delicate and too sacred organs for such treatment. One is always afraid of leading people to fancy that they do believe what they do not believe, and so of propagating hypocrisy under the name of faith. I am not afraid for any of the accessary details of Scripture, if one is led to recognise the meaning and coherency of its laws and its facts; but I tremble greatly for those who dwell on those details as mere exercises either of skill or of what they call trust and reverence; while the laws and facts are more and more escaping, or their minds are becoming too sensual and frivolous to take them in.

But the story proceeds. Balaam learns that there was an Angel in the way. He is again a humbled man; he is assured that God will not let him speak any words but His own. Still he tampers and traffics with the inward voice. He allows Balak to build the altar, and offer the bullocks and the rams. He practises the usual arts of the diviner. But as he looks down upon the hosts of Israel, a mightier inspiration than any he has known yet, takes possession of him. The vision of a divine kingdom, of a society in which God shall really be the King, in which all ranks and orders shall be subject to Him and witnesses of His presence,—a vision which may have dawned upon him in the better and purer days of his childhood,—now comes upon him as one that is actually to be realized. '*From the tops of the rocks he sees them, from the hills he beholds them. Lo, the people shall dwell alone, and not be reckoned among the nations!*' I say, that it was a *new* inspiration, not because he was now for the first time speaking at God's bidding and uttering the words of the Almighty, but because heretofore he had thought of himself as the inspired man, as the divine prophet,—of all other people, as excluded from the divine communications except as they were imparted through him. And now the marvellous spectacle opens upon him, of a *people* whom God has blessed, of a *nation* which is called by His Name. With this there comes a belief which had been hidden from him before, of God, not merely as the giver of wisdom to favourite men, but as the righteous Being, the Author of a divine order. Out of that thought another unfolds itself; a deep sense, if it were but a transient one, of his own unrighteousness. What has he been living for? To be called a prophet ; to be praised, glorified, sought after by people and rulers ; to have the delight and anguish of feeling himself raised above other men, separated from all others.

It has been weariness and vexation of spirit. Oh, for the possibility of being right and true, of being like Him whose words he has uttered ! Oh, if he might but get that gift at last, when Balak's gifts and all his own will look to him even more paltry than they looked then! Oh, that he might ' *die the death of the righteous, and his last end be like his !* '

That deep cry came from the inmost heart of a man conscious of his hollowness as he had never been conscious of it before. You may think that when his soul swells into poetry, when he looks upon the goodly tents of Israel and sees them spread forth as the valleys, as gardens by the river-side, as lign-aloes which the Lord had planted, as cedar-trees beside the waters,—the personal conflict has ceased, and that the outward prospect is occupying him altogether. No! there is a deep melancholy in the tones of that song which shows you what is passing in the mind of the singer. The vision of a body of men marshalled in their hosts by God Himself, having the shout of a King in the midst of them, brings indeed into his heart a sense of life and joy. But it is the sight of spring to one whose spirit is wintry. The nation has a strength within it which must conquer; God has blessed it; no enchantments that are formed against it shall prosper. It shall be higher than Agag; the Kenite must fall before it; all that seems great now must be broken; there are victories in the distance which the prophet sees dimly, and can only express in words rising far above his own conceptions. But what has he to do with these triumphs of God? '*He will see them, but not now; he shall behold them, but not nigh.*' A Star he sees is rising upon the world, a light that shall one day fill it. '*But who shall live when God doeth this?*' What would he give if he could sympathise with the great purpose which will be accomplished in the world; if he could care to see righteousness and truth established in it, if he could feel as he supposes each one in that Israelitish host must be feeling, while it advances with predestined and invincible might, '*with the strength of a unicorn,*' to put down the tyrannies of the earth, and proclaim God as the King. But there is a barrier of pride and self-exaltation which will not be broken down. When he saw that it pleased the Lord to bless Israel, he could abandon for a moment his prophetical machinery: '*he went not, as at other times, to seek for enchantments.*' Truth triumphed for that hour in his heart, as it would one day triumph over the nations. But the evil spirit returned to the house that was empty, swept, and garnished, and took with it seven spirits more wicked than itself. The magician could not bear to gaze upon the broken wand; to part with power, even the reputation of possessing it, that he might die the death of the righteous. He had felt sin at the core of his life, without seeking to have it cast out;

he had known God as a righteous Being. Henceforth they were at war. He is filled with a deeper spite against the people whom he might not curse than it was possible for Balak to feel; he has been permitted to know the secret of their strength ; he sees how it may be sapped. 'Curse them not, but tempt them to lust and cor-'ruption; then they will be as weak and contemptible as ' yourselves.'

We have found, brethren, what a good pretext there is for both the theories, which I was compelled to reject at the beginning of this discourse. Balaam *was* a deceiver; one who tried to impose his divinations upon rulers and people. Balaam did become a most faithful servant of the Spirit of evil. What I could not admit,— what reverence for the words of Scripture forbad me to admit,—was, that Balaam got his wisdom by tricks of his own, or from the devil. To think so is to subvert all moral order, and to deny the very principle which the Bible is written to assert. *All* good is from God ; *all* power, *all* wisdom, is from Him ; only the direction and the use of it come to us from ourselves or from the tempter. I know that there is a kind of sacredness attaching in our minds to the mere word and name of inspiration, and that we are afraid to speak of evil men as being the subjects of a divine inspiration,—even though Scripture authorizes and enforces the opinion. Nay, we are afraid to speak of any gifts and powers except those which were used in the composition of the Scripture-books as being inspired. I rejoice and give thanks that during the last week that most dangerous and ungodly prejudice has been in a very solemn manner broken through and set at nought by an authority to which English Churchmen owe all respect. The sentence has gone forth as the profoundest expression of our English faith, in the presence of the representatives of all nations, that knowledge of every kind, that which leads to the creation of railways and steam-carriages, as well as the most spiritual, is of God; 'that the spirit of man is from Him, 'and that his understanding comes from the *inspiration* 'of the Almighty.'* That is a phrase which inferior ministers might have shrunk from using, lest it should give offence to their weaker brethren. But if they yielded to that excusable cowardice before, they are bound now to proclaim aloud a truth, which was never more needed to preserve nations from sinking into Atheism, in proportion as they become stewards of ampler treasures and mightier powers.

Do you ask what security there is for the special dignity and authority of Scripture, if the doctrine which has received this sanction gains currency? I answer, there is no security for the special dignity and authority of Scripture while you are content to rest them upon an arbitrary limitation of a word which Scripture itself instructs us to employ in a very wide and general sense. If you would know what the special claims of Scripture are upon your reverence and love, let it instruct you how to distinguish the false prophet from the true. You will not find that Isaiah is true and Balaam false, because the one received communications from God and the other did not, nor because Isaiah belonged to the covenant people and Balaam did not; for we hear continually of false prophets amongst circumcised men

* The prayer of the Archbishop of Canterbury at the opening of the Great Exhibition, May 1st, 1851.

who frequented the divine schools. But you will find that Isaiah lived for his people, and not for himself; that he did not value himself upon his gifts, or upon his holiness, or upon anything whatsoever that belonged to him as an individual. His eyes had seen the King the Lord of Hosts, and that sense of God's holiness which made him know that he was an unclean man and dwelt among a people of unclean lips,—yet enabled him to go forth and declare His truth and His kingdom, to testify that if the kings of the house of David were ever so unbelieving, ever so tyrannical, He would raise up a King who should be a refuge from the heat and storm; who should judge the poor, who should gather together the outcasts of Israel, and in whom the Gentiles should trust. The certainty, under every possible discouragement and conflict, that the righteous God would prevail over all that was unrighteous and anarchical in the universe,—the delight in this assurance,—the willingness to be made an instrument of carrying out God's purposes, let what would come of him or his character, let him be honoured as a prophet, or cast out as the offscouring of the earth,— this, this is the sign of the true man, this is what separates him from the solitary self-seeker who shrank from the thought of God appearing to set the world right; who only wished, when his wishes were purest, that *he* might die the death of the righteous.

But the faithful man, Isaiah or Jeremiah, did not come to this state without passing through internal struggles which Balaam never knew, without having to experience all the temptations which he did know and to which he yielded. The books of their prophecies are no mere records of words put into their mouths, of sudden overpowering inspirations. They tell how the man struggled with the divine Teacher, how he said he would speak no more words in His name, till the fire could not keep itself pent in his heart any longer; how he complained that the Lord had deceived him; how the precious and the vile had need to be separated in him by the severest discipline, that he might know assuredly that he was not speaking the thoughts of his own heart, but words which God desired him to speak for the good of his age and of generations to come. This is the Scripture,—not merely an inspired book, as we sometimes call it, thinking to pay it great honour,—but an actual discovery of God Himself and of His ways with His creatures. If we consider it only as a collection of inspired sentences or oracles, we may accept it as divine; but we shall gradually lose sight both of Him who is speaking in it, and of those by whom and to whom He is speaking; its godliness and its humanity will disappear together. We shall be continually stumbling at one sentence and another, trying to force them into some strange meaning of our own; then violently outraging the conscience which God's Word itself has been cultivating in us, calling in His Omnipotence to dispense with His righteousness,—when it is the very characteristic of Scripture that it makes Righteousness the root of God's being,—power only its instrument and accident. If we take that other view of the Bible,— the errors, sins, false or imperfect judgments of its best and wisest men, will be no scandals to us; we shall accept them as foils which enable us to see His character more clearly, in whom is light and no darkness at all. We shall perceive that men could only apprehend truth, just so far as they saw it in Him after whose image they were formed. Every step in the history will be a step into clearer illumination, God showing Himself more fully, that the thoughts and actions of men may be capable of a closer correspondence to His. At the same time, it will be no perplexity to us, but an infinite comfort,—that the powers, and energies, and kindly affections, and right desires of every man whatsoever, in every part of the earth, whether yielding to the right or resisting it, should be vindicated for Him from whom every good and perfect gift comes down. This will not hinder us from recognising His gracious purpose, in calling out a family, a nation, a church, to be the heralds of His great Name, to show forth His kingly and fatherly rule over men. For we shall see how dangerous all His most precious gifts are likely to become, if those who are entrusted with them do not know that they are but holding them as dispensers to a great household; and that they can have no blessings of their own, except so far as they feel that they are meant to give each member of that household his own portion of meat at the due season. The Bible, so considered, becomes an orderly expanding history. The Star which Balaam saw afar off emerges more and more out of the darkness. At last it is seen how God could raise up a Prophet to men; one of their brethren, who should be with them in all their sorrow and affliction, because He was with His Father in heaven, and perfectly delighted to show forth His name, to declare His kingdom, to do His will upon the earth. At last it is seen how His Holy Spirit, which had been bestowed without measure upon His well-beloved Son, could come down and make men's bodies His temples; could bind men of every nation and tribe in one; could inspire them with all gifts; could consecrate all their gifts to the service of their Father in Heaven and their brethren upon earth.

I must say one word more, which is closely connected with the application of this whole subject to our own selves. Though the writers of the New Testament cannot have held an essentially different opinion respecting Balaam from that which was common among their countrymen, yet they certainly dwell upon the dark side of his character more than it is dwelt upon in the book of Numbers. They especially represent him as the type of a false prophet, and this not for the purpose of condemning him, but of showing how his evil tendencies might be more prevalent and more fatal in the new dispensation than the old. The reason is evident. They had been taught to refer all gifts and powers, which appear in particular men, to that Holy Spirit, who was now manifested as the indweller in human hearts, as the bond of human fellowship. Those whom St. John in the Apocalypse describes as followers of Balaam were men who believed most strongly in a Spirit, and boasted that they were possessors of it, but who forgot altogether that He was the Spirit of Holiness; who blessed Him for enduing them with powers,—who did not ask Him to renew and remake *themselves*, the wielders and exercisers of those powers. Such Balaamites there have been in all ages among those who minister at God's altar, among those who perform different offices in His household and His vineyard. In whatever form self-exaltation comes into the heart of man,—in the form of craving for popularity, of intellectual pride, of spiritual pride, in the desire for dominion over others, in the secret triumph of our own superiority,—the Balaam sin is working underground, the fruits of it may some day become apparent. Let no one of us say that it is not his sin, that it may not penetrate into him and diffuse itself through him, when he seems to himself to be engaged,—nay, when he is in fact engaged,— in the most godly services, and receiving the most godly inspirations. Let our trust be in God and not in ourselves, to deliver us from this root of bitterness. Let us ask Him that we may not value ourselves upon gifts, or tongues, or prophecies, but may be filled with that love which shall remain when they cease, and when He is all in all.

SERMON XIII.

PROSPERITY AND ADVERSITY.

(Lincoln's Inn, Third Sunday after Easter, May 11, 1851.)

Lessons for the day, Deuteronomy IV. and V.

DEUT. v. 33.

Ye shall walk in all the ways which the Lord your God hath commanded you, that ye may live, and that it may be well with you, and that ye may prolong your days in the land which ye shall possess.

THERE are certain popular maxims and phrases respecting the difference between the Old and New Testament which we accept, as if they were parts of holy Scripture, and which affect all our judgments of it. The rewards of the Jewish dispensation, we are told, were temporal; those of the Christian, eternal. The Israelite was taught to respect blessings in the world that is; we are bidden to set our minds upon the world that is to come; prosperity was the sign of God's favour to the chosen nation; adversity is one of the seals of adoption in the Church. If these sayings really expressed the deepest thoughts of those who use them and repeat them; if divines were not compelled again and again to forget them when they are dealing with the facts of the Scriptures, or applying them to the consciences of men; if humble wayfarers when they are in want of a guide for their lives, or help in their sorrows, did not continually set them at nought; I should consider it a perilous and rash enterprise to dispute their authority For though they cannot, so far as I know, allege decrees of any church in their favour, and though on the face of them they look as if they interfered with some by which we profess to be bound, there is, no doubt, a sanctity in customary notions which should not be rudely violated. Their currency is evidence that they carry a truth within them, and that truth,—however we may think it has been perverted by the elements with which it is surrounded into a cause of error and unbelief,—should be diligently sought out, and reverently acknowledged, before we dare to reject the opinion in which it is enshrined.

I have chosen a passage from the lesson for this afternoon which seems to afford a strong justification for the view which is ordinarily taken of the Jewish economy; it is a passage the importance of which can scarcely be overrated; it may help us, I think, to understand better the whole book from which it is taken. The words which close my text, '*That ye may live, and that it may be well with you, and that ye may prolong your days in the land which ye shall possess,*' are likely to fix your attention first as bearing most directly upon this subject. I have no desire to avoid the most literal interpretation of them; any other I should hold to be entirely unsuitable to the context, and to the character of the person who spoke them. But I must defer the consideration of them till I have examined those which precede them, without which they are unintelligible upon any hypothesis, '*Ye shall walk in all the ways which the Lord your God hath commanded you.*'

I. One of these clauses is commonly said to enjoin

a duty, the other to promise the blessings which those might confidently look for who performed it. Whatever worth there may be in this division, it cannot be considered a satisfactory one by any thoughtful reader of the book of Deuteronomy. Let me recall to you two or three passages from the chapters which we have read to-day. Take for instance this: '*For what nation is there so great, who hath God so nigh unto them, as the Lord our God is, in all things that we call upon him for? And what nation is there so great, that hath statutes and judgments so righteous as all this law which I set before you this day?*' And this again: '*But the Lord hath taken you and brought you out of the iron furnace, even out of Egypt, to be unto him a people of inheritance, as ye are this day.*' Once more: '*Ask now of the days that are past, which were before thee, since the day that God created man upon the earth, and ask from the one side of heaven unto the other, whether there hath been any such thing as this great thing is, or hath been heard like it? Did ever people hear the voice of God speaking out of the midst of the fire, as thou hast heard, and live? Or hath God assayed to go and take Him a nation from the midst of another nation, by temptations, by signs, and by wonders, and by war, and by a mighty hand, and by a stretched-out arm, and by great terrors, according to all that the Lord your God did for you in Egypt before your eyes? Unto thee it was shewed, that thou mightest know that the Lord He is God; there is none else beside Him.*'

Now what is the effect of all these passages? (and there are hundreds like them; they embody the very spirit of the book.) Do they not declare in the most plain and direct manner that the main, characteristic, fundamental blessing of the Israelite, consisted in this, that God took him into covenant with Himself; that He delivered him out of the hand of human oppressors; that He brought him under His own government; that He revealed to him what manner of Being He was? Would not your natural conclusion be on the first perusal of these passages,—would it not be strengthened by all subsequent reflection upon them, by comparison of one with the other, 'Whatever ' other advantages the Israelite may have enjoyed, I am ' taught here that his relation to God, his national position ' which is grounded upon that, the fact that he was placed ' under a divine law and made acquainted with its nature, ' were his great gifts and privileges, to which all others ' were subordinate?' Is there anything new or surprising in such statements? Could you have doubted, after reading the books of Genesis, and Exodus, and Numbers, that the highest mercy God could confer upon men was to make them conscious of His presence and of His order; that want of belief in that Presence, want of submission to that order, were *the* curses of human beings,—from which all slavery to men and to natural things, all division, all suffering, proceeded?

We fall then, I conceive, into a very inaccurate method of speech, when we say that the prize which God proposes to His people is set forth in one of these clauses; the duty, or performance by which they are to earn that prize, in the other. Moses teaches his countrymen that God *has* conferred upon them the highest prize which man can conceive, freely and without any merit on their part. When they were bondsmen of Pharaoh, He claimed them as His servants; when they trembled before the powers of the visible world, He showed them that these powers were His instruments, and that He used them for their good;

when they fancied that the Ruler of the world was indifferent to them, or hated them, He proved that He was watching over them and caring for them, even in their meanest condition, though they were not thinking at all of Him; when they supposed that He was capricious, He proved to them the evenness, regularity, equity of His government; when they fancied that He was unmerciful, He declared Himself as the Lord God, forgiving iniquity, and transgression, and sin. Was this knowledge of the living and unseen God nothing in itself, but only valuable in virtue of some results that were to come of it? Moses tells his countrymen that it was everything. This knowledge was *the* good thing which they had received from the Source of all Good. To hold it fast, was to be a nation; to lose it, was to sink back into the condition out of which they had been raised,—not by their own might,—and which if they trusted in their own might, would assuredly overtake them again.

Will any one say, brethren, that this was a *visible* blessing? It was the discovery to them of an invisible Being. Moses said to them, ' *Take ye therefore good heed to yourselves; for ye saw no* MANNER OF SIMILITUDE *in the day when the Lord spake unto you in Horeb.*' Or was it a *temporal* blessing? It was the discovery to them of a Being who is and was and is to come, the same from generation to generation. Surely the word temporal' must be the most inappropriate to describe it that we can conceive. If the knowledge of God is eternal life, eternal life was offered to the Israelites. Our Article cannot be too strong in its denunciation of the doctrine that the old fathers looked only for transitory promises. One who could not pass away or change was the ground of all their belief, the object of all their hope. They came into a region of transitoriness and change when they forgot Him, or began to draw their notions of Him from the vicissitudes of the world around them and the fluctuations of their own hearts.

II. Is there no duty then enjoined in the words of my text? Does it *merely* speak of a blessing or a privilege? Certainly when it is said, ' *Ye shall walk in all the ways which the Lord your God hath commanded you,*' it must be meant that there was something required on the part of the creature as well as something bestowed by the Creator. What I wish you to observe is, that we cannot understand what is required unless we understand what is bestowed. If we believe that a way has been made for us, and that we have been put into that way, we can apprehend the force of the precept to walk in it; we can feel what is meant by transgression and revolt. If we believe that an actual living Being to whom we are related has put us in this way, and that it is a way of dependence upon Himself, we can understand how the preservation of it becomes a duty to Him; we begin in fact to know what duty is. If, finally, we believe that He who puts us in this way is the only person who can keep us in it, or prevent us from going out of it, we may feel that His command is itself a power; that it does not merely say, ' Thus and thus you ' must do, thus and thus you must not do;' but, ' This ' will I enable you to do, this will I prevent you from ' doing.'

The more you read the book of Deuteronomy, the more you will feel that these are the principles upon which all the exhortations of Moses to the Israelites are based. He repeats, as you heard this afternoon, the Ten Commandments to the people,—to those Israelites who were born in the wilderness. These commandments begin as they did at first with the words, '*I am the Lord thy God, which brought thee out of the land of Egypt, out of the house of bondage.*' They are not literal copies of the former precepts; in one instance there is a memorable alteration. The Sabbath is ordained, not as before, because God rested on the Sabbath-day. The Israelite who keeps it is to remember that God had delivered him out of the land of Egypt. Thus the belief of a redemption already effected underlies every institution, every precept, the whole economy. Moreover, the commandments are represented as God's covenant: it is not merely said amidst thunders and lightning and fire, 'Whoso trans-'gresseth shall die.' God out of this thunder and lightning and that fire proclaims that His own will and power shall go forth to hold up the nation and all the members of it in their obedience; that they are people of inheritance to Him, that He will be with them and guide them, and support them by night and day. Accordingly the exhortations and warnings of this book are not directed against the rebellions of a people who are told to do certain acts and who neglect them, or who do acts which are forbidden. They are directed against a people with whom God is in covenant,—who deny that He is among them, who do not trust Him to keep them as He has promised to do,—who think they can do right, and be right without Him; who set up other gods in the place of Him, because they do not like to retain Him in their knowledge; who become the worshippers and servants of visible things, because the presence of an invisible Being is terrible and hateful to them; who worship unrighteous and unmerciful beings like themselves, because they shrink from the recollection of the righteous and merciful Lord. The effects of such wilfulness are set down in very appalling language, some of which we may consider hereafter; language illustrated and fulfilled in the history of that people, and, as I think, in the history of every nation in the ancient and modern world of which we have any records. And so also the effects of obedience are set down with the like breadth and clearness; these effects being order; prosperity; union among themselves; victory over enemies,—the honour and reputation of a true and understanding people in the sight of nations; all the material blessings which accompany and follow such a state of society.

III. We come then at length to this class of blessings which are shortly gathered up in the words: '*That ye may live, and that it may be well with you, and that ye may prolong your days in the land which ye shall possess.*' It is here signified in very simple, clear language, which admits, I conceive, of no double sense, that a people in a right, orderly, godly state shall be a well-doing people; a people with all the signs and tokens of strength, growth, triumph; a people marked for permanence, and indefinite expansion. I cannot put another meaning upon these words; I should think that a wish to dilute their force was a proof of the greatest carelessness about the authority from which they proceed, as well as of the most shocking inhumanity. If it be the distinction of saints and spiritual men, that they do not trouble themselves about the external prosperity of a land, that they do not care whether the oxen are strong to labour, whether the sheep are bringing forth thousands and ten thousands, whether there is no complaining in the streets; if they are so occupied in the future as to have no interest in the present, too busy with their souls to have leisure for thinking about the ruin which may be threatening the bodies of their fellow-men,—then I say at once Moses, David, Isaiah, Jeremiah, were not saints and spiritual men. They had no pretension to the title; every word they have left is a disclaimer of it. They never fancied that the desire that their nation should have all possible outward blessings was a proof of indifference to the unseen Source of these blessings; they considered it an act of homage to Him,—that any other feeling would have been a practical denial of Him. If natural things were not His, if the bodies of men were not His, then it would have been right to put on a contempt of the external world and of all which merely concerned man as an animal. But since they rejected any such notion as idolatrous or atheistic,—since they believed the one Lord, their God, to be the Lord of the whole universe,—they had no choice but either to forget Him altogether, or to see tokens of His wisdom and power in all events whatsoever, whether voluntary or involuntary creatures were the instruments in bringing them to pass. Since they held that God's order was the perfectly right and living order, they could not but think that all disorder, all wrong and death which had invaded it, must have come through man's neglect to fulfil the part which had been assigned him;—through his unwillingness to till and subdue the earth which he was meant to till and subdue; through his idleness and distrust and self-seeking, his refusal to walk in the ways which God had commanded. They knew too well, for they felt in themselves, how strong the disposition in all men was to choose a way of their own, and to forget the covenant of God. They could only look up to Him to overcome this tendency, in them and in their countrymen, by whatever discipline or punishment He knew to be needful.

IV. And therefore, brethren, it cannot be true,—the whole history of the Jews declares it not to be true,—that the blessings of adversity were unknown to them, were reserved for a later period. Which of the good men of the Old Testament was not proved in a furnace? Into whose soul did the iron at some time not enter? It was not because they believed in God's promises to their nation, and were sure that its outward prosperity must and would at last correspond to its inward health and vitality,—it was not because they longed for the earth to bring forth and bud, to have heaps of corn upon it, that its presses might burst forth with new wine,—it was not on this account that they had to endure less of inward sadness, or fewer reproaches from the kings and priests and people to whom they spoke. No; the more strong their feeling was that God had chosen their nation and made a covenant with it, the greater was the struggle with their individual selfishness, their desire of great things for themselves; the more need had they of God's fires to purify them. The more they believed that the nation could only be what it was intended to be when it was remembering the covenant of its God, the more had they to reprove those who were living to themselves and glorying in themselves,—not caring for the privilege upon which all the outward blessings of Israel depended,—not caring to know Him who executed righteousness and judgment upon the earth. These reproofs brought, as they were certain to bring, reproaches, shame, persecution upon those who uttered them. No men could be more taught than the Jewish seers were, that punishments are necessary for individuals and nations, and that '*whom the Lord loveth He chasteneth.*'

I have thought it necessary to examine these often-repeated dogmas respecting Old Testament history,— because they seem to me to have just the same effect in hindering the right and manly investigation of it, as the idols which Bacon denounced and overthrew, in hindering the fair investigation of nature. But I have felt even more anxious to discuss them upon another ground, because, if I am not mistaken, they are as hurtful to the rightful understanding of the New Testament as of the Old. They prevent us from seeing the difference which does exist between them, by inventing one which does not exist; and they both indicate and foster tendencies, which in our day I fear are ripening and are bringing forth very evil fruits.

For it is surely a perilous and an almost fatal notion, that Christian men have less to do with the present than the Jews had, that their minds and their religion are to be projected into a region after death, because there only the Divine Presence is dwelling. Is it possible that this is what the writers of the New Testament meant when they proclaimed that the Son of God had taken flesh and become man, and that thenceforth the Lord God would dwell with men and walk with them, and that they should be His children and He would be their Father? Do such words import, that the world in which God has placed us has lost some of the sacredness which it had before; that the visible has become hopelessly separated from the invisible; that earth and heaven are not as much united as they were when Jacob was travelling to the land of the people of the east: that now earth is merely a forlorn place, in which men are forced to stay a certain number of years, engaged in a number of occupations with which Heaven has nothing to do, while yet it is held that the preparation for Heaven is the great business of those who dwell here? Surely there must be terrible contradiction in such language, a contradiction which cannot fail to exhibit itself in our practice, to introduce unreality, insincerity, heartlessness into every part of it.

This unreality, insincerity, heartlessness, may remain hidden for a time, though its mischiefs will be at work. There may be a sort of compromise and understanding in the upper and middle classes of society, that certain persons shall have religious tastes and indulge them, while the majority shall be given up to their farms and merchandise. The hollowness of the arrangement will often come to light; it will divide those who feel and know that they ought to be at one; family obligations, family affections will break it down, or will be destroyed by it; at length those whose consciences tell them that they must work in the world feel themselves excommunicated, and act as if they were; while those whose minds are in the future declare that they must separate themselves and form a world of their own, or their souls will perish. Such things have happened again and again in all societies,—are happening now. But still, as I said, these social conventions, often broken, may be renewed; there may be truces if there can be no solid peace, so long as what are called the respectable classes have the power of settling the terms. But from the moment that the men of toil and suffering, the real stuff of which every country is composed, claim to exercise any direct and independent thought upon such subjects, from that moment it becomes absolutely impossible that arrangements which are grounded upon the notion of a part of mankind having certain religious propensities, and a part belonging to the world, should last. The alternative *then* is a faith which shall belong to men as men, which shall concern *all* their ordinary pursuits, toils, relations; which shall not only bestow upon them an artificial sanctity, a passing benediction, but which shall show that they are holy according to God's eternal purpose and order,—the alternative, I say, is between such a faith and absolute Atheism. We must settle it in our minds clearly and decisively,—not that we may come to this point hereafter, but that we are come to it now,—here in England and in every country of Christendom. The revolutions of three years ago announced this crisis; oh! do not let us delude ourselves with the notion that any plots or devices of ours have suspended it. God in His mercy is giving us a brief respite, during which we may decide on what ground we will take our stand. If we hope anything from a conventional religion adopted to keep the existing system of the world together, we shall find ourselves utterly deceived; the fabric and its props will fall together. If we hope anything from a religion having no deeper foundation than a wish for our own personal security, we shall find that the protest against selfishness which Christianity has borne for 1800 years will prove the destruction of the counterfeit which usurps its name. But if we believe in our hearts that the New Testament is not contrary to the Old; that our Covenant is larger, deeper, more social than the Jewish,—not narrower, more individualizing, less rooted in the Nature and Being of God; that every maxim of trade or government, however sustained by custom, opinion, authority, which is opposed to Truth and Righteousness, is doomed to perish; then we have a Gospel which men will listen to in the nineteenth century more than they did in the sixteenth or the third; a Gospel that will uphold all ranks and orders of society so long as they do not interfere with a more fixed and everlasting order; but which will derive fresh evidence and authority from their dissolution if they should claim for themselves some independent worth, and set at nought the blessings which God has intended for all His creatures. '*I said, Ye are gods, and are children of the most High,*' your authority is God-given, and deserves all reverence while you use it as if it were. But if you will be gods in yourselves, if you pretend to some absolute right over your fellow-creatures, if you will not acknowledge that they, the meanest of them, are children of the most High, redeemed by the blood of His Son, endued with His Spirit, then shall ye fall like feeble men as you are, and die like one of those princes whose fate has been set before your eyes as a spectacle and warning to yourselves. The Book we have begun to read to-day is full of terrible threatenings and prophecies; let us not forget them or apply them to others rather than to ourselves. Assuredly they will be executed upon us if we choose some separate way of our own; not that way which God has intended for us all. But if we will walk in that good way, His word remains sure. The land which the Lord our God has given us will be a good land. We shall be able to rejoice in the prosperity of it. We shall be able to leave it an inheritance to our children's children. And with it we shall leave them also the blessing which God in

His old covenant and His new pronounced upon the poor; the sign of fatherly love which Solomon and St. Paul alike saw in God's chastisements; the assurance that here we are in the presence of an innumerable company of saints and angels, and of God the Judge of all, and that Christ desires that we shall enter into the fuller enjoyment of that society, into a deeper apprehension of His Redemption, when death is swallowed up in victory.

SERMON XIV.

THE NATION AND THE CHURCH.

(Lincoln's Inn, Fourth Sunday after Easter, May 18, 1851.)
Lessons for the day, Deut. vi and vii.

DEUT. VII. 22—26.

And the Lord thy God will put out those nations before thee by little and little: thou mayest not consume them at once, lest the beasts of the field increase upon thee. But the Lord thy God shall deliver them unto thee, and shall destroy them with a mighty destruction, until they be destroyed. And he shall deliver their kings into thine hand, and thou shalt destroy their name from under heaven: there shall no man be able to stand before thee, until thou have destroyed them. The graven images of their gods shall ye burn with fire: thou shalt not desire the silver or gold that is on them, nor take it unto thee, lest thou be snared therein: for it is an abomination to the Lord thy God. Neither shalt thou bring an abomination into thine house, lest thou be a cursed thing like it: but thou shalt utterly detest it, and thou shalt utterly abhor it; for it is a cursed thing.

IN my last Sermon I tried to show you that the Old Testament does not differ from the New, because the rewards which it proposes are transitory or earthly, or because it exalts prosperity, and does not recognise adversity as a blessing. But I did not deny that there was a very striking difference between them. I hinted that one evil of these widely-diffused notions was, that they concealed the true character of it. The obvious and admitted distinctions, that one contains a partial, the other a complete revelation of the Name and nature of God; that one presents to us a peculiar Nation, the other a universal Church unfolding itself out of that nation,—explain, it seems to me, the facts which the inventors of these theories have unsuccessfully attempted to explain. I am quite aware, however, that questions of a very serious kind arise out of this view of the subject. Have we any right to say that the Christian Church is a mere expansion of the Jewish nation, a perfect flower coming out of a bud? Are they not contradictory in their very nature? Are not exclusion, war, persecution, extermination, set forth as principles of the one; comprehension, peace, forgiveness, regeneration, of the other? Is it possible to speak of the same Being as the Author of both? Is it possible for any one heartily to sympathise in the fruits of the Gospel, who does not shrink with a kind of horror from the acts enjoined by the Israelitish Law? Have not the great evils of the Church, in fact, arisen from the effort to combine in itself two opposite natures, to be at once loving and hateful, destructive and life-giving? Is not the time come, when this unnatural combination must cease, when the new must expel the old, or be swallowed up by it?

The lessons which we have read to-day force these inquiries upon us. They bring out before us in all their strength and fulness those characteristics of the Jewish dispensation which one class of our popular teachers openly denounce as cruel and hardhearted; which another rejoices to think were right once, but have become utterly wrong now; from which a third seeks to derive reasons for holding no communion with the members of an idolatrous Church, though it shrinks from adopting the Jewish precedent as an actual guide to ourselves. I wish to consider, first, what, according to the statements we have been reading, the Jewish nation was to be and to do; secondly, how far its principles and acts are in accordance with those which our Lord enjoins upon His disciples; thirdly, in what sense we inherit or do not inherit Jewish obligations.

I. There can be no doubt that these passages represent the Jewish nation as bound to a perpetual conflict with idolatry. The resistance was primarily an internal one The members of the nation were not to meddle with the accursed thing; they were never to bow down to natural or human symbols. This was the tenure of the nation's existence; losing this it lost itself. So Moses teaches in these chapters; the doctrine comes out still more distinctly, minutely, awfully, afterwards. But the Israelite was not merely to be tenacious of the true worship, and watchful against any intrusion of the false; he was to go forth against the idolatrous people of Canaan, to break in pieces their gods, to destroy their altars and high places. The language on the one subject is as clear and imperative as on the other. There is no room for the plea that the Jew was to defend his own position, without assailing that of his fellows. He was to feel that he had a commission to fight, not chiefly for his own borders, though these would be extended, but mainly as the soldier of God, to put down that which exalted itself against Him. And not only the idol or the idol-temple was to be destroyed; the inhabitants of the idolatrous country, their wives, their children, their sheep, and their oxen, were to be put to death. The leader of the hosts was to set his foot upon the necks of their kings.

What is this, it will be said, but a religious war of the most ferocious kind, a war for establishing the tenets of

Judaism, and putting down the tenets of those who differed from it; a war not justified upon the ordinary excuses of lands invaded or threatened, of commerce interrupted, even of fears that such results might happen if no steps were taken to hinder them? How can any war whatsoever, any crusade, be denounced or considered otherwise than praiseworthy and exemplary, if these are defended?

It will be seen at once that such phrases as 'the tenets of Judaism,' the 'tenets of Heathens,' are not scriptural expressions, or equivalents for any that are to be found in Scripture. They are struck in a different mint. Some may think them much better, belonging to a much more advanced state of civilization. Whether that is so or not, one cannot be substituted for the other; they have nothing in common. We merely read ourselves into the Bible when we introduce them there; and it is an idle thing to pronounce judgment upon a case which we have invented.

Without taking that course, we may consider a few facts which ordinary history makes known to us. If we examine the condition of any people in the old world, we shall, I think, perceive that some apprehensions of a just and righteous Power, the ground of law and order, the protector of boundaries, the avenger of wrong, lay near the heart of them all. In proportion as the people we read of was strong, concentrated, triumphant, so was this feeling strong. But near it lay an element of weakness, division, falsehood. They connected this righteous and avenging Power with some visible objects. Such objects had different aspects in different places, produced different effects on different minds. The worshippers of them became divided, narrow, local. This was one inevitable result. But besides this, they became animal and sensual. Their gods had been formed in great part by their animal and sensual instincts. Every day the thing worshipped became more coloured and perverted by the low habits of the worshipper's mind; every day that mind became grosser from the objects which it reverenced and which it had debased.

But presently there comes in a new cause of corruption. The priest,—the witness that there is a Being, or that there are beings above man, whom he is intended to worship,—promotes the growth of these downward tendencies. He becomes their minister. As the conscience grows indifferent to actual transgressions, the religious acts which he enjoins keep up in it a sort of morbid sensitiveness. Its pains must be removed, though its sins cannot. Hence a whole system of practices, each of which tends to make the belief in God more confused, to make that which is divine more and more in the likeness of the corrupt human, of the animal, of the devilish. It has *not* been a mistake or delusion into which men have fallen, when they have traced all the moral evils of the world, all its political evils, to its superstitions; that is to say, to its false notions of God. They have only gone wrong when they have failed to see that all these hateful superstitions are the denials of some precious truths, of which the national conscience, the national constitution, even the national idolatry, was testifying. They have only gone wrong when they have refused to see that all the strength, the order, the truth, which have been in any people, must have come from above; because the weakness, disorder, untruth, which were in them, so certainly have come from beneath.

Now what the Scriptures say is this, that the God of the whole earth declared or unveiled Himself to the members of one family, because it was His purpose that in that family all the families of the earth should be blessed; that in due time He raised this family into a nation, revealing to the members of it His righteousness and truth, through laws, ordinances, and institutions; renewing the covenant which He had made with their forefathers; preserving most carefully the distinctions of their families; treating each as an integral portion of the nation. To this nation it is said He gave the command that they should go forth against certain tribes, the cup of whose iniquities was full, —that is to say, in whom idolatry had produced its ultimate effects, in whom it had reached its full consummation, who had lost the very sense of righteousness and order and truth, who were preying upon each other, who had sunk into all unutterable crimes,—for the purpose of sweeping their gods, themselves, and everything that belonged to them, from the face of the earth. However we judge of these facts, this we must at least admit to be the statement of them. And therefore the difference between the Jews and other people is precisely this: All the great nations that we read of have effected extensive, and on the whole, salutary, conquests. Their triumphs have been the means of spreading law, government, civilization, where they would otherwise not have reached. They have swept away feeble, corrupt, sensualized people, who had become animal-worshippers or devil-worshippers, and had lost all sense of their human dignity. But we feel that the nations who have done these works, have done them in great part for their own glory, for the increase of their territory, at the instigation and for the gratification of particular leaders. All higher and more blessed results of their success, which it is impossible not to recognise, have been stained and corrupted by the ignoble and selfish tendencies which have mixed with them and been the motives to them; so that we are continually perplexed with the question, what judgment we shall form of them, or what different causes we can find for such opposite effects. There is *one* nation which is taught from the very first that it is *not* to go out to win any prizes for itself, to bring home the silver or gold, the sheep or the oxen, the men-servants or the women-servants, that it is to be simply the instrument of the righteous Lord against those who were polluting His earth and making it unfit for human habitation. If this people were represented as a particularly exalted and virtuous people in themselves, their history would throw little light upon that of others They would be merely rare exceptions, from whose successes or failures no inference could be drawn. But being throughout affirmed and proved to be a hard-hearted, stupid, stiff-necked people, we perceive whence all their strength, vitality, courage proceeded. We see that they were great, and brave, and united, as Moses tells them they would be,—just so far as they believed that God was in the midst of them and going forth with them, that this gave all the heart to their enterprises,—and that just so far as they lost this, they were meaner and more selfish than all other people. The confusion then that we see elsewhere, is explained and removed here. If we could believe Moses's statement, it would be the greatest help in understanding and interpreting Greek, Roman, and all other histories; it would explain to us why all ancient history is *national* history; why the history of two or three little nations is really the history of the whole world. At the same time it would show us how a nation, which seemed at first the enemy of all others, was really doing their work; was warring with their evils as much as its own; was acting as the punisher of evils, which, if they are left in a land, destroy the inhabitants of it by inward consumption and by mutual executions.

We have all some method of accounting for the stories we read of destructive wars; but they are often tortuous, confused, immoral methods. We talk of good coming out of evil; as if that which was bad did or could of itself produce any fruits except bad ones. We speak of the great advantages of a more civilized nation meeting a less civilized, even if one exterminates the other; a conclusion to which we are certainly driven in many cases by facts, but yet in which I think we are all at times shaken by other facts of a very humiliating and painful kind; and which, when we have arrived at it, is not altogether consolatory or satisfactory. We believe that a people utterly defiled by its own immoralities and superstitions is destined to perish, and generally perishes by the hand of some other race;—those words, 'is destined,' or 'generally,' either merely announcing certain observations of experience, or introducing some vague, dark, unknown fate, to relieve the oppression which they cause us. All these are either contrivances to escape from the belief in God; or else the trembling, convulsive efforts of shipwrecked men to grasp at that belief. Suppose now they dared say to themselves, 'This was ordained. God intended this, and appointed
' the persons who were to carry it out; the blessing came
' from Him; what they did as His agents, they did bene-
' ficially, effectually; whatever they did merely to carry
' out a scheme of their own, to gratify their own lust of
' vengeance, to build up greatness for themselves, was

'rebellion against Him, and led to misery.' If we had courage to use this language,—that is to say, if we had courage to follow the letter of the Bible, and to believe that it was giving us a rule for our guidance as to the course of the world,—we should, it seems to me, face undoubted facts and series of facts with far more honesty and with far more hope. For consider what we have gained. We have not merely substituted one name for another. When we speak of GOD, we mean the Righteous Being, the defender of Right, the opposer of Wrong. We mean that there *is* such a Being. One, of whose nature Right is the ground; of whose acts Right is the end. We distinctly affirm that that which contradicts His being, that with which He is at war, is every form of oppression, injustice, falsehood; whatever has undermined human society and made the earth miserable and accursed. We affirm that all this came not from Him, but simply by abuse and perversion of that power with which He has entrusted His creatures; by the insurrection of beings whom He had endued with wills against His will. We affirm that He calls out men to be His agents and fellow-workers; to understand the purposes which He has at heart. We affirm that whensoever these instruments of His become self-seekers,—and aim at turning the commission which He has given them to their own personal ends—that moment they are punished upon the same principles as all other people, and with greater severity.

II. I have merely assumed hitherto that we are considering the condition of the old world. It may seem to you that many facts which meet us every day are of the same kind with those to which I have been alluding: but I do not urge that thought upon you at present. We are asked whether the Gospel has not introduced quite another view of human duties and of the divine character, from that which we find in the book of Deuteronomy; whether we can apply the maxims of that book without setting aside all that we have learnt from the Sermon on the Mount? Now we surely have not learnt *this* from the Sermon on the Mount, that there is *not* a Righteous Being, —One whose Will is to all good,—One to whom Injustice and Wrong are opposed. Our Lord did not open His lips to repeal that fundamental principle of the Old Dispensation. On the contrary, He came,—so His whole discourse, so all His parables and His acts intimate,—to show forth the Righteousness of God, to bring it out in its fullest and innermost meaning. Neither did He say that henceforth men were not to be the instruments in doing his work, in carrying out His purposes. On the contrary,—He said that they were to be like His Father in heaven; that they were to be as He was, and do as He did. Nor can we say that He proclaimed a doctrine which would less interfere with the local gods of the different people of the earth; on the contrary, He more distinctly announced a one Father of all the families of the earth who was claiming the homage of all. Supposing the Gospel to diffuse itself, it must be quite as assertive and intrusive as Judaism. Its very comprehensiveness involves it in a more direct and deadly hostility with all partial and divided objects of worship. The ends of the two dispensations then do not appear to be different any more than their principle. The difference must be sought for in the means by which the principle is manifested and the ends effected. Here we certainly encounter a very marked opposition; but I believe no contradiction. Hatred and love in all cases are opposites; but the hatred of evil is so far from being contrary to the love of good,—that one cannot exist without the other. They must have different ways of expressing themselves; one can never be merged in the other. Each must have its own province and work, or both will suffer and at last perish. Christ brings out the all-perfect, universal, absolute Love of God in His acts and His sufferings, His life and His death. So far as it can be proclaimed in words, He sends forth His disciples to proclaim it. He ordains sacraments which shall be witnesses that it is really gathered up in a Person, that it must be received from Him.

As this message or revelation concerns the exhibition of the Divine character in human images, those must be the best and most perfect instruments and messengers of it who exhibit this character in their own: loving their enemies; doing good to those who hate them; in all things building their lives upon sacrifice, not selfishness. But the evil fruits of selfishness must meet with their own appropriate recompense. The sword of justice, not words or acts of tenderness, must cut off these. He who being entrusted with it, fails to use it through any weakness or faintness of heart, yields to selfishness,—refuses to be God's minister, allows that which is hateful to God and destructive to his fellow-creatures, to live and multiply. He who is seized with a sudden fancy that he is to forgive enemies when he is called upon to punish wrong, will not forgive them when they injure him. The judge who is too tender-hearted to sign a warrant for the execution of a criminal, will very probably end by being the head of a committee of safety, and will defile the land with the blood of innocent men.

The Sermon on the Mount then is in peril from those who insist that it shall abrogate one tittle of the Law. But it may limit the functions of the Lawgiver, if it point to some more effectual method of accomplishing His purposes than any which he can use. He must always be interested in putting down idolatry, because it interferes with the invisible authority upon which Law stands; and because it is the fruitful source of crime. He is interested therefore in finding the most effectual means of extinguishing idolatry. Our Lord shows us that the punishment of the idolater is not now the best means. The proclamation of Him is a more perfect one. It was proved to be so. Idolatry was more directly assaulted in its high places, received more deadly wounds, in the three centuries during which the Gospel of the Son of God was opposed by all the swords of the Roman empire, and when it had no earthly sword of its own, than by all the battles of the Israelites. Henceforth, therefore, the magistrate may confine himself to the punishment of the unrighteous acts which idolatry produces. He may, just because he hates it as much as Joshua or David hated it, leave it in its own naked form to be encountered by a power which has been proved to be mightier than his own.

III. The distinctions which I have attempted to draw are not artificial; they belong to the nature of things, they are deep and radical. They must affect all the relations between the magistrate and the herald of the Gospel, between the Nation and the Church. We acknowledge generally that to punish wrong and to remove the causes which hinder the *well-doing* of a community, is the characteristic work of the one; that the diffusion of good principles, the advancement of the *well-being* of a community, should be the great aim of the other. But then these distinct tasks so often involve and cross each other, that men say they must at last be identified; they so continually interrupt each other and interfere with each other, that men cry they must be wholly separated. The process of identifying them takes place in two different methods. The civil power in a particular nation may look upon itself as divine, and therefore as bound to claim spiritual functions; the ecclesiastical power may claim to itself all civil functions. In other words, Christianity may be resolved into Judaism; the Church may be looked upon as only a part of the Nation. Or Judaism may be taken up into Christianity, the Church may affirm that it has no need of the Nation. The former system has had able advocates in all times, some very recent ones. The Scotch Covenant, afterwards our own Commowealth and Protectorate, were very vigorous attempts to realize it in practice. The whole history of Romanism is an illustration of the other. The study of both experiments throws great light upon the relation between the Old and New Testaments; but receives back a greater and more brilliant light from them. A very intense honest hatred of idolatry characterised those who dwelt exclusively upon God's covenant with the nation; a feeling of God's actual government, and of his righteous war with evil, gave a healthful strength and manliness to their minds. But the Gospel of His good-will to men was strangely narrowed by these bold wielders of the sword of the Lord and of Gideon. They could not look upon Christ's incarnation and death as actual witnesses of God's reconciliation with mankind. They could only look upon them as the deliverance of a few from that evil, which they came by degrees to regard as more essentially the ground of things than God Himself. When they did try to think of Him as the ground of all things, it was hardly possible for them not to consider Him the author of the curses, which the Old Testament represents as the consequence of departure from the state which He established. It was not possible to avoid the sinking of God's righteousness in His sovereignty, or to prevent His election of some from being regarded as implying a want of love, if not hatred, for the rest. Thus not Christianity only, but Judaism, was outraged by this Judaical Christianity. The fundamental principle of the Old Covenant, that the choice of one people was to be for the blessing of all,—its fundamental doctrine that the revelation of a God of righteousness is that blessing,—were put in peril by the good men who held this faith as a true and solid possession, were absolutely subverted in the minds of numbers to whom they bequeathed it.

The other experiment is, I believe, equally decisive. The Latin Church has valiantly and zealously asserted the Name into which we are baptized, as a ground of fellowship between all nations and kindreds. It has put forth the Incarnation and Sacrifice of Christ as declaring an actual union and reconciliation between heaven and earth, between God and man. It has declared the highest authority to be a spiritual authority. And, apparently in zeal to maintain these great principles, it has claimed a right to crush the individual nations; asserting one general language for devotion; affirming Christendom to have one place and one man for its centre. What has come of this? The hatred of idolatry has ceased. Every old form of sensual and divided worship has been adopted and naturalized by the Church; everything which the Jewish nation was to count accursed, it has blessed. And yet it *has* become local, partial, and narrow. The Universal Society, in order to put down the nations, became itself, not indeed in any high and noble sense a Nation, but, a petty principality; a court with all the worst, most corrupt, most selfish habits incident to a principality and a court. Instead of showing its superiority to the nations by dispensing with their swords in the propagation of its faith, it has craved for their aid, and this while its better men were proving continually how much more they could do by acts and words of love, and how ineffectual persecutions were. And when the nations have given it this help,—instead of going forth, like the Jews, to put down immoral superstitions which interfered with the confession of God's righteous and universal name, and corrupted the earth,—they have become the agents in establishing superstitions; therefore in fostering in the heart of nations the crimes which the righteous punishments of the civil legislator and judge must afterwards exterminate, if they can. Such have been the results of trying to sink the Church in the Nation or the Nation in the Church.

The cry for separating them which is so loud in our day, supports itself by two opposing arguments. One set of them proceed upon the notion that beliefs are involuntary, indifferent, belonging to a region with which the legislator has nothing to do. The other affirms that belief to be all-important, imperative, enjoined by divine authority; therefore it must be preserved from all interference with a power by its nature incompetent, yet, as experience shows, apt to be intrusive. I quite agree with those who take the first ground,—that belief in all its shapes and forms is a very subtle principle, which requires a kind of treatment entirely unlike that which legislators and magistrates can afford time or wisdom to bestow upon it; only I should say that it lies out of their reach not because it is *involuntary*, but because it is concerned with the innermost *will* of man; whereas their transactions must be chiefly with his outward acts. But if they fancy that these outward acts are not affected and determined by the processes which go on within, all experience belies and contradicts them; they must encounter the effects of belief, whatever it is, at every turn; they must acknowledge them as its effects, whether they like it or not. And therefore their notion that it is indifferent, becomes in practice a very poor and insincere pretence, which is dropped in a moment, when its results become palpably inconvenient; the doctrine, in fact, coming at last to this, that all beliefs may be tolerated while they are not beliefs; while they are negative, feeble, inoperative. The moment they come forth with any positive energy,—the legislator who adopts this theory is confounded, and finds that he must persecute in fact, though not in name.

Such inclinations and acts on his part seem to afford great justification for the eagerness of religious men to be exempt from all State cognizance, so far as their religion is concerned. But unless they are prepared to deny that a false religion does produce evil and corrupt moral effects, such effects as the makers and executors of laws must take cognizance of; unless they are prepared to affirm that their religion does not bear at all upon human life, or that it has a set of maxims altogether peculiar to itself, which are not meant for human beings as such; that is, unless they are ready to take up all the maxims which are most utterly disparaging to the Gospel, and which have in all times been checking its influence and perverting its nature, they cannot rationally maintain their theory of separation; least of all can they enforce it in practice.

These conclusions might be very distressing and unsatisfactory, if there were not evidence that while men have been trying to identify the Nation with the Church, or to sever them utterly, God has been using each for His purposes,—has been claiming each for a distinct part of His kingdom. However selfish the plans of kings may have been, they have been witnesses against the idolatry which priests have been promoting. He has made the assertion of royal supremacy a bulwark against a supremacy which was undermining His own. He has used nations, as of old, to punish and destroy others more corrupt than themselves,—though they might not feel that they were acting by His command, and might covet the silver and gold which He forbade the Jew to touch. He has infused into little insignificant communities an irresistible might, with which they have overthrown long-established tyrannies. He has taught our rulers, at various periods of our history, that it is our vocation to resist every power, papal, imperial, democratic, which strives to destroy the peculiarities of race, family, individual,—and to construct a society which shall be an artificial corporation, not a living body. At the same time He has raised up witnesses for the unity of His own nature, and of mankind, which He has formed in His image. Priests, in spite of their own sin and exclusiveness have kept alive a testimony in the world, that a Spirit has come down to establish a universal communion, with which the diversities of feeling, opinion, temperament, constitution, shall not interfere.

And now the time is come when we must either understand these purposes of God, and work together with them; or when that separation of Nation and Church, which decrees civil and ecclesiastical have been unable to effect,—shall be effected, as far as we are concerned, by the separation of all that is meant to be united and harmonious in our hearts. The notion has been working for a long time among us, that indifference is another name for charity; that zeal for Truth and the name of God is identical with exclusiveness and narrowness. If we yield to that notion, for us there will be no Nation, no Church; each will succeed in robbing us of the other. But if we have learnt to believe that the Spirit of love is a consuming fire which must destroy the idols and high places that we ourselves have set up, and then all those which are withdrawing men anywhere from the living and true God,— we shall find that the command to drive out the debased people of Canaan, is an utterance of the same gracious Will which bade the disciples go into all lands and preach the Gospel to every creature, baptizing them ' *in the Name of the Father, and of the Son, and of the Holy Ghost.*'

SERMON XV.

THE TEST OF PROPHECY AND MIRACLE.

(Lincoln's Inn, Sunday after Ascension Day, June 1, 1851.)

Lessons for the day, Deuteronomy xii. and xiii.

DEUTERONOMY XIII. 1—3.

If there arise among you a prophet, or a dreamer of dreams, and giveth thee a sign or a wonder, and the sign or the wonder come to pass, whereof he spake unto thee, saying, Let us go after other gods, which thou hast not known, and let us serve them; thou shalt not hearken unto the words of that prophet, or that dreamer of dreams: for the Lord your God proveth you, to know whether ye love the Lord your God with all your heart and with all your soul.

THE thought will certainly come to us when we hear these words; 'But is not this the test by which I have 'been taught to try the divine prophets? Has not the 'fulfilment of their predictions been the reason which has 'been given me for believing in their mission and autho-'rity, nay, for believing the Revelation of God in the 'Scripture altogether? If the test fails in any one case,— 'if I have the highest authority for thinking that it will 'fail,—if I am warned that the guesses of a lying and 'mischievous prophet may be successful, and that yet 'I shall be guilty of a sin if I pay heed to them, what 'is the worth of this evidence and of all the arguments 'that have been grounded upon it?' For many reasons it is exceedingly desirable, even necessary, that we should consider this question at the present time. Let us desire that we may look at it humbly and fearlessly, not shrinking from any acknowledgment of our own mistakes and insincerities, and sure that nothing is safe but Truth.

One objection to the language of the text, which would seem to many very formidable, will not, I trust, have much weight with you. 'Did not the whole commission and 'work of Moses, it might be asked, rest on signs and 'wonders? Did he not go into Pharaoh with power to 'turn a rod into a serpent and water into blood? And 'was not the faith which these signs awakened in his own 'power, the reason for obeying him and for letting the 'people go? Was it not by signs and wonders, in like 'manner, that he asserted this authority over the Israelites 'in the wilderness? To diminish the trust of the people 'in signs and wonders,—was it not to shake all their trust 'in himself, all their assurances that God was with him?'

The consideration we have bestowed upon the previous books of Moses, and upon this last, has, I trust, shown us clearly what the answer to these questions is. He *was* to exhibit signs and wonders before Pharaoh; but the signs and wonders were for the very purpose of breaking that trust in charms and portents and in the tricks of magicians, which had crushed in the tyrant's mind all trust in a living, righteous God. These acts proved that a God who cared for the outcast and slave, was King and Master of the Universe, that its powers were His powers ; that Pharaoh in doing homage to them was giving himself up to false gods. They were demonstrations of this fact to him and to mankind : but instead of its being affirmed that these powers exercised a salutary and gracious effect on the mind of Pharaoh, we are told expressly and repeatedly that they hardened him. The commission of Moses to Pharaoh then did not rest upon signs and wonders, or consist in them. It rested upon a revelation of the Righteous God to his own conscience; it consisted in a message from the Righteous God to the conscience of the Egyptian. The signs and wonders were most valuable accidents and accompaniments of the message. But they denoted a foregone conclusion. If they were regarded in any other light than as a declaration of an invisible King to men who were serving visible things, that they were His subjects, the purpose of the sign was not accomplished · its effects were evil, and not good.

The case was still stronger in respect to the Israelites. All the signs and wonders which Moses wrought in their eyes when they were murmuring against him in the wilderness, were signs that God Himself was in the midst of them; that He was caring for them, watching over them, supplying their daily wants. There is not one of the miracles which is not distinctly affirmed to have this object. We may say, if we please, Moses was permitted to break the ordinary laws of the universe that he might prove he had a special dignity and a right to be obeyed. He says no such thing. He says, 'You shall see by this 'and this act whether the Lord is among us or not, 'whether He is regularly and habitually our King, 'whether He is governing the daily, hourly events of our 'lives.' The miracles were assertions of a permanent order against the inclination of the Israelites, exhibited in all their doubts and complainings, to suppose that they were under a capricious ruler, under an irregular government; such as it was the curse of the people round about them to confess and believe in,—if I may apply such sacred words as 'confess' and 'believe' to a condition of mind which implied the absence of all confidence, a perpetual fluctuation and uncertainty.

These conclusions, which were involved in all the history of the earlier books, form the staple doctrines of the book of Deuteronomy. There they are drawn out with the greatest care; they are forced upon us again and again; all Moses' lessons from the past and concerning the future turn upon them. The meaning and use of the manna, as Moses expounds it in this book, is a key to all the other cases of divine interference, as we call it. They received it, he says, day by day, that '*they might learn that man does not live by bread alone, but by every word that proceedeth out of the mouth of God doth man live.*' The particular instance was the discovery and exemplification of a universal law. One mode of illustrating it had been appropriate to the wilderness, another would be appropriate to the promised land: the first was not a better, diviner state of things than the second ; it was inferior, transitional, always intended to issue in the blessing promised to their fathers; the blessing, not of being left to themselves, but of no longer doing that which was right in their own eyes; of being brought into a more fixed national order. But the words of Moses go further. The Israelite was not only instructed that *he* did not live by bread alone, but that *man* did not. The lesson of the manna was a lesson respecting the whole race which God had formed in His image. It was an assertion that *all* were under an invisible government, were sustained by an unseen hand; it was a witness against that dependence upon chance, or upon the spontaneous fruits of the earth, which made cultivation of the land,—the fulfilment of God's law and blessing,—impossible ; it was a solemn record that the Egyptian was not subject to one giver of corn, and the Assyrian, the Greek, to another ; but that there was one Lord over all ; first and chiefly the Lord of human beings, then the Lord of the earth and its productions.

Signs and wonders then,— either such as were shown before Pharaoh to tell him that he was not the King of kings, and could not rule subjects according to his pleasure, or such as told the Israelites that a deliverer and not an enemy was constantly governing them,—do not in the very least degree interfere with the principle laid down in the text. They established no obligation in a Jew or in any man to believe a prophet, or a dreamer of dreams, because he showed a wonder, and because the wonder came to pass. They supplied him with a law which, if he obeyed it, would be a protection against that danger; which would not allow him to wait for the results of a dream or a prophecy before he pronounced judgment upon it; which would make the question one of great indifference to him, whether the issue accorded with the guess or confuted it.

The prophet came to the faithful Israelite with a burden of the Lord. There would be a hurricane or an invasion, or great victories and prosperity. 'Well what then? In 'either case what is it you bid me do? Is it to trust in 'the Lord God of Israel, to make Him my dread and Him 'my confidence? Is it to repent that I have so often 'neglected the duty which lay before me, and chosen a 'bye-path of my own? Is it to determine in God's 'strength that I will be more simple and manful in my

'obedience henceforth? Then you are a prophet of the
'Lord; whatever happens I shall be right in giving ear to
'you. I am certain of your credentials. God has sent
'you to me; it is His voice which is speaking to me; I
'shall be rejecting Him, not you, if I do not heed it.'

'Or do you come to persuade me that I am *not* to trust
'God, *not* to act as if He had made a covenant with me?
'Do you wish to frighten me out of my confidence, to set
'me upon inventing new plans of my own, or adopting
'new plans of yours? Do you wish me to add some
'practices to my worship, which the law of my fathers has
'not prescribed, that I may recommend myself more to the
'divine favour, or avert the divine wrath? Do you wish
'to make me feverish, restless, discontented, by your
'announcements of evil to come, or easy and satisfied
'with the condition of myself and of my land by your
'announcements of good to come? Do you want to make
'me tremble as the trees tremble in the wind, or would
'you make me think that all is peace and security? You
'are no prophet of the Lord; you would turn me away
'from following Him; you would have me bow down to
'false gods, gods who can be bribed to give me help or
'success, or to let me go on in my bad courses. I do not
'care the least whether the event corresponds to your
'words or not. There may be a famine, there may be
'plenty of corn or wine, there may be a defeat, there may
'be a triumph,—anyhow *you* are a deceiver; you would
'lead me into wrong or falsehood, if you have ever so
'much knowledge of what is going to take place in the
'world. Begone with your dreams and prophecies, your
'signs and wonders; I am not afraid of them, but I am
'afraid of you and of myself, because you are come

'speaking out of that which is evil in you to that which
'is evil in me. I know what it is in my heart which
'answers to *your* language. It is that which does *not*
'answer to God's language, it is that which makes me
'unwilling and unable to hear that and obey it.'

So a man or woman of Israel, whose heart was sound in God's covenant, would have spoken. It did not require any skill in sifting evidence, any capacity for reasoning about the inspiration of the prophet, any power of weighing likelihoods as to the accomplishment or non-accomplishment of his predictions. The wayfarer who was a fool in all trials of this kind, but was striving to be true and to do the work he had to do, would have laid bare the pretensions of a lying prophet, and confessed a real one. Those who would not have done either,—those upon whom each mere trickster could always calculate as a sure prey,—were the sons and daughters of Sion who led wanton and luxurious lives, who fancied they were wittier and wiser than their neighbours; who knew by heart all the criteria by which the divine seer could be ascertained. The diseased, morbid consciences of such Israelites, their self-conceit, and their desire of being different from the vulgar, their love of novelty, their belief in tests which are infallible on paper— most fallible when brought to bear in the actual business of life,—tempted and rewarded every man who sought to establish a dominion over them himself, and to make them traffic with the gods of the people round about. From these came the worshippers of Baal and Ashtaroth ; these offered their children to Moloch; these burned incense to the Queen of Heaven. All moral abominations followed from their religious practices; all political ruin, all direct outrages upon law. It was not, therefore, a hard saying,—

however it may sound so,—that the Israelite was to have no pity upon them who seduced him into such courses; that he was to consider the idolatrous son or wife an enemy; that he was to go forth to destroy any city among the tribes in which idolatry had established itself. I explained, the last time I addressed you, why we are not bound by these precedents, why it would be a sin in us to act upon these commands; not because the evil is less now than it was then, or that it affects nations and undermines law and morality less, but that a greater and more effectual remedy has been discovered to us for it; that the Gospel of the Son of God has more power to destroy false worship than the sword of the civil ruler; that when he tries to do it, he finds that he can strike off branches which soon grow again, but cannot reach the root. The wisdom of experience forces him to abstain, because it shows him that he is weak. The wisdom of God, the Supreme Reason, commands him to abstain, because it shows him what is strong. So far, thanks be to God, the precepts of this book have been set aside by the revelation of the principles upon which they are grounded. But be it never forgotten, that though Christians have no right or authority to engage in a religious war, even for the putting down of any false system; though, even in countries which we possess, the civil magistrate must only in outrageous cases, where crime is the direct and palpable result of a religion, as in the burning of Hindoo widows, interfere with the free exercise of it; yet that God did call forth the Mahometan armies in the 7th century, to do a work by vulgar arms, which the Christian Church was not accomplishing by its mightier weapons, because the hand which wielded them was palsied through contact with the accursed thing. The Eternal

Righteousness will assert itself in one way or another,—with us or without us,—by a full declaration of the Truth and Law which draws all that is partial into itself, or by a visible proclamation of its own eternal hostility to the material religions which divide human beings, and make them crawl upon earth instead of rising to heaven. But if subject to this observation—I have joyfully confessed that a portion of the lesson we have read this afternoon has lost its application to us, I cannot make that admission with reference to my text and the doctrine which we have seen to be contained in it. I think it does bear very directly upon our thoughts and conduct, and that in several ways.

I. If the text teaches us how the true Jewish prophet would speak to his people, and in what spirit they were to hear him, it teaches us who read him, how we are to receive his words. That events have answered to particular predictions which we find in the Bible, may increase our interest in studying it and may strengthen our faith. But there is a deeper instruction to be gained from the prophecies than the observation of these coincidences can impart. The real significance of these is felt when they are viewed in connexion with the course of the divine government. The search for them alone, is a mere exercise of dexterity,—of a dexterity which is found deceitful and dangerous in its application to the affairs of the world,—which is useless, fallacious, and most irreverent, when it is resorted to for the interpretation of Scripture. The facts of our Lord's life do indeed beautifully fulfil, as the Evangelists bid us observe, the intimations and indications of the prophets, but that is because the Word who was speaking by and in the Prophets, whose character and office they were permitted in glimpses to behold, was fully manifested when the Virgin bare a Son, and His name was called JESUS. Such fulfilments we might trace with ever fresh delight in His acts and words, though the writers on the evidences of prophecy should have mistaken its application in a hundred cases or in every case. If any new historical information were to disprove all that has been advanced by these writers, the truth of Christianity and of Prophecy would not be affected in even the slightest degree. We should only be thrown back from Bible commentators upon the Bible itself, and there we should find treasures for which we have, as yet, only begun to dig; yet which are not far from any of us, and may reward the search of the ordinary reader, and of the practical statesman, quite as much as that of the scholar. A man who has learnt from the Prophet to acknowledge a guide of his spirit,—who rebukes his errors, calls forth his faith, turns all events into discipline,—does not want proofs of that prophet's veracity. A student of the causes of a nation's well-being and of the steps which lead to its ruin, is much more impressed by a few such passages as those which record the early visions of Isaiah respecting the state of Jerusalem, — its luxuries, its bribes, its idols, the faithless race of priests, the extortions of the rich, the eagerness of proprietors to lay house to house and field to field, the feebleness, at last the confessed, feebleness of rulers, their eagerness for power passing into a cowardly dread of it, lest the ruin should be under their hand— than by all the arguments drawn from events which are supposed exactly to have carried out the denunciations against Egypt, or Tyre, or Babylon. That these denunciations were carried out and will be carried out against every country and city in the state to which the inspired man refers, all history will teach us, whether we can point to the special incidents which proved their truthfulness or not. And such lessons must surely be more solemn and profitable to ourselves and ultimately more convincing to gainsayers, than those upon which a certain class of modern divines seem inclined to dwell so earnestly and exclusively.

There is another class which cares little for these arguments from the past. 'Let us ask the prophets,' they say, ' what they have to tell us of the time *to come.*' Much assuredly: yet the interpreter is not to be heard if he does not speak to us first of a Present God, of one who is in covenant with us as He was with our fathers, who is calling on us every hour to turn from our idols to Him. If this is not the substance of his teaching; if all his predictions do not flow out of it; if he begins with arguing about events that are to be, and about the when and the where and the how; he is not speaking in the spirit of Scripture: though he may quote it ever so profusely we may be sure he does not understand it. To us, at all events, he is speaking falsely. He is leading us away from our actual Judge and Lord; he is making the conceits of our intellects or our imaginations the objects of our fear and our hope. We must not wait for the year or day which he has fixed for the occurrence of some portentous judgment or great blessing, to determine whether we will give heed to him or not. If he would make one action or thought or belief of ours depend upon a contingency; if he would make our faith in God and in the certain fulfilment of every word that he has spoken, vary with the changes in his conclusions and calculations; the principle of the text applies to him. The Lord our God is using *this* prophet, this dreamer of dreams, to see whether we love Him and can trust in Him; or whether we trust in events and circumstances and our own theories.

II. What I have said of Prophecy applies also to Miracles. The text does not separate them, nor can we. We turn to the signs and wonders in the New Testament as in the Old, to prove that God was speaking them. Do we not rather need the assurance that God is speaking to explain the signs and wonders? The leper who heard Christ speaking with authority on the Mount, said as he came down, ' *Lord, if thou wilt thou canst make me clean.*' He confessed the voice of the Deliverer and the King. He came to Him trusting that He would exercise the power, which belonged to Him in both characters, on his behalf. How simple does the record of every sign of our Lord seem, when it is looked at as the expression at once of His love and His might, of His divine sympathy with suffering, and His divine will to restore health! If we try to ascend from the sign to Him, do we really ever find Him? Do we discover His close relation to ourselves? Do we recognise Him indeed as the brightness of the Father's glory? The Gospel of the Son of God to men, that He came to make them children of his Father in heaven, would be imperfect if the Lord had not asserted his claim to be ruler of winds and waves, of the souls and bodies of his creatures. How meanly do we think of it, when we suppose that it cannot be presented at once to the hearts and consciences of miserable and sinful men, but must be ushered in with a long array of proofs, which the great majority of people, in our day at least, find it much harder to receive than that which is proved, nay, which I suspect they never do receive till they have first embraced that.

III. And lastly, this consideration becomes very important, when not only we ourselves, but the poor people of our land, are continually assailed with arguments intended to show, that the signs and wonders recorded in recent ecclesiastical history are not different in kind from those which are spoken of in Scripture. We ought not to dream that rules, however valuable in themselves, for testing the evidence of a miracle, will be of the slightest avail in removing impressions of this kind from the minds of honest and humble people, who have only a slender knowledge of facts, and have never been trained to any habits of judicial investigation. Is it fair, is it right, to demand of them a culture which we know that they cannot possess? And suppose they did, are we sufficiently sure of our historical inferences, to insist that a course of practical conduct shall be made dependent upon them? We may see good reasons to think that devout men have overlooked intermediate agencies in their zeal to refer all events to God, and that indevout men have played with the weakness of their fellow-men for the sake of drawing reverence to themselves. But there may still remain many stories for which we cannot account, and a multitude more which we cannot require other people to account for in our way. We want some safer and more comprehensive rule than we can arrive at by any such methods. The text offers one. A person who takes it for his guide may make answer to his tempter, 'I shall not debate with you 'about the reality of this or that sign or wonder. Let 'it have all the worth or credit you can give it. But 'for what end do you bring it before me? What am 'I to do, because the eyes of this statue are seen to 'wink; or the blood of that saint, under the pressure of 'priestly prayers and popular curses, undergoes liquefac-'tion? You say, if it be so I must abandon the ground 'I have held up to this hour. What ground? My 'belief that God has made a covenant with our fathers 'and us, my assurance that God has reconciled Himself 'to us in His Son, and that in that Son we may draw 'nigh to Him with clear consciences? Yes! that is 'what you mean, in whatever words you may disguise 'your meaning. Here then is my reply. Your advocates 'say that a habit of faith is better than a habit of 'unbelief; on that plea they call upon us to believe 'these miracles. On that plea I repudiate your exhorta-'tions. I believe in God the Father who has exalted 'His Son with great triumph to His kingdom in heaven. 'I will not risk that faith by declaring that I cannot live 'without a visible father on earth. I believe in the Son 'who has ascended on high that He may fill all things, 'and present His perfect Sacrifice before Him who has 'accepted it for me and all mankind. I will not ex-'change that faith for the acknowledgment of an 'incomplete sacrifice and local intercessors, who can 'awaken no reverence and fill no hollow in my heart. 'I believe in God the Holy Ghost, the Comforter, who is 'able to exalt us to the place whither our Lord is gone before 'us. I will not give up that faith for faith in prophets 'and dreamers, in workers of signs and wonders, who

'would bring down Christ again from above. I believe
'in the Father, the Son, and the Holy Ghost, the one
'God into whose name I am baptized, in whom I am
'united to the whole Church on this side of death and the
'other. I fear for myself and for my age lest you
'should take this faith from us, leaving us a phantom
'Church instead of a real one, a dead system for a Living
'God.'

SERMON XVI.

PENTECOST.

(Lincoln's Inn, Whit Sunday, June 8, 1851.)

Lessons for the day Deut. xvi. 1—18, and Isaiah xi.

DEUT. xxx. 19, 20.

I call heaven and earth to record this day against you, that I have set before you life and death, blessing and cursing: therefore choose life, that both thou and thy seed may live: that thou mayest love the Lord thy God, and that thou mayest obey his voice, and that thou mayest cleave unto him: for he is thy life, and the length of thy days: that thou mayest dwell in the land which the Lord sware unto thy fathers, to Abraham, to Isaac, and to Jacob, to give them.

You will have felt I think by this time, how well the book of Deuteronomy answers to its name. It is most strictly a *Law* book. It sets forth the Law under which the Israelites were living, and which they could not violate without losing their life as a nation. But it is not a book of *Statutes*. It does not contain a set of decrees which the chosen race were to observe, like those which are found in the latter part of Exodus. It rather explains the very meaning and principle of their social existence. It is what we might call in modern language, a constitutional treatise; an exhibition of the grounds upon which their polity rested. This is the *second* Law, or that which was implied in the terms and denunciations of the first.

In a former Sermon I noticed a very memorable difference between the form of the Fourth Commandment, as it is delivered in the twentieth chapter of Exodus, and as it is repeated here. I consider that difference to be significant of the object which the later record keeps steadily in view. The Sabbath was to be kept, not merely because God rested on the seventh day, but because the Israelites had been bondsmen in the land of Egypt. It commemorated a *Redemption.* That fact of a redemption lay, I said, beneath all the institutions which the chosen people were enjoined to preserve. Apart from the faith and acknowledgment of it, their institutions, —one and all,—became unreal, unintelligible. They could not observe them, if they did not receive them as witnesses that they had been delivered from a tyrant and taken under God's immediate government. That truth was the foundation of their society. It would hold together so long as that truth was remembered. It would perish when that truth was lost. The book of Deuteronomy is nothing but a continuous assertion and illustration of this maxim; an application of it to the condition of the nation in all periods.

The lesson we read this morning supplies us with a memorable instance. It has been chosen to-day because it records the appointment of the Pentecost, or Feast of Weeks. Let me repeat to you the words in which that appointment is set forth: '*Seven weeks shalt thou number unto thee. Begin to number the seven weeks from such time as thou beginnest to put the sickle to the corn. And thou shalt keep the feast of weeks unto the Lord thy God, with a tribute of a freewill offering of thine hand, which thou shalt give unto the Lord thy God, according as the Lord thy God hath blessed thee. And thou shalt rejoice before the Lord thy God, thou, and thy son, and thy daughter, and thy manservant, and thy maidservant, and the Levite that is within thy gates, and the stranger, and the fatherless, and the widow, that are among you, in the place which the Lord thy God hath chosen to place His Name there. And thou shalt remember that thou wast a bondman in Egypt, and thou shalt observe and do these statutes.'*

The last words, ' *You were bondmen in the land of Egypt*,' we should have supposed must be meant for the Passover, since that was instituted on the night of their liberation, and was to be a perpetual celebration of it. But no! *This* feast, which was to begin when the sickle was put into the corn, this feast which was a thanksgiving for what we call the blessings of nature, was, just as much as the other, a feast of Redemption. They could not keep it, except they had been made free; they could only keep it with any gladness, when they received it as a token and pledge of their freedom. The poor idolater would seize the fruits of the earth, would feel that they had in some way dropped upon him; that if he did not perform certain services, they might another year refuse to come to him. The blessing of the Israelite was that he could understand all the regular and mysterious processes in the ground and in the mind of the husbandmen, to be appointed by his invisible Lord and Friend. He could wait in faith their coming at the season which the gracious Ruler had fixed; could hail them when they appeared as blessings the more new and marvellous for their orderly recurrence; could look upon interruptions, failures and disappointments as warnings to remind him of God or of his own neglects and transgressions. That was the spirit of one recollecting that he had been a bondman in the land of Egypt; that he had been under the rod of a tyrant who might decree one thing to-day and another to-morrow, who cared only for obtaining results, and nothing for the human creatures who were to produce them; that he had lived among men and had shared their ignominious delusion, who fancied that all their wealth came from the river or its inundations, or from some animal powers, and that these must be flattered or appeased; that he had looked upon the earth as a hard and partial mother, pouring her dainties into the lap of some of her children, refusing a bare subsistence to the great multitude of them. And now it was his privilege to feel and know that he was not at the mercy of the earth or of a man, that He who had brought him out of slavery was the life-giver, the giver of strength and wisdom to man; then the giver of the fruits which rewarded the use of his powers. He was to regard the earth and those fruits as blessings to the manservant and the maidservant, to the widow and the fatherless. They were to take part in the great festival; for they were sharers in the meaning of it, in the good-will of Him who was praised in it.

I have not chosen this passage for my text to-day, but one from a chapter which the Church reads on Whit Tuesday, because I think it embodies the spirit of the whole book, and throws great light upon the Jewish and Christian Pentecost. It is a recapitulation of principles which I have dwelt upon already; but one clause of it brings out a topic most needful for the illustration of the Pentateuch, upon which I have not yet found opportunity to speak. I do not dread the charge of repetition, and I should consider the omission of that subject a very culpable one.

When I say that the book of Deuteronomy is a book of laws and maxims, I am using language which, though true, is not satisfactory. Do not let such phrases cause you to forget that a living man is speaking in it. We do not miss merely what some would call the dramatic interest of it,—we miss its inmost sense and intention,—if we lose sight of the old man standing before a mixed multitude of people, whose fathers he saw carrying burdens in Egypt, and whom he had been leading for forty years towards a land which he was not to enter. Not a single precept is, in the proper sense of the word, intelligible, if you consider it as a precept, without remembering that it came out of the mind and heart of the Teacher, and was charged with all his experience, his sympathy, his sorrow, and his hope.

If any one should say, 'But these are divine words; 'why need we think of the mere human agent who was 'appointed to deliver them?'—I answer him, You will never know what divine words mean, if you strive to separate what God has joined together. They will become mere letters to you, which you may worship as you may worship a stock or a stone, but they will not be God's words to that generation or any other. If you would think of Him as a Person, if you would believe that He can and does speak to men, then let Him explain to you the nature and method of His own speech. Look at the sympathy and the love and the sorrow, as well as at the hope and foresight of the prophet, as expressing to you, feebly but most really, the mind of Him whose servant he was, whom he was representing whenever he truly fulfilled his office as a guide and lawgiver of the people. I do not say that we may not derive very great blessings from a book though we overlook the accidents and circumstances of it, or only hear some of its sentences apart from their context. '*The wind bloweth where it listeth; you cannot tell whence it cometh, or whither it goeth.*' God's voice may speak to a man's heart through any phrase or symbol. But if we profess to study a book, we must follow the course it points out, not take one of our own. And the loss is very great, if through dread of being too human in our thoughts and feelings, we learn to think that all human thoughts and feelings have not their original in God.

I. '*I call heaven and earth to record against you,*' says Moses. This was no idle rhetorical formula. The open sky was over his head, the same sky which was over Abraham when he left his father's house not knowing whither he went; the same to which he looked up that he might know by the multitude of the stars what his seed should be; the same under which Jacob had slept when he saw the ladder; the same which had been over his descendants when they were making the bricks in the land of bondage; the same which had looked down upon them in the hot day, in the clear night, all the time they had been journeying through the desert; the same which their children's children would behold in the land of promise. It was the witness and pledge of permanence, the sign that in the midst of perpetual change there is that which abides.

And the earth was at their feet; the earth which received its heat, light, quickening power, from that heaven; the earth which might be a garden such as Egypt was, or a wilderness such as they were passing through; the earth which might be changed from the one to the other; the earth which needed something else than sun or shower, which asked for some hand to put the seeds within it, and for some hand to destroy the thorns and thistles that grew upon it; the earth which was given to man that he might dress it and keep it, and bring food for his race out of it. Moses then could call heaven and earth equally to testify to his words. The one said to man, ' Thou art meant to ' look above thyself. Only in doing so canst thou find ' endurance, illumination, life.' The other said, 'Thou art ' meant to work here. Thou must put forth an energy ' which is not in me, or I shall not yield thee my fruits.' The one said, ' The sun, moon, stars, are shining upon ' thee; but if thou askest sympathy from them thou wilt ' not find it; if thou askest power from them thou wilt ' learn that what thou receivest from them is not what ' thou needest; it is not akin to thy own. To find help ' from them thou must suppose each of them to be ruled ' by some Person. And that is a pledge and proof that ' there is a Person ruling over them who is claiming thy ' obedience, who is desiring that thou shouldest know Him.' The earth said to him, ' If thou wouldest govern me and ' subdue me, work with Him who is governing thee and ' seeking to subdue thee ; for my Creator is thy Lord and ' King. He who understands all my secrets, and can ' make thee understand them, is the same who knows the ' secrets of thy spirit, and would make thee know them.'

II. But he says, '*I have set before thee life and death, blessing and cursing.*' You have heard how he had done this. There is not one exhortation in this book, as I said before, which would lead an Israelite to think that he was to aim at obtaining a life which had not been freely given him, or to avoid a curse from which he had not been already delivered. He is warned in the most fearful language of *forgetting* the things which his eyes had seen, of not believing that the Lord God had really taken His fathers and him, his brethren and his children, to be a people of inheritance to Himself; he is told what misery will come upon him if he goes after the gods of the nations, or makes them for himself out of the things above or beneath. There is no hint given him upon which he can build a dream of security; the past is invoked to remind him of his temptation to faithlessness and murmuring; he is not encouraged to expect that any circumstances will diminish that temptation,—that it will assail him less in the promised land than in the wilderness. But all the terrible warnings and prophecies of what he and his descendants may do hereafter imply that he *is* in a blessed condition and that they *will* be; the condition of men whom God has claimed to be His servants and to know Him, the condition of men who may trust Him to the very utmost to uphold them, bless them, protect them against their enemies.

III. And therefore he goes on : ' *Choose life*,' ' Say
' distinctly, deliberately to thyself, I do not mean to give
' up the ground on which I am standing. I do not believe
' that there is any power in earth or hell which can
' compel me to give it up. God has placed me on it; all
' which is contrary to God may say it is not mine; but all
' that is contrary to God will not prevail against God, and
' therefore need not prevail against me.' This stedfast resolution each Israelite would find it needful to make, and having made it, continually to repeat. For death would come in the form of life, the curse would put on all the attractions of a blessing. Earth would fill her lap with pleasures to draw away her master from his dominion, and

make him lose himself in her embraces. He would be tempted to become a slave by the hope of independence; and when once he had tasted the cup and been transformed, not only those who had presented it, but those who should raise him, would conspire to tell him that his rights as a man were gone; that he was no longer in any relation to God; that he must thenceforth count himself one of the creatures into the likeness of which he was reduced. This 30th chapter of Deuteronomy is especially an answer to that lie. It presumes the Israelite to have fallen; to have incurred the deepest curse which this book pronounces. And still it addresses him as a child of the covenant; still it bids him act on the assurance that God has not forgotten it, and is at hand to lift him out of the abyss of unbelief and falsehood into which he has sunk. ' *Choose life,*' is still the command at all times; is still a command which at all times could be obeyed; because it is not in the power of man to convert his own falsehood into a truth, or to convert God's truth into a falsehood.

IV. I urged, in a former sermon, that the blessings of the Jewish covenant were first of all inward and spiritual blessings, though all outward good things flowed from these. The words before us abundantly confirm that assertion. The great reward of choosing life is, '*that thou mayest love the Lord thy God, and that thou mayest obey His voice, and that thou mayest cleave unto Him.*' The recompense for not distrusting and suspecting a friend, for assuming that he means you well even when you cannot understand him, even when his acts would bear a hard construction, is, that you come to be acquainted with him, to enter into his character, to discover all the deep hidden sympathies of it. ' You must 'love him,' says the poet, 'ere to you he will seem worthy 'of your love.' It is a paradox in human friendship, and yet every one may have proved it for himself. We might hesitate to apply the paradox to our relations with God, because they are grounded upon the principle, 'not that we 'loved Him, but that He loved us.' And yet it *is* applicable there also. For He himself awakens in His creature a blind trust, a faith of expectancy, grounded upon the acknowledgment that He is that which by degrees He will show Himself to be. And therefore the growth of love and knowledge, and the power of cleaving more strongly because the attraction is stronger, are always proclaimed in Scripture as the rewards and prizes of a man who walks in the way in which God has set him to walk, who chooses life and not death.

V. '*For*,' says Moses, '*He is thy life and the length of thy days.*' 'From Him comes the power which enables thee 'to trust Him and cleave to Him. In Him who is the 'unchangeable and immortal One thou wilt find thy own 'immortality. The land of thy fathers, of Abraham, and 'Isaac, and Jacob, will be the perpetual symbol and 'witness to thee that He continues the same from gene-'ration to generation, that He is present with the whole 'race of which thou art a member. Dwelling in that 'land, and remembering that it is His, you will learn 'what it is to have Him for your everlasting dwelling-'place and home.'

VI. And here comes in another strong moral compulsion to this course, '*that it may be well with thee, and with thy* SEED *after thee.*' In the fourth chapter of this book, the precept to teach the things which their eyes had seen to their sons and their sons' sons, is repeated with great emphasis and solemnity again and again. When they are told that it shall go well with them if they shall keep God's covenant, it is added in the same chapter, '*and with thy children after thee.*' Though I have not yet spoken expressly upon these words, you will have seen, I hope, how the sense of them has been coming out through all the lessons we have been considering. The five books of Moses are emphatically the history of a family. I have tried to show you that they are the history of an education. We have seen that God is Himself set forth as the teacher of the family from generation to generation; as the teacher of each new member of it,—by means of the circumstances in which he is placed, with a view to the work which he is appointed to fulfil. What I wish you specially to observe here is, how inseparably the divine and the human education are blended. The fathers are to teach their children that which God has done for them, that which he will be doing for those who come after them. The great lesson of all which they have to impart is,—that He will be the present and living guide of each succeeding race as much as He had been of Abraham, Isaac, and Jacob. They were not to indoctrinate their children with a great many notions about a distant Being dwelling in some far-off, unknown region; they were to tell them that the Lord was their God, that He was dwelling in the midst of them, that they were the children of His covenant. Nowhere is this lesson conveyed more strikingly and beautifully than in the chapter from which my text is taken: '*For this commandment which I command thee this day, it is not hidden from thee, neither is it far off. It is not in heaven, that thou shouldest say, Who shall go up for us to heaven, and bring it unto us, that we may hear it, and do it? Neither is it beyond the sea, that thou shouldest say, Who shall go over the sea for us, and bring it unto us, that we may hear it and do it? But the word is very nigh unto thee, in thy mouth, and in thy heart, that thou mayest do it.'*

This doctrine of a God nigh to them, a God of the heart and reins, an ever-living teacher, was the soul of Jewish education, as it was the soul of Jewish history In the second commandment, the Jew was told what would be the consequence if that education was forgotten. God, it is said, is a jealous God, visiting the iniquities of the fathers upon the children unto the third and fourth generations of them that hated Him. The words are startling and terrible. We shrink from them with a kind of horror. But these are the facts of history. The Jews did forget the unseen and righteous God; they did forget that He had made a covenant with them and with their children. And the children did become more corrupt than the fathers, more superstitious, idolatrous, divided, slavish. The curse must be a real one. The commandment which affirms it carries its own witness. And it also carries within it, the comfort that is needful to sustain us under the oppression which the mere fact nakedly contemplated must cause us. There is a jealous God, jealous over his creatures because He loves them,—who is watching over them when they are wandering furthest from Him, when they are most forgetting and distrusting Him. He has not caused or decreed their superstitions, their divisions, their slavery. All have come from their not choosing the state which He intended for them; from their going out of the good way, from their liking death better than life. Hence came the primary curse, hence the entail of curses, each more terrible and degrading than the last. How such an entail should ever be cut off, how men can ever be preserved from sinking deeper and deeper into the abyss which they make for themselves, this is the information which we ask from ordinary history, and ask in vain; this is precisely the information which the Scriptures are written to give us; that ordinary history may become to us not a dark, but an illuminated, scroll.

VII. I said that these words of the text interpret what has preceded them in the books of Moses; and the more we meditate upon them, the more we shall get that help from them. But I said also that they belonged to the Whitsuntide festival. We have not far to seek for the connexion. We hear the words '*choose life.*' They sound promising, cheering words. We persuade ourselves that they are not only reasonable, but that they tell us where the power is which can enable us to obey them. But in the sore conflict with actual temptations that confidence disappears. It seems as if after all we were under a law of death, as if we had little to do but to cry, 'Who shall deliver us from it?' In the midst of that strife, some of the words which we have read in this chapter open a prospect of relief. But it is lost in the tumult of our thoughts. It seems as if we *must* be climbing to heaven, and crossing the sea, and going down to hell. There is a haste and fever in us, which will not let us be still to hear the Divine Word, though it be ever so near us. Then comes that other speech from the lips of One who knew what was in man, '*I will send you another Comforter, even the Spirit of Truth, who shall abide with you for ever. For He dwelleth with you, and shall be in you.*' If we hold that that promise has been fulfilled,—that the Comforter has actually been manifested as the guide, inspirer, sanctifier of human hearts, the author of sevenfold gifts, the light and fire of love,—then God is indeed calling Heaven and earth to record against us this day, that nothing can be done for His vineyard which He has not done for it; that He has brought us within a circle of blessings, that He has made us partakers of a Divine Life, that He has given us the power of choosing that life; that we are resisting the Holy Ghost if we do not cleave to Him and love Him, and claim the blessings of His new and perfect covenant.

We have need to remember that this gift appertains to the most inward and radical part of our being. It is not a gift which is dependent on feelings and tempers of our mind; but is to be the source of those feelings and tempers. The Holy Spirit is an indwelling Person, not a vague and transitory influence. We have need to remember this, because the fight which we have to fight is a harder one than that of men in the old time. Evil came before them more in its outward and gross forms. To us it presents itself in its inward power and essence. The words, ' *We wrestle not with flesh and blood, but with principalities and powers, with spiritual wickedness in high places*,' were spoken not by a lawgiver, but by an Apostle; not to a camp of Israelites, but to a baptized Church. He felt the full power of his own words. It may be, brethren, that we are to feel the power of them more than our fathers did. It may be that we shall have to understand, in this latter age of the world, that there is indeed a battle going on between evil and good in their most naked and absolute natures. It may be impossible for us to shrink from the confession, if we attempt it ever so, that a Spirit of evil is claiming us for his subjects, is demanding our undivided worship. The words, '*I have set before you life and death, blessing and cursing,*' may come for us to mean, ' You must either secretly and ' openly confess the Father of our Lord Jesus Christ to ' be God, or you must in your inward hearts and in all ' your outward acts confess the devil to be God.' And if so, what need is there that we should fall back upon the fact and the mystery of this day, that we should say boldly, ' Christ our Lord has proved that the Spirit of ' good is mightier than the Spirit of evil; that the one can ' and shall cast out the other.'

And oh! brethren, let us not forget that it is a blessing for us and for our seed after us. This is the meaning of all our festivals; this is, above all, the meaning of our Whitsuntide festival. I hail it as a testimony that not God's outward gifts only,—the blessings of spring-time and harvest,—but the treasure of His own Spirit, is for the manservant and the maidservant, for the widow and the fatherless, for the stranger that is within our gates. I hail it as breaking down the barriers which our selfishness as members of a nation has drawn between different classes, between those who are breathing the same air, speaking the same language, governed by the same laws; which our proud religious selfishness has drawn between those who are heirs of the same covenant. But I hail it still more as a proof that that covenant is the same from age to age, as a witness against our neglect in handing down to those who shall come after us the torch which our fathers handed to us. We have not dared to tell the children of this land that they are redeemed by Christ's blood and endued with God's Spirit. That sin is visited upon us, and may be visited upon our children. Many of *us* are seeking,—*they* may seek,—help in superstitions and idolatry, because we have not held fast the belief that the living and true God is in the midst of us. Whitsuntide proclaims that truth in spite of us. The loving and jealous God is still saying to us, 'The promise is for you and for your 'children, and for multitudes from the east and from the 'west, from the north and from the south, whom I shall 'hereafter call.'

SERMON XVII.

JOSHUA AND ST. JOHN.

(Lincoln's Inn, First Sunday after Trinity, June 22. 1851.)

Lessons for the day, Joshua x. and xxiii

JOSHUA XXIII. 1, 2, 3.

And it came to pass a long time after that the Lord had given rest unto Israel from all their enemies round about, that Joshua waxed old and stricken in age. And Joshua called for all Israel, and for their elders, and for their heads, and for their judges, and for their officers, and said unto them, I am old and stricken in age: and ye have seen all that the Lord your God hath done unto all these nations because of you: for the Lord your God is he that hath fought for you.

THE command which Moses gave the Israelites to go and smite the Canaanites with the edge of the sword, was touched upon when I was considering the book of Deuteronomy. I do not wish to repeat what I said at that time. But the lesson we read this morning brings the subject before us again under a different aspect. If we have been ever so much convinced that a war is justifiable, the details of actual battles,—especially when they are given so broadly, with so little attempt to gloss over the most frightful circumstances of them, as in the book of Joshua,—may well cause us some perplexity. And the compilers of our services seem as if they had been anxious to increase rather than allay it. They have not only chosen as a specimen of the book the chapter which contains most records of conquest and slaughter, but they have brought this chapter side by side with an Epistle of which the burden is, '*God is love; he that loveth not knoweth not God.*' Can anything be more startling than the contrast of these two documents? Nothing, certainly; that I conceive is the reason for placing them both before us at the same time. The Church knew, that the readers of the Old and New Testament must be struck with the opposition. She wished her ministers not to shrink from a fair and manful examination into its nature and cause.

Perhaps the course which has been taken for presenting the difficulty to us, may suggest the right method of considering it. Joshua and St. John stand out, as if in direct hostility to each other. We know that the book of Joshua must have been read by the Apostle in his childhood, his manhood, his old age. Let us inquire, how at different times of his life he must have regarded it.

I. We find him first a mere Galilæan fisherman. We may take it for granted that he heard the Scriptures read in the synagogue, that many thoughts and impressions about them came to him as he worked by day or by night upon the lake. At that time,—before he had listened to any diviner voice, when his best outward teaching must have been that of the scribes,—it may be supposed that this book of the wars of the Lord will have had some attractions for him. No doubts respecting the spirit of it will have been suggested to him by others, or probably will have occurred to himself. But it is a very rash conclusion that the absence of doubts involves the presence of interest. Though we cannot of course tell, in any instance, what personal and special influences may lead any particular child or man to pore over one book rather than another, all general reasons would lead us to think that at this period the history of his country must have been nearly lost upon him. He will have received it as coming from divine authority, but there will have been nothing which bound it to his actual human sympathies. What was there in what he saw and heard, that could make any Jew feel he belonged to a chosen, vigorous, triumphant people? How much less could a Galilæan dream that *he* had any share in the glories of a land from which he seemed cut off by his dialect and by the contempt of all whom he encountered? The dead words may indeed have kindled into life in some minds. The present may have seemed to explain the past. Some Judas or Theudas appearing to call upon the peasants of the land not to pay tribute, but to assert their rights as the old people of God, might give those who followed him a momentary delight in the story of Joshua's victories over the sons of Anak. Without this, no comments of doctors will certainly have made the story an intelligible or practical one to them.

II. It is a common notion, suggested by his own words, that the Apostle was a hearer and disciple of John the Baptist. That would be a new and most memorable æra in his personal life. It must have been the commencement of a change in all his feelings respecting the country to which he belonged. The words, '*The Kingdom of Heaven is at hand*,' believed with however much of strange wonder and questioning, will have broken down the barrier between the ages gone by and his own, and have given him an assured hope that the God of Abraham was with him and his brethren. Still more thoroughly will the teaching which was to exalt the valleys, and level the hills, have destroyed the separation of places, dialects, and castes. In Jordan was a common flood for the dwellers in the capital, for Galilæans and Idumæans. The fisherman had the privilege of repenting; the Scribes and Pharisees were told that they needed repentance equally, though they were less likely to seek for it. The hearts of the children were turned to their fathers;· all the records of God's dealings with them will have acquired a freshness and significance. But though this must have been ultimately the effect of John's preaching upon all who faithfully listened to it, its immediate appeal was undoubtedly to the individual conscience. Each man was awakened to a sense of his own evil; he felt that he could not have contracted it from without if there had not been a root of it within; the axe must be laid to that; he wished, first of all, a baptism for the remission of sins. Such a thought absorbs, for a while, a man's being; the disciples of John will not in general have found leisure to think of the book of Joshua.

III. Another period came. Jesus saw James the son of Zebedee and John his brother in a ship with Zebedee their father mending their nets, and He called them. They were with Him when He opened His lips and said, '*Blessed are the poor in spirit;*' '*Love your enemies;*' they were with Him when He was healing the sick; they were with Him on the Mount of Transfiguration; they were with Him in the garden of Gethsemane. You would conclude, probably, that while John felt the immediate presence and power of His Master, he must have turned away with involuntary, if not confessed, displeasure from such passages in the Hebrews' books as we have been hearing to-day. I believe it was just then, that he began to feel any hearty sympathy with them. The impression which was left upon the disciples and upon the multitude by the Sermon on the Mount, is fully expressed in the words with which St. Matthew finishes his report of it: '*He spake as one having authority.*' There might be exquisite gentleness and benignity in the language of the speaker, in His countenance and His manner. No doubt the people felt that there was. But what they felt chiefly and most distinctly was, 'He is a king, He can command 'us. He is not spelling out the letters of the law, He is 'announcing it as one from whom it has proceeded, who 'knows what it is.' If you read the Gospels, you will see that it was this impression of authority, of kingship, which the disciples received from all the acts and words of their Master. He said that He was come to establish a kingdom, and they were sure that He did not deceive them. They might be slow to discover the conditions and principles of it; about the reality of it they could have no doubt. They were sure also that they were to be ministers in this kingdom, that the fisherman would not have less to do with it than the ruler of the synagogue, that it was meant for poor men. And now all that they had heard in the old Scriptures of a kingdom which was to put down the tyrants and giants of the earth, came to life in their mind. It was no longer the story of an unknown region; it was to be fulfilled in their own. They walked with Christ through the very towns and villages which Joshua had portioned out to the tribes of Israel. Every step of the ground which they trod bore witness of some triumph of weakness over strength, of the feeble and degraded over the mighty

And He who led them was surely asserting and proving that this kind of power was His, that He could and would exert it. The carpenter's Son could bid the winds and waves be still, could break the fetters of ancient disease, could set men loose from the dominion of evil spirits. Why when possessing such powers, He did not at once shatter in pieces the power of centurions and Roman governors, and make Judæa or Galilee the seat of a glorious empire, was, of course, a marvel to them; as so much of His conduct and His language was. But because they could not penetrate this mystery, they were not to doubt, they could not doubt, that His purpose was the same as that of all leaders, lawgivers, kings, who had preceded Him, or that He was come to do what they had left undone. And while that faith continued, it was absolutely impossible for them not to dwell upon all the battles of Joshua and of David, with an earnest delight, with a confidence that they were battles fought on their behalf,—in the like of which they might one day be permitted to engage, with a prospect of a more complete and permanent victory.

If you say, that nevertheless they must have shrunk from the thought of the bloodshed and destruction that accompanied these battles,—for what could they see in their Master but grace and goodness to all manner of people?— I answer, I do not know anything about their feelings except what I can gather from direct statements in the evangelical narratives, or through legitimate inferences from those narratives. And here it happens, that both are directly at variance with this conclusion, plausible as it looks. There are comparatively few statements respecting St. John in the Gospels; but every one which we have, shows that meekness and tenderness were *not* the qualities which he first learnt to appreciate in his Lord, and that he was not hindered by any sense of these from desiring to renew the severities of the older time. He would have called down fire upon the village of the Samaritans, as Elias did. *So* he would assert Christ's right to govern and to be obeyed. He forbade a man who was casting out devils in Christ's name, because he followed not with them. *So* he thought he was maintaining the distinctness of the calling of the disciples, as Jews were taught that it behoved them to maintain their privilege as a covenant people. He wished that he and his brother might sit one on the right hand, and the other on the left, in their Master's kingdom. He was sure that they were able to drink of the cup which their Master drank of, and to be baptized with the baptism which He was baptized with. *So* he showed that he looked upon their Master's throne as no imaginary or metaphorical one, but as one which was to be established like that of David, through struggle and conflict and garments dyed with blood. Now I am not denying that there was much of ignorance, and confusion, and selfish feeling, mixed with all these thoughts and apprehensions. What I say is (and those who take the opposite view to mine, if I understand them, say the same) that it must have been a mighty step in the education of these Galilæan fishermen, to be taken under the direct guidance of Christ. His discipline may have brought their errors and follies to light, as all true discipline does: but it must have brought them into a much higher position than that in which they were previously. It would be a monstrous outrage upon our reason and conscience to say, that they were not raised infinitely above the state in which they were when they were mending their father's nets, or even when they listened to the Baptist preaching in the desert. And yet the effect of this greater elevation of character, the effect of their intercourse with the Son of Man, was to make the history, which we regard as so sanguinary, look far more real and divine in their eyes than it had ever done before.

IV. But there came a fourth stage in St. John's life. He had leant upon his Lord's breast at the last Supper, he had stood beside the cross, he had borne witness to the blood and water which flowed from His side, he had heard the words, '*Woman, behold thy Son,*' '*Son, behold thy mother;*' he had gone to the sepulchre, he had looked in and seen the linen clothes lying, he had heard the words spoken to him with the other disciples, '*Peace be unto you. As the Father hath sent me, so send I you.*' He had heard the words spoken of himself, '*If I will that he tarry till I come, what is that to thee?*' He had stood on the mountain of Galilee where they worshipped, but some doubted; he had seen his Lord ascend on high; he had waited at Jerusalem with the other Apostles for the promise of the Father; he had been one of those on whom the cloven tongues of fire had sat; he had been one of those who spoke with other tongues as the Spirit gave them utterance; he had seen the 3,000 baptized, and had become one of the pillars of that church in Jerusalem, the members of which counted nothing they had as their own. Will he not now have regarded those qualities of his Master, which he was scarcely able to discern before, as the most characteristic of His Person and office? Will not his dreams of an actual sovereign have been dispersed? Will he not have found himself separated by a whole heaven from Joshua and the warriors of the old dispensation? 1 will reply to each of these questions separately.

I cannot doubt that when St. John was endued with that Spirit which dwelt perfectly in his Master, he felt and understood as it was impossible for him to do till then, the force of the words, '*Come unto Me, all ye that labour and are heavy laden. Take my yoke upon you, and learn of Me; for I am meek and lowly of heart, and you shall find rest to your souls.*' The Spirit no doubt convinced him of his own want of meekness, of his uncharitableness, of his exclusiveness, showed him how different the mind of which such qualities form a part is from the mind of Christ; what need there is of hard conflict with ourselves, that the one may take the place of the other,—that the true Lord of our spirits may ascend His throne and cast out the evil power which has usurped it. Yes, brethren, unless the Scripture deceives us altogether, St. John had need of hard inward struggles, to become a gentle, gracious, loving man. That soft feminine countenance,—unmarked by a single furrow,—which painters have chosen to ascribe to him, can never have been his actually, is not his ideally. The man who would have called fire from heaven upon the Samaritans, the man who was sure he could endure Christ's baptism of fire, had no soft features, no sentimental expression. If he was the apostle of love, it was love in a different sense from this. '*Blessed is he that overcometh,*' are the words which rang again and again in his ears, when he saw the vision of his glorified Master. He had been taught, through the bitterest inward strife, what such words meant. And therefore, though he delighted to dwell upon the graciousness and gentleness of his Master, he did not forget that He made him a scourge of small cords, and drove them that sold and them that bought out of the Temple, or that he told the proud religious men of Jerusalem that they were claiming the devil for their father, and doing the deeds of their father. Such stern sentences did not seem to him inconsistent with the divinest grace and mercy. He could not conceive of a grace and mercy which tolerated evil, which did not seek for the extirpation of it.

And this being the case, brethren, I must utterly deny that St. John looked upon Jesus less as an actual King when He had ascended on high that He might fill all things,—than when He was sitting on the lake of Gennesareth, or walking in the streets of Jerusalem. This was to him the sign and pledge that His Kingdom was an actual one; the descent of the Spirit was the sign that He was actually setting it up on earth, as He had promised He would. No doubt the kingdom which was thus beginning was very different in most respects from that which he had anticipated. The paradox which had seemed so incomprehensible when it was first uttered, that in this kingdom the chief of all should be servant of all, now interpreted itself by his own experience, and by all the discords and contentions which arose from the neglect of it. He learnt from his Master's sufferings, he was learning gradually from his own, that the garments dyed in blood were the garments of the Conqueror Himself; that endurance and death are the greatest and divinest manifestations of the power of good,—the mightiest instruments in casting out evil. He found that that which provokes the bitterest opposition and raises against itself all the restless factions in the heart of man and in human society, is not a law but a gospel; not the proclamation of punishment, but the proclamation of forgiveness; not the assertion of God's pity for a few, but of His love for all. But that discovery only made him more certain that,—before God establishes His righteous and loving kingdom upon earth, and brings human wills into captivity to it,—there must be a mighty resistance; such a one as would justify the seeming contradiction, that the Prince of Peace came not to bring peace upon earth, but a sword.

To the third question then,—how far St. John at this stage of his life can have entered into the history of the wars of Joshua,—I answer, It is quite possible that his strong belief in Christ as a conqueror through suffering,— and of this being the highest method of conquest,—may for a time have made him unable to understand the triumph with which the old Israelite leader records the discomfiture and extinction of the Canaanitish hosts. I do not know whether this was the case or not. I can quite conceive that it was. But then I think this feeling would have been accompanied by two others. First, with a very distinct acknowledgment that Joshua's battles were tending to the establishment of a righteous kingdom upon earth,—steps, though perhaps almost incomprehensible steps, to that victory of the weak over the strong which the Gospel and the Church, by other instruments, and with greater success, were achieving. The second feeling is, that the Christian man is in as literal a sense a warrior as the Jew ever was; that spiritual wars are not fantastic wars, but rather contain the concentrated essence of that struggle and effort which we see outwardly exhibited in the battles of individual heroes or of disciplined armies; and therefore that the language which describes such battles is one which the churchman is obliged, even in spite of himself, to adopt as the only exact and satisfactory one, for describing the work in which he is or ought to be engaged, both when he is alone, and when he is in the midst of his fellows.

V. But the words which I have quoted already, '*If I will that he tarry till I come,*' remind us that there was still another stage in the history of St. John. He was not merely to take part, as the other Apostles did, in the establishment of the universal kingdom upon earth, but he was to see the kingdom which had preceded it pass away. Before he died, that city which he had been wont to call the holy city, the city of peace, was to become the most unholy and turbulent of all cities. The doom of that city which his Master had announced, was to be fulfilled in his day; to him was vouchsafed the vision of another Jerusalem descending from God out of heaven. Thus it was not possible for St. John, if he desired it ever so, merely to contemplate a society that brought members into itself by an inward attraction, that fought only with spiritual weapons. He was forced to think of armies compassing the homes of his fathers, and the Temple in which God had been worshipped. He was forced to see not Palestine only, but the whole Roman empire, given up to revolution and anarchy. There was the horrible spectacle of the generals of legions contending without a principle, which should have the right to torment the world; there was the still more horrible spectacle of religious sects persecuting and supplanting each other in the name of the God who had called them out to testify of Him as the Lord that executeth righteousness and judgment in the earth. Was a Christian man to be

indifferent to such sights as these? Was he to say, ' All
' this has nothing to do with me. These are the strifes of
' the *World*. I belong to the *Church*; I have secured my
' salvation. What signifies it to me if these unbelieving
' heathens or Jews tear each other in pieces?' Yes,
brethren, a Christian in our day may use this horrible
and blasphemous language, and may compliment himself
upon the high spiritual state of mind which it indicates.
St. John could not, for he believed that '*God so loved the*
WORLD *as to give His only-begotten Son for it*.' He believed
that that Son of God had actually taken the nature of
these unbelieving heathens and Jews. And therefore how
utterly appalling these facts of the world's history must
have been to him, if he had had no help to the solution of
them! It could not have been enough for him to know
that there is something *besides* wars and sieges, the overthrow of kingdoms, distress of nations, with perplexity.
He must know that there is a meaning in *these* very things,
that *they* do not go on without God, that the devil has not
his own way with respect to *them*. Will he not then have
turned with another kind of interest than he ever felt
before, to the records of his country's history, to that very
one which we have been reading this afternoon?

Joshua said to the elders and officers and people of
Israel, ' I am old and stricken in age. You have seen
' what the Lord God hath done for you. He hath driven
' out these nations before you. He Himself hath fought
' for you.' Will not the Apostle, old and stricken in age, as
he sat alone in the island to which he was banished for the
Name of Jesus Christ, and for the Word of His testimony,
and meditated on all the sorrows and confusions of the
earth upon which he was dwelling, have found in the old

leader of his country's hosts, a teacher, and a friend? He could learn from him that there is a divine and gracious purpose in that which looks saddest and darkest; he was told that nations are not swept out of the earth for nothing; he could read in the destruction of them the assurance that no long possession can confer a right upon those who do wrong; that the earth is God's, and that He will reclaim it from those who lay it waste and make it a den of robbers. This is comfort which no lapse of ages could weaken, which no change of circumstances or sins of men could take away. For thus he knew why Jerusalem was doomed to fall, though God's temple was in it, though One greater than the temple had hallowed it, and walked in it, and wept over it. Thus he knew why the great city which had trampled down Jerusalem and was the appointed instrument of her punishment, would herself perish in the greatness of her pride and her luxury; and why every form of godless power which might establish itself there or elsewhere,—whatever names it should assume, whatever disguises it should wear,—would fall in due time by God's sentence, because it measured its power against His; because it crushed the earth which He had redeemed, and raised an idol of falsehood to mock His truth. Thus he knew assuredly that whatever Dagon, or Moloch, or Mammon, should be set up in any land or in any time for men to worship,—and should command them to receive its mark and its image and the number of its name,—would be thrown down. His nation had existed to testify of that truth by its words and its arms. The Church which was unfolding itself out of his nation would exist to testify of it more completely. For it had been revealed to him that the foundations of the universe stood upon Love; that God is Love, and that whosoever dwelt in Love, dwelt in God. Therefore all which was contrary to Love was a lie, and would perish utterly and for ever.

Thus, I think, will St. John have been instructed that the new commandment,—which is true in Christ and true in us, which He has fulfilled and which we may fulfil,—is the same old commandment which was heard from the beginning. The old commandment and the new are both for us. To our elders and judges and officers God is saying, 'I have fought for you and your nation. Therefore only 'it has prospered. See that you do not set up strange gods 'in place of me. Be strong and very courageous to fulfil 'even my sternest precepts, to put down the wrong and to 'maintain the right.' To us,—our Bishops, our Presbyters, our Deacons, our people,—He is speaking as He spoke by the mouth of the old apostle the last time that he was borne into the church at Ephesus, '*My children, love one another.*'

SERMON XVIII.

THE BOOK OF JUDGES.

{Lincoln's Inn, Second Sunday after Trinity, June 29, St. Peter's Day, 1851 }

Lessons for the day, Judges IV. and V.

JUDGES v. 1, 2.

Then sang Deborah and Barak the son of Abinoam on that day, saying, Praise ye the Lord for the avenging of Israel.

A PERSON who thinks that a divine Lesson-book should present to us exclusively or chiefly high maxims of morality, or perfect models of character and behaviour, finds the book of Judges a great stumbling-block. He would rather pass it over; he would wish it were found in some other place, not as a part of Scripture; he feels that only extracts carefully selected from it can be safely set before a Christian congregation. For the tribes of Israel are exhibited not as specimens of excellence, proofs of the blessed results of the divine government which had been established among them, but disorganized and barbarous; in strife with each other, the victims and slaves of the nations round about. In their extreme need, we hear of champions rising up in their defence. The historian seems to wish that we should sympathise with them; to a certain extent we are obliged to do so. But are we not often ashamed of our sympathy, and afraid to indulge it? Are not these champions prone to ordinary vices? do they not sometimes seem as if they indulged them in a more gigantic way than their fellow-men?

If there is one of the judges for whom we are inclined to feel a more than common interest and reverence, it is Gideon. The different scenes of his life form as clear pictures, as the eye or imagination can desire. You see him threshing wheat to hide it from the Midianites; trembling lest he should die because he has seen an angel of the Lord; rising up by night to throw down the altar of Baal; watching his fleece to know whether the dew will rest upon it while the ground is dry; gathering thousands about him and sending away all but the three hundred who lapped the water with their mouths; going out to see the hosts of the Midianites, the Amalekites, and the children of the East, as they lay along the valley asleep like grasshoppers for multitudes; listening to the dream of the soldier which cheers him for the work of the morrow; arousing his company with their trumpets, their lamps, and their pitchers; leading them forth with the shout, '*The sword of the Lord, and of Gideon;*' putting the hosts of the Midianites to flight; coming over Jordan with his little band faint but pursuing; taking vengeance on the men of Succoth and Penuel, slaying with his own hand Zebah and Zalmunna whom his sons dared not look upon;—all these visions rise brightly before the minds of children, and sometimes return to grown men as if they had once been parts of themselves. But after all it may be asked, 'Does 'the child accurately distinguish between the impressions 'which are made upon it by these sacred histories and those 'which it receives from classical or middle-age tales? Is

'Gideon essentially a different man from Diomed? Are his
'acts more strictly conformable to an ordinary ethical,—not
'to speak of a Christian,—standard? If Gideon's prowess
'is referred to an invisible power, so is that of the Greek.
'Why should one be invested with a halo of sanctity, and
'the other be called profane? Why are we encouraged to
'study the one for examples, and told that the other is a
'legend of paganism?' These questions present themselves
to the man as he reflects on the lore of his infancy. They
give rise to a vast amount of perplexity and scepticism.

One common way of solving these difficulties is to say,
'We have been mistaken in supposing that the Bible is a
'divine history at all. It is an ordinary human history.
'There are continual references in it, no doubt, to super-
'natural beings; so there are, and must be, in every human
'history, because men in all times and places have believed
'in such beings. The Hebrew belief was, no doubt,
'different from the Greek belief, as that was from the
'Egyptian. Hence a difference in the accidents of the
'story. In kind they are the same.'

Another course which commends itself to persons who
are not willing to take this extreme one, is to say, 'There
'are divine elements in the book assuredly; doctrines which
'must have come from God, illustrations of those doctrines
'in the lives of holy men. But along with this there is
'a common, earthly history, which must be treated like
'every other.'

In these lectures I have not, as you know, used either of
these methods, of explaining the Scripture-books, and of
removing the difficulties which occur to the student of
them. I have adopted in its fullest sense the ordinary
belief of our country, that we are dealing with a divine

history; that the Bible is the record of God's revelations of Himself; that each distinct part of it has a worth of its own; that these portions together constitute a real, not an imaginary, whole. Our mistakes originate, I have tried to show you, not in the rigidness with which we have adhered to this belief, but in our careless deviations from it. Sometimes we confound a revelation of God with a revelation of certain notions and opinions about God. Sometimes we think that a history of God's revelations means a history of certain exceptional heroes. Either of these suppositions is in direct contradiction with the express language, with the inmost spirit, of the Bible. God promises to declare Himself to us that we may believe in Him, trust Him, love Him,—not that we may hold a certain theory concerning Him. God tells us that He has made Man in His own image; not a few particular men who are different from their kind, but the kind itself. And he assuredly who is the most perfect specimen of it, in whom the divine image is fully manifested, will be he who is most entirely at one with the whole race,—who the least separates himself even from the most miserable and degraded portions of it. The characteristic of all the books which we have yet examined, has been this; each man who is brought before us, instead of being a picked man, different in his natural qualities and tendencies from his fellows, raised above them by some accidental advantage, is precisely like all others,—his infirmities those which belong to men generally, those which belong to his own class specially. Such infirmities, instead of being hidden, are carefully noted; more pains are taken to exhibit them in those who are the founders of the nation than in others. Jacob is set forth in disadvantageous contrast with Esau; the first presumption of Moses, his subsequent unwillingness to obey God's commands, the unbelief which excluded him from the promised land, are all industriously brought out before us. If we choose to say that these Scripture saints are great by reason of some inherent greatness of theirs, that is our fault. The Bible has laboured to deliver us from an opinion, so very mischievous to ourselves, so destructive of the truth which it wishes us to receive. It has tried to convince us, that it is making us acquainted with men of the same nature with ourselves,—not exempt from our temptations, but sharing in them, frequently yielding to them. And what then are these men good for? Why does it concern us to hear of them? They are good for precisely this. God calls them out that they may act as His servants, as deliverers of their country, as benefactors to mankind. So far as they yield themselves to that calling, so far as they give themselves up to do the work which they are called to do, He speaks in them, He shines through them; men see His image, and are raised by it to know what they are meant to be. So soon as ever these men begin to act and speak for themselves,—to use the strength or the wisdom which God has given them on their own behalf, to set themselves up as heroes or tyrants separate from their brethren, the moment they yield to the attractions of the earth beneath them, to the impulses of their lower nature,—that moment they become witnesses for God by their rebellion, as they had been by their obedience; making evident the truth of their assertion, that He governs the world, since if these His servants governed it without Him, they would soon make a desert of it.

Suppose this principle should not forsake us at the end of the book of Joshua, but should be carried on into the book of Judges, what would follow? Would it be a very puzzling fact that Gideon, and Jephtha, and Samson, should not be more free from the passions and temptations incident to human beings, incident to men of their tribe and race,—of the peculiar age into which they were born,—incident to special gifts and a special position, than all those whom we have heard of before? The conscience of mankind has answered this question. It has said very decidedly, 'This 'would not have been a true book, and therefore certainly 'not a divine book, if it had been otherwise. Above all, 'it would not have been a book for men. We should have 'had no sympathy with it; it would have given us no warnings. It might have been useful for the people of 'another planet; it would have proved itself not to be 'intended for ours.' 'Oh!' but then it is asked, 'are not 'these *inspired* men? And are not *inspired* men to be 'different from other men?' Alas, that we should cut ourselves off from God's great mercy to His creatures for the sake of an epithet. Alas! that when He raises up men to teach us what He is and what we are, we should turn round upon Him and say, 'Thou oughtest to have so 'constituted these men that they should not have been our 'teachers, that they should have had no relations with us; 'otherwise Thou dost not satisfy our notion of what an 'inspired man should be.' Brethren, it does not signify one jot, whether God satisfies our notion of what an inspired man ought to be. It does not signify one jot whether we have a notion upon that subject or not, further than this, that if it interferes with our learning what is good for us to learn,—and recognising truth where we meet

with it, and being true ourselves,—the sooner we part with
it the better. Depend upon it, the inspiration of these
men was not something which was imparted to them that
they might not do us good, that they might be more
separate from us. It was given to them to bind them more
closely to those among whom they dwelt, to make them feel
for them and act for them, because God was feeling for
them and acting for them. It was given to them, that they
might be helpers to all men in all times to come, who must
be taught of God, yes, and be inspired by God, if they are
to do any true act, or utter any true word. It was given
them, that they might teach men in all ages to come, not to
think themselves safe because they have a calling from God
and gifts from God, but to understand and believe that the
greatest perils attach themselves to that honour; that they
are only safe in holding it when they refer it all to God,
and use it wholly for their brethren, believing that there is
not one, the very lowest of those brethren, who is more
likely to fall than they are, who has not as great capacities
for the highest knowledge as they have.

But I wish to consider the question I proposed just
now, more directly. If this is so, where lies the difference
between these and the Pagan heroes? If you mean to
ask, 'Since the Scripture refers *all* powers whatsoever to
' God, how are we to prove that the powers which Pagan
' heroes or those who recorded the exploits of those heroes
' possessed, and which they said proceeded from some god,
' did *not* in fact proceed from Him?' I frankly own, I
cannot answer you. With the Scripture in my hands,
telling me in every page that I must attribute every good
gift to the Source of Good, I will not and dare not argue
for any exception. I have said very often that I look

upon the Scripture as a law-book, a book which tells us the principle on which the whole world is governed. I do not think that I should prove my reverence for it, and my sense of the difference between it and Pagan records, if I said that they established a case of deviation from those laws. If again you mean to ask whether the portraits of heroes in Pagan stories resemble those which the Bible brings before us? I answer, Just so far as they are faithful descriptions of human beings, and of the good and evil which is in them, just so far they do resemble the characters which the Scripture presents to us; because those are the faithful and veritable characters of men. But I find this especial difference between the Pagan and the Scripture stories. The former, as we all confess, are pictures of *heroes*, of men apparently exalted above humanity, while they offer no standard by which we can measure what humanity is, or *what* is above it. Where all begins from the one eternal God, all is tending to bring forth the one Man in whom all men may feel and realize their own glory. Where all begins from man, and only works up towards God, that which is general and common necessarily becomes associated with the mean, that which is separate and rare with the celestial. This is the inverted order of Paganism, this is the secret of that self-exaltation which mingles with and defiles the patriotism and self-sacrifice which God has taught men in every land to exhibit, and which He has never suffered to become extinct amidst all the contradictory and destructive elements that have been working beside them.

I do not think, brethren, that it is necessary to teach our children that they should try the acts which they read of in different books by different standards. I think that if we do this, we shall very grievously confuse their minds, and utterly destroy their belief in the Bible, which, if it has any effect upon us at all, must lead us to feel that there is the same right and wrong in all cases whatsoever. You are not bound to check a child's sympathy or your own with a story in any Pagan book, because you wish it to reverence, or because you yourself reverence, the sacred books. If that reverence is real and not affected, it will extend your sympathy in all directions, it will attach your sympathy to whatever is good and real, sever it from whatever is artificial and dishonest. Our forefathers were not so wrong as we sometimes fancy, in bringing Pagan associations, and even Pagan divinities, into fellowship with Hebrew and Christian truths. So devout a poet as Edmund Spenser, so stern a hater of idolatry as John Milton, would surely not have sanctioned that practice, if they had not felt that the Scriptures throw light upon all the surrounding world, that they claim all things for God, and redeem all the subordinate agencies in the creation which men have set up against Him, for His service. On no other principle, is it possible to reconcile the classical studies in our public schools with their evidently Christian foundation and object. On the other hand, this principle fully recognised and carried out, would, I believe, do more than anything else to harmonise the different parts of our education, and to show that it is intended to call forth the powers, the conscience, the reason of human beings made in the image of God,—not to fit them to be rivals of each other in the miserable service of Mammon. But if we set that object before us, we must labour above all things that we may not use the Bible itself, to destroy the object for which it was written, abstracting out of it a capricious instead of an immutable morality.

The lessons we have read this morning and afternoon have been turned to this most dangerous use. I cannot sufficiently admire the wisdom and courage of the Church, in choosing them to illustrate the character and spirit of the book of Judges. No passages of it could have served the purpose nearly so well. All the characteristics of this part of the history are to be found in them. The Israelites do evil in the sight of the Lord; the Deliverer and his covenant are forgotten; they give themselves up to the worship of visible things. The consequences which Moses had so solemnly predicted, follow. They are sold into the hands of Jabin king of Canaan. For twenty years Sisera the captain of his hosts, who has nine hundred chariots of iron, mightily oppresses them. This is the principle which proves itself in so many different cases. Faith and freedom are pronounced and found to be inseparable. Idolatry is the necessary forerunner of slavery. Then comes an inspiration,—in the strictest, simplest sense of the word. A woman feels that God has called her to speak words of hope, reproof, encouragement to the people. She stirs up Barak to help her; one tribe after another gathers about them; the man will go against the enemy if the prophetess will go with him, else he will not go. The inspiration has been communicated to the people; they know that God is in the midst of them; they put Sisera to flight; he escapes on foot. Jael the wife of Heber the Kenite tempts him into her tent, promising him safety. While he sleeps she takes a nail and drives it into his temples. She shows him dead to Barak and Deborah. They sing a song of triumph to the Lord for the discomfiture of their enemies. Deborah not only exults in the fall of Sisera, but pronounces Jael 'blessed among women,' for the deed which she has done.

Here we have the very puzzle to which I have been alluding, brought before us in another form. Deborah is an inspired woman; you cannot read the story of her acts without feeling that she is. You cannot read her song without recognising in it the tone and power of a prophetess. And Deborah, thus speaking, praises a woman for persuading a man at peace with her father and the Kenites to take refuge with her, that she may privately and deliberately murder him. This is the case, and the question therefore arises in a number of hearts, Are we bound to commend Jael's act because Deborah commends it? Should we not call it an act of very detestable treachery if we read of it elsewhere? Are we to give it a different name, because we meet with it here? I say at once and without hesitation, It is at the peril of our consciences if we do this. We cannot venture upon such trifling with eternal laws which God hath established, and not man. The moral law recognised in an Arab tent condemns an act of this kind; if we in any wise sanction it, we are saying, not that we possess a written law, but that we have the privilege of casting aside one which, as St. Paul expressly declares, *is the work of God written in men's hearts.* Think how terrible this result is; how fatal to all reverence for Scripture, and for the righteousness which it reveals! I have heard indeed of one desperate method of cutting the knot to which some divines have resorted in despair of untying it. They have said that Jael meant to be faithful to Sisera when she beckoned him into her house, but that she received a sudden intimation from heaven of her duty to commit the murder, and committed it accordingly. I only mention this horrible solution of the riddle as an instance of the strange frauds we may practise upon ourselves. We desire to justify God's ways; that we may do so we cast the whole blame of human evil upon Him! We cannot feel comfortable while we believe that the thought of an act which we feel to be treacherous arose in the mind of the wife of Heber the Kenite; we are quite happy if we can believe that it arose in the Divine Mind! I know that when the interpretation presents itself in this form it will make us all shudder. I desire that it should. A number of such blasphemous notions dwell within us in a confused twilight. They must be brought into the clear open day that we may see what they are. Else they will work in some an utter unbelief in all moral distinctions, an unbelief which must terminate in Atheism; they will tempt others, who receive the Bible as the guide of their judgments and their lives, to think that Ravaillac was, after all, the worthiest champion of Christendom. Brethren, whether we see our way on this subject or not, let us solemnly resolve that we will not abandon the least particle of what we feel and know to be true, for the sake of getting satisfaction upon it. If you trust God, you can wait, you must wait, for light about a thousand perplexing passages in His providence. If you think that the Scriptures record His word you can wait till He makes you understand it. You will then have often to be thankful for perplexities, as the physical student has in his department, which destroy crude theories and bring you into a more quiet and humble investigation of facts. But if you begin with undermining the divine character, for the sake of explaining more easily and rapidly events which you see or read of, you have purchased a temporary,—very temporary,—repose to your intellect by the sacrifice of the principles upon which your existence as a moral and spiritual creature rests.

'But then the BIBLE applauds the act of Jael.' No! not the Bible. The Bible tells me frankly that Deborah the prophetess applauded it, and I am sure that it tells me the truth. I am sure that a woman inspired with an intense sense of her country's miseries and wrongs, burning with a desire for the destruction of the oppressor, certain that when he fell he would fall by God's righteous judgments, and not by any achievement of hers or Barak's, struck with the retribution which had overtaken one who had trampled upon other men's rights, and practised base frauds, as all tyrants do when open violence fails,—I am sure that such a woman could not appreciate the merit or demerit of the instrument who had wrought deliverance for Israel; that in her thanksgiving to God she would mingle gratitude to Jael, without the least pausing to consider whether she had been prompted by the same inspiration which led *her* forth to hazard her life for God's people, or by a very different and diabolical one. That at such a moment, any person,—a woman especially,—should lose all other feelings in one indiscriminate emotion of rapture,—should treat all persons who had helped to produce it as worthy of admiration and benediction,—we should all think exceedingly natural. And I ask you whether the habit of mind which leads you not to expect that which is simple and natural in the Bible, is not a very false and dangerous one? Should we not suspect ourselves when we find we are indulging it? I should think this a very genuine description of strength and weakness if I had read it elsewhere,—but in the book of God,— that is quite different! What! because you think it is God's book you look for something unreal! You are startled and scandalised because you meet with that which is thoroughly in accordance with facts and experience! You will have to be shocked and scandalised by such discoveries, the further you read in it. You must go elsewhere if you want to see human beings dressed out for show and effect; here you will see them as they are, in all the greatness which they derive from a high calling and purpose, in all the littleness which belongs to them as mere creatures of flesh and blood. And this, this is the witness that you are studying the work of a Divine Artist; this is the proof that the Bible is not a collection of fragments, but that it has a living unity. We in our wisdom desire a picture in which there shall be no perspective; where each person shall stand out as full and large and prominent as every other; where light and shadow and proportion shall be wholly wanting. You cannot be satisfied that Deborah should be a brave, noble woman, that she should go forth in the name of the Lord of hosts, that she should trample down strength, should praise the Lord for the avenging of Israel. You must instal her as a teacher of ethics, though she makes no pretensions to the character, though the Bible nowhere claims it for her. I do not ask Deborah to explain how an act which I recognise as the judgment of a righteous God upon an evil man should be effected by the deed of a person more evil than himself. I doubt not that when she was judging Israel under the palm-tree, she would have been led,—by her reverence for the law of God and by His teaching,—to inflict the most summary and decisive judgments upon such acts as she then commended. At that instant, all other thoughts were absorbed in joy for the rescue which she ascribed to its true source.

I think God, and not man, is the author of the Bible; I believe that He is teaching me through Deborah much that I have need to learn. I gladly receive the lessons which He imparts through her. But I shall not allow my reverence for her to interfere with my reverence for God. I shall not insist that she must be right, when she contradicts lawgivers, prophets, apostles, the Son of God. I shall not in that neological spirit, cut the Bible into fragments, and insist that it is without coherency, without a purpose. I shall regard it as a book of gradual discovery, of growing Revelation; and I shall believe this to be its final and most certain revelation, that God is light, and with Him is no darkness at all; that He never calls good evil, or evil good; that every false act done by saint or sinner, man or angel, proceeds from the father of lies. Since the Son of God has been manifested, the works of the devil have been manifested also; it is a monstrous contempt of God's blessed teaching to say that we cannot know them; an awful denial of it to say that in certain instances we may identify them with His works who has come to destroy them.

Brethren, in what I have said this afternoon I have not been encouraging you to interpret Scripture in a lax, careless method, according to some notions of your own. I have wished you to feel that you are studying a holy and divine record, and therefore that you are to be very watchful, lest you should substitute rude and vulgar conclusions of mortal judgment for that which is higher than mortal judgment, and is to correct them. God teaches us in His Scriptures by the errors, confusions, contradictions of His best and stoutest servants. Was not Job an inspired man? Might not even his three friends claim some supernatural teaching? Their words are recorded in Scripture. Thank God that they are! Not for the world would we dispense with them. But if we receive them as authoritative, we contradict God Himself, for we are told He was angry both with Job and his friends because they had justified themselves rather than Him. We must be content to learn in His way, not in ours; to be trained as that apostle was, whom we remember to-day, by the experience of our own mistakes, presumption, vanity, cowardice; to be trained by the records of the mistakes, presumption, vanity, cowardice, of those whom we venerate most, who have been the greatest pillars of the Church; that so we may learn what that eternal rock is upon which it rests, and against which the gates of hell shall never prevail.

SERMON XIX.

ELI AND SAMUEL.

(Lincoln's Inn. Third Sunday after Trinity July 6, 1851.)
Lessons for the day, 1 Samuel II. and III.

1 SAMUEL III. 14.

And therefore I have sworn unto the house of Eli, that the iniquity of Eli's house shall not be purged with sacrifice nor offering for ever.

OUR Lessons have brought us to a new stage in the history of the chosen nation. We begin to-day the prophetical and regal period of it. That is a subject upon which I do not intend to enter now.

I have chosen a passage from the lesson of this afternoon, not so much because it is an opening to the later books of the Old Testament, as because it throws back a light upon the earlier. I regard it as the most suitable conclusion to these Lectures. The questions which have so often occupied us in the course of them, whether the character of the Bible as a divine history interferes with its claims to be a faithful human history; whether the divine kingdom which the Scriptures speak of means merely a priestly kingdom; whether the real maxim of Jewish records is utterly inapplicable to us, or whether we are as much under an actual divine government as they were;—all come before us in the story of Eli and Samuel. The priestly order, as we have seen, was an essential part of the Jewish commonwealth. It dwelt in a particular family; the rebellion of Korah, Dathan, and Abiram, had been an attempt to take it out of that family; the suppression and punishment of their rebellion vindicated the limitation. Eli inherited the office which had belonged to Aaron; his sons offered the daily sacrifice. They were sons of Belial, we are told; they knew not the Lord. They valued the portions which it procured them; they made it vile in the eyes of the people by showing how vile it was in their eyes; having lost all sense of God's presence in the acts which most avouched His presence, there was nothing to restrain them. They became openly and brutally corrupt; gloating, it would seem, in the thought of turning consecrated places into places of sin. Thus they made the sacrifice of the Lord to be abhorred. This is the special charge against them. The people loathed the whole service. It not only lost all reality in their minds, it became positively hateful to them. Unbelief in anything true began to mix strangely and awfully with honest detestation of a lie. This is a description, the liveliest and most faithful possible, of a nation becoming atheistical through the atheism of its priests; learning to think that whatever is divine is with them; inwardly convinced at the same time that in them there is nothing divine, something very devilish.

Old Eli, the high priest, might have kept some of them from this persuasion. There must have been in him a real sense of the sacredness of his function. No one could dream that he thought of what he was to gain by it, or ever used it for any base ends. Whatever reverence a man can inspire by showing that his heart is personally engaged in his work, that it caused him inward delight, he will have inspired. But there is a limit to this kind of respect, and moreover a mischief in it. Eli was a pious or devout man; he was evidently a kind-hearted, amiable man; but he was not, strictly speaking, a righteous man. He did not care that God's order should be established, that wrong-doers should be punished. So long as he could keep his internal quietness, all was well. He wished his sons to be better, no doubt; he told them so. To preserve the commonwealth from pollution, to make the Tabernacle a fit place, not for his devotions, but for God to dwell in,—this did not come within the range of his religion. This good man exhibited in himself one side of that atheism, which was coming forth in heartlessness among the people, in depravity among his own children. He honoured God as an individual man; not as a father, as a member of a nation, as a high priest. Whatever honour therefore he attracted to himself, did not go beyond himself. He was the specimen of a departing age; he was sincere, no doubt; but his sincerity would die with him. His sons seemed to be the regular natural specimens of the priestly character. 'That was what 'the mysterious consecration, and the holy oil, and the 'vestments for glory and beauty, and the Urim and 'Thummim, and the words upon the forehead were coming 'to at last!'

All this the Scripture does not make the slightest attempt to conceal or to palliate. The case is stated broadly. Eli is condemned as well as his sons. And what then has become of that order of which we have heard so much? Is it nothing? Has it proved itself to be the empty thing which the nations round about always thought it was; which the people of the covenant are beginning to think that it is? The order is just where it always was; not shattered or shaken in the smallest degree; confirmed and established by the unbelief of the people, the crimes of Hophni and Phinehas, the imbecility of their father. If it was not of God, it was false from the first; if it was of God, He would prove it to be His, and prove that He was not dependent upon the order, but the order upon Him. This is the great and blessed truth which the story brings out before us. It is not, as some would say, that a *dignus vindice nodus* had occurred, and that then God interrupted the ordinary course of His Providence to set things right. Man, not He, is the interrupter. Man breaks the course of his obedience; he will not believe that God is with him of a truth. Then God shows him that He is. He does not allow him to remain in his delusion, to shut his eyes and fancy that he is unseen.

I. There are two methods in which we are told this revelation or discovery of the reality of things was made to the people of Israel at this time. Both are *methods* in the strict sense of the word; not sudden miracles, but a series of acts producing an impression by their conformity with a law, by their continuousness and relation to each other. A child is born to a woman who had for many years been longing and praying for one. In her joy and thankfulness for the gift she devotes him to the service of the Tabernacle. He is brought up as a child under the eye of the priest. As he lies in his little chamber, near the place where the Ark of God was, before the lamp went out, a voice called him which he thought was Eli's. He learnt by slow degrees that another than Eli was calling him, and that he had words to utter which would make both the ears of the whole house of Israel to tingle. Eli perceived that there was something in the heart of the child. He forced him to declare it. Then the boy told him that the Lord would not cease till he had made an end of the house of Eli, and that sacrifice and offering would not purge away the evil which it had committed.

Does it seem to you that this communication to Samuel was something strange and irregular, not in conformity with the regular course of God's dealings. I think a moment's reflection will show you that you are mistaken. A Jew who believed in God's covenant, could never think it a strange event that God should hold converse with a man. The feeling that this was possible was no doubt exceedingly weak at that time; just because faith in the covenant was exceedingly weak. The routine of daily services and sacrifices will have seemed to the Israelites in the days of Hophni and Phinehas a mere muttering of addresses to God, or attempts to move His mind; which ordinarily they will have regarded with indifference or contempt; which in critical and extreme moments they will have hoped might be successful. The thought of God ordering the sacrifice,—God communicating Himself to the creature, God uttering Himself to him and by him,—will have become a faded traditional thought in their minds. Why? Simply because their minds were out of tune, ready to exchange unbelief for superstition and superstition for unbelief, incredulous of an invisible Presence, and therefore credulous of visible powers and influences; turning all things upside down, supposing that it was easier for the meaner being to ascend to the higher, than for the higher to stoop to the meaner. Now if it pleased God to correct this false and vicious state of feeling, and to show that He does educate His creatures; that He knows what is passing in their inner minds, and can awaken those minds to perception and to action;—can you think of any simpler and quieter method than that of training a child,—already dedicated to a mysterious service,—to feel and know that he was actually under an unseen guide, and was to be the spokesman of His purposes?

Something of what is implied in the very idea of a prophet I have hinted at in former sermons. The full development of the character and office belongs to the later books. But thus much is clearly intimated in the passage we have read this afternoon, that he whom all Israel from Dan to Beersheba knew and felt to be a prophet, was under an education and government which obliged him to feel that his words were not his own, and yet that he was in the highest degree responsible for them; that they were given him, but given him in trust; and that he must seek for continual help neither to hide that which he was to publish, nor to mingle with it notions and fancies of his own. These three characteristics meet in this simple child-prophet. He knows that God is his teacher; he knows that He is teaching others through him; he knows that he is to foretel the inevitable results of ill-doing to priests and to people.

II. This is one of the methods. I have indicated the other in the last sentence, the method of *retribution*. The righteous Judge of the world shows that the world cannot go on without Him; that priests who try to establish their rule as if they had one of their own and were not merely His servants,—must above all men pay the penalty of their sin and unbelief. The people whom they have perverted into godlessness must taste the fruit of their godlessness. Those who have fancied there could be a routine of ordinances without the God who appointed them,—and that some independent charm was in them,—must be stripped of all signs and pledges of the Divine Presence, till they confess that Divine Presence without them, and so are fit to be trusted with them again. The Philistines came against Israel. The elders of Israel in their terror thought that the Ark of God might save them if it was carried down to the battle; the atheistical priests went with it. They were slain, the host discomfited, the Ark taken. Eli fell dead at hearing the news. The glory of the land was departed. If He who had made His Presence known in the Ark, had been confined to it, the land must have indeed perished. There was nothing left to keep it alive. But God was the same, wherever the Ark might be. He still spoke out His judgments and His prophecies by Samuel's voice. In due time, having proved that the nation lived only in Him and by Him, He gave it health and restoration.

Now imagine the earnest Dominican, Savonarola, in the days of Alexander the Sixth, reading this passage. Do you think he could have supposed that it belonged only to the times when the judges judged Israel? Must he not have said, 'It belongs to my time and my country. The 'abominations which the priests of the Christian Church 'are committing in the city which boasts to be the centre 'and mother of all, are such as Hophni and Phinehas 'never perpetrated. And the cause of them is the same. 'These Italian priests of ours, like the Jewish, can go 'through their routine of services without the slightest 'belief in God, without the least sense that He is a righteous King and Judge. They think that they are to 'speak a great many words, and to go through a circle of religious acts, but they have no dream that He is

speaking or acting. These men who are sent into the
' world to testify that He lives, think in their hearts that
' He is dead. And therefore it is certain that they will
' commit crimes in the darkness of night, nay, in the face
' of day, which ordinary men, which heathens, would
' tremble at.' Now when a man, overwhelmed with these
thoughts, felt an irresistible compulsion to proclaim aloud
in the ears of his countrymen that God would come forth
out of His place to punish the simonies, and murders, and
incests which He had seen, and to prove that Italy and the
Church had another ruler than those who were defiling and
destroying them, do you think he could doubt that the
same divine voice which Samuel heard as he lay near Eli's
chamber, was bidding *him* testify of present sins and
coming destruction? I cannot conceive how a man could
shake himself free from the influence of that Art Worship,
which was banishing all other in his day, and could defy
all terrors of the visible and invisible world, that he might
speak what he knew to be true, if he confessed any lower
call than this. I know well that Savonarola did mingle
fanaticism, sometimes grievous fanaticism, with his manly
and noble protest for righteousness. I allude to his case
partly for that reason. It seems to me that any extravagant
pretensions which he put forward for himself,—any errors
into which his mighty influence as a preacher, and the
belief of the people in his prophetical powers betrayed him,
—was the consequence, not of his studying the history of
Samuel, and accepting it too simply as a guide for the
times to come, but of his omitting to draw from it some of
its deepest and most helpful lessons. The temptation of
Savonarola and of every man possessing remarkable
endowments and feeling certain of the purpose to which

he should devote them, is to think of himself as under some economy different from that of other men. Though in his moments of highest inspiration he claims them all as fellow-heirs with him,—though the very secret of his power lies in his sympathy,—yet he is continually apt to fancy (and how fearfully does the adoration of crowds increase and perpetuate the delusion!) that he is an altogether different being from those who hang upon his lips. Hence come the pretensions, and sometimes the dishonourable efforts to support them, which have defiled the lives of men essentially true and brave, and have caused them their greatest sorrows and humiliations. Now the moral of Samuel's story, standing as it does, not alone, but as part of a history altogether in accordance with it, is surely this; that the man is right, and the child is right, just so far as he acknowledges that God's voice is speaking to him secretly and inwardly, preparing him for whatever work he has to do; that the man who is conscious of special powers and a special commission, is emphatically to assert that God is the author of them,—in order that he may encourage *all* his brethren to feel that their gifts and their callings are also divine. Why was Samuel raised up except to tell a people who had forgotten God's ancient covenant, that it was true and no lie? Why is any teacher raised up in the Christian age except to tell baptized men that God's Spirit is with them, and that the greatest and the least of them must give account for a trust so awful; for the presence of a Guide whom they may trifle with and grieve, but whom they cannot banish, and who is speaking to them continually, whether they heed His voice or despise it?

I cannot feel, brethren, that we, the priests of the

English church, have borne this testimony to you the members of it as we ought, by our deeds or by our words. All praise be to God, if the open scandals among us are not what they may have been in other days; not such as may enable us to find an exact parallel for our own case in the lessons we read to-day. But I dare not say, that we too have not made the offering of the Lord oftentimes to be abhorred by the people. Whenever we represent the great atoning Sacrifice in the language of heathenism, and not in the language of the Gospel,—as an offering to make God loving, and not as the fruit of His love, as an effort of Christ to obtain that which the Father was unwilling to grant, not as His perfect surrender and submission to the Will of the Father,—we make the very principle of sacrifice to be abhorred; we destroy all apprehension of its true nature in the creature, because we have denied the ground and original of it in the Creator. When we do not proclaim the gospel of a finished sacrifice for mankind, but draw limitations and distinctions which shut out multitudes from the blessings of it; we cause the offering of the Lord to be abhorred. When we show in our services or our worship, that we care for the rich more than for the poor, and that we think the one exist for the sake of the other,—that one main business of the priest is to preserve the barriers of classes, and to assert wealth as the great barrier, not to proclaim a universal communion;—we cause the offering of the Lord to be abhorred. When we dispute with each other, and rail at each other, and show that we do not believe the Spirit of love has power to overcome the spirit of wrath and hatred, even in ourselves; we cause the offering of the Lord to be abhorred. When we use cant phrases to which no realities correspond; we cause the offering of the Lord to be abhorred. When we tell men that they are to make great efforts, and to overcome great temptations, and do not tell them that they have God Himself helping them and striving with them; we cause the offering of the Lord to be abhorred.

I speak, brethren, as feeling the infinite peril which those are in of forgetting God, who are continually speaking of Him to others, and whose privilege and calling it is to set forth the tokens and sacraments of His Presence. Eli and his house needed a Samuel; it will go ill with us, the priests of this day, if we think that children—and that hundreds and thousands who are without the innocence of children—may not speak words of awe and warning to us. In one sense, every man whom we meet in the streets, with the image of God defaced and crushed through our indifference, is a prophet to us. But yet it may please the Lord of the vineyard to send different teachers from these, men really taught by Him to see the evils we are committing, and what will flow from them. Oh! may we not stone them and cast them out! And may they be preserved by His grace from setting up themselves, or fancying that they have any right to be honoured, or have any glory except in uttering the word which He has committed to them, and in doing the acts which He has sent them to do! Christ said to the twelve fishermen whom He was sending forth with words of blessing and warning to publicans and sinners, to priests and rulers, '*He that heareth you heareth me; he that despiseth you despiseth me. He that despiseth me despiseth Him that sent me.*' From that contempt of Himself may He of His mercy deliver us and our land. And may He deliver us also from the great curse and unbelief, of fancying that His Church rests upon those who temporarily minister in it; or that the sentence which must go forth against them, if they are faithless and godless, affects its stability. The ark may be taken captive; the priests may die in their sins; the witness and relic of the old world may fall down with the weight of age and sorrow. But amidst thunders and earthquakes, the Tabernacle of Testimony will be opened in heaven; and He will be revealed who has the covenant of an everlasting priesthood; the Living Word who is the Teacher of prophets, the King of kings and Lord of lords.

THE END.

www.ingramcontent.com/pod-product-compliance
Lightning Source LLC
Chambersburg PA
CBHW050331230426
43663CB00010B/1816